D1080288

MEN'S COOKING

From hot starters to dangerous desserts (all variations and flavours)

First published May 2010

A catalogue record for this book is available
from the British Library

ISBN 978 1 84425 869 7

Haynes Publishing,
Sparkford, Yeovil,
Somerset BA22 7JJ, UK
Tel: +44 (0) 1963 442030
Fax: +44 (0) 1963 440001
E-mail: sales@haynes.co.uk
Website: www.haynes.co.uk

Haynes North America, Inc.,
861 Lawrence Drive, Newbury Park,
California 91320, USA

Printed and bound in the USA

Author	Chris Maillard
Project manager	Louise McIntyre
Designer	Richard Parsons
Copy editor	Ian Heath
Indexer	Alan Thatcher
Photography	Carol Sharp (cover, chapter openers, step-by-steps)
	Alamy (pages 75, 137, 154)
	istockphoto.com

Author's Acknowledgements

A large portion of thanks to lovely Carol for the lovely
images; the incredibly patient and unflappable Louise
for excellent editing; design gurus Lee and Richard for
their visual skills and breakfast suggestions; and my
Mum for allowing me to nick her lemon meringue pie
recipe. This book is dedicated to Clem, Gabe, and
anybody else who has eaten my cooking and survived.

MEN'S COOKING

From hot starters to dangerous desserts (all variations and flavours)

Owners' Kitchen Manual

A no-nonsense guide to buying, cooking and eating great food

Chris Maillard

Contents

Welcome to the Men's Cooking Manual

Isn't cooking women's work? Well, no

Even setting aside the fact that most top professional chefs are blokes, just think about it. It's the perfect chance to play with dangerously sharp knives, naked flames, volatile liquids (both flammable and drinkable), big bits of dead animal, and a whole variety of noisy and complex gadgets. All in the comfort of your own home.

What's more, it's a basic survival skill. A bit less flashy than being able to wrestle grizzly bears or build a family-sized tepee out of twigs, admittedly, but far more likely to get used regularly.

And it's sexy. Right from a sharp-dressed Michael Caine acting suspiciously cosmopolitan by knocking up a little European-style something for his dollybird in '60s spy thriller *The Ipcress File* to today's smouldering hunks of celebrity chef beefcake, being able to make a meal is guaranteed to give any man a dash of sophisticated savoir-faire and sex appeal.

But there's more. Not only will women fall head-over-heels in love with your culinary prowess, other blokes will be quietly envious of your abilities. Particularly if you can lash together something tasty and filling after the pub or before the match.

If you've got a family to feed, you'll probably be climbing the kitchen wall with boredom at the usual beans-and-fish-fingers diet. Well, break the system. Learn to make something that the tinies will enjoy which isn't the usual kiddy stodge.

And the best thing of all? Cooking usually gets you out of doing the washing up. You can feel justified in settling into a relaxed post-meal slump, while someone else wrestles with soapy cutlery.

What are you waiting for? Get in that kitchen and rattle those pots and pans, as legendary blues singer Big Joe Turner (a man who'd seen a fair few decent meals) put it so nicely in *Shake Rattle and Roll*.

So here's how to do it. This is your manual. Not a recipe book full of glossy photos of stacked, drizzled, manicured dishes with tiny bits of exotic herbs balanced on the top, but a book full of basic skills and straightforward information.

After reading this, you should be able to feed yourself and anyone else, and clued-up enough to take a decent stab at cooking almost anything. By the way, the recipe for roast camel's hump is on page 174. Good luck.

How to use this book

Start at the beginning. There's some handy stuff in those bits. Don't just head straight for the recipes, or you'll miss quite a bit of vital info. When you do get there, though, here are a few hints. Measurements are all metric, and temperatures are in Centigrade. If you need to convert them, check the tables on page 171. We've given total time, which is from the moment you decide what to cook to the second you start eating it, and how many minutes of actual work is involved – that's stirring or chopping rather than watching the telly while something's in the oven. They're also graded for difficulty, like this:

Dead easy. A toddler could do it

Very straightforward. No worries.

Pretty unchallenging, but with the odd quirk.

Basic competence would be handy.

Keep your wits about you and it'll all be fine.

CHAPTER 1
TOOLBOX

All truly interesting blokes' activities have their own specialist tools. From stud pullers to chain splitters, fly-tying vices to solder suckers, there's a set of specialist kit you need if you're half-serious about anything.

And cooking's the same. Having good equipment will make your life easier, will enable you to do a whole range of stuff that would be hasslesome otherwise, and will fill you with that inexplicable satisfaction that comes from looking at a well-stocked, well-ordered toolbox.

Of course, you don't have to go to stupid lengths – there's no real need for a full pegboard wall with every bit of kit outlined in magic marker and labelled in Dymo tape, and F1 pit-style Snap-On tool chests may be a little extreme – but you won't have much fun if you're stuck with one of your Mum's cast-off aluminium saucepans and a blunt charity shop knife.

You can outfit yourself with the basics pretty cheaply and easily, then add bits as you need them or can afford them. As with everything, buy the best you can, but there's an awful lot you can do with a few smart, low-budget buys.

But as with everything, it's easy to get interested in the kit rather than the activity. It's all too tempting to start building an arsenal of impressively shiny bits and pieces, but when you get to the point of owning three sizes of melon baller it's probably time to remember that it's about cooking great food rather than owning a ton of dust-gathering machinery.

Mind you, there's a great new pasta machine just out...

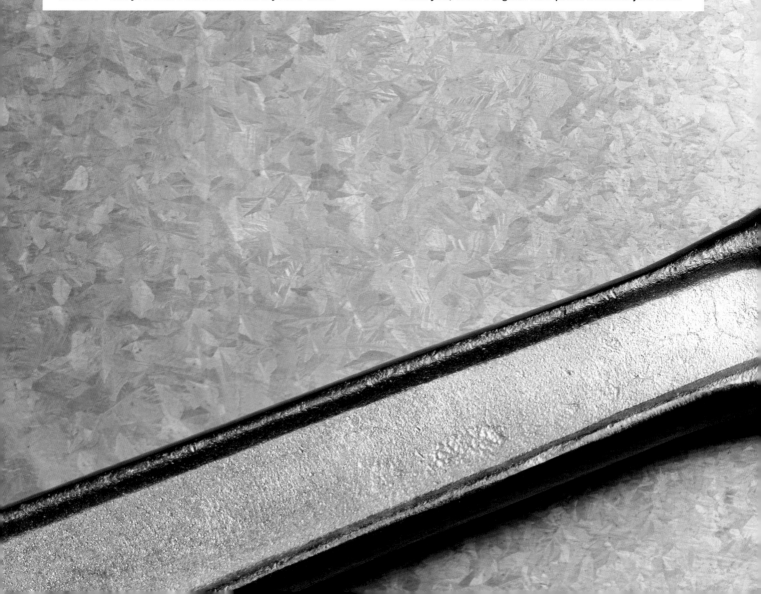

Essential equipment: stuff you need

Whether you're buying kit for the first time or upgrading from some horrible, battered old rubbish, here are all the facts on all the gear you'll need.

POTS AND PANS

You will need pans. But if you're just starting to build up your kitchen arsenal, you don't need many.

- Start with a large one that will work for stew, soup, and so on, and preferably fits into the oven to do duty as a casserole – so make sure the handles are heatproof.
- Then you'll need a couple of smaller saucepans – somewhere between 15 and 20cm would be fine. And to save on space, if they fit into each other that's good.
- Look for solid construction – but they needn't be too heavy; the cast iron Le Creuset-style pans are fine, but a big one full of, say, potatoes is a real handful.
- Make sure the handles are heatproof (not nasty cheap plastic) and ideally separated from the pan slightly so they won't get quite as hot.
- Aluminium is generally not a good idea. There are scare stories about it gradually poisoning you, but the main reason is that it's not a good, even conductor of heat, so will develop hot spots for food to stick and burn.
- Copper pans are the professionals' choice, as it's an excellent conductor, but they're a nuisance to keep looking decent. Some pans have a layer of copper enclosed in steel for the base, which is excellent.

- Steel is the mainstay, and a heavy-bottomed steel pan with a sturdy handle will last a lifetime. Buy fewer, not cheaper, though. Get the best you can. Having said that, IKEA do a reasonable range, though they're often unusual sizes so other makes' lids and so on may not fit.
- Non-stick is not a bad idea, but don't buy cheap non-stick pans, as the coating will flake off. However, there are plenty of midrange pans with a good thick non-stick coating.
- You'll need oven pans too. Baking trays are fine, but something with higher sides like a roasting tin is more useful. Make sure they're sturdy enough to cope with being walloped on to the stove and scraped with a metal spoon. If you can get small enough ones to fit two on an oven shelf, that'll be handy when things get congested in the cooker.
- Mixing bowls, pie dishes, and serving bowls can be picked up here and there pretty cheaply, but make sure anything that's going to go in the oven is properly heatproof – Pyrex or similar. At minimum you'll need one big bowl (25cm or thereabouts) and a couple of medium-sized (15cm) ones.
- Pyrex do a brilliant measuring jug that holds one litre, which will double as a mixing bowl or even an oven dish.

weight and see: solid, heavy-bottomed pans are crucial

Keep it simple: you don't need heaps of gadgets

Other stuff

- You'll need a chopping board. Wood is best, end grain (usually looks like lots of small squares) is better still. Big, thick, and solid is good, though you may want to lift it sometimes. Plastic ones can be OK, but glass is noisy and hard on knives.
- A colander – or at a pinch, a big sieve – is invaluable for draining veg, pasta, etc. Try to get one that will stand up on its own, as juggling the other kind is a pain.
- A wire-mesh cooling rack – though the grill out of a grill pan will do if you're stuck.
- One or more trivets or mats to prevent hot pans scorching surfaces.

CROCKERY AND GLASSWARE

- You need plates and bowls, unless you like eating out of a paper bag. Get plenty – at least double the amount of people who'll regularly use them – because they'll get used for other things while cooking, and you'll end up frantically washing up if you don't have enough. A good basic set consists of dinner plates (around 25cm), side plates (around 15cm), and bowls – one type could work for everything, but you could also get wide, shallow bowls for salad or pasta, then smaller, deeper ones for sloppy desserts and soup. And don't forget eggcups if you like boiled eggs.
- The same principle applies to mugs and glasses – get double the amount that there are regular users. A good solid selection is mugs, wine glasses, and half-pint (approx 250ml) tumblers.
- Don't forget a good-sized teapot if you drink tea, and a small milk jug if you ever have posh guests.
- If you want to go for ice buckets, water jugs, decanters, fancy coffee pots (see page 157), toast racks, place mats, candelabra, and doilies, it's your life. Carry on.

Hand tools

These are essential:
- Knives (see page 16).
- Wooden spoon and/ or spatula.
- Large metal spoon or ladle.
- Can opener.
- Bottle opener/corkscrew.
- Grater.
- Kitchen scales.

These are useful:
- Fish slice, or flat metal spatula.
- Biggish tongs.
- Whisk.
- Hefty scissors or kitchen shears.
- Small, fine-mesh sieve.
- Food processor or mixer.
- Vegetable peeler.
- Rolling pin.
- Bottleneck-sized funnel.
- Measuring spoons.

These are optional:
- Small blowlamp, pasta serving spoon, cherry stoner/ olive pipper, lemon zester, butter curler, melon baller, solar-powered nutmeg crusher, etc etc.

Mug your mum: old but handy gadgets

There are some tools that just don't date, or wear out. You'll run across them in charity shops, car boot sales, on eBay, or in an aged relative's loft. Just don't actually steal them from Granny, eh?

■ Earthenware mixing bowls
The classic big cream bowl is brilliant for all manner of things, from cakes and dough to marinading meat and even covering dishes while you're doing something else.

■ Kitchen scales
Those old-style balance-beam scales often pop up, with a motley selection of pound and ounce weights, half of them missing. But they work perfectly well, and a full set of metric weights is dirt cheap. Plus their batteries won't run out halfway through a tricky bit.

■ Pressure cooker
This is an aluminium or steel pressure vessel which seals the food in, then uses high pressure to cook it fast. They make threatening gurgling noises, blow superheated steam out of pressure relief valves, and if it all goes wrong could turn into a powerful bomb. What's not to like? They've gone out of fashion here, but are ideal for cooking beans, pulses, stews, curries and so on quickly; that's why they're still well used in India and thereabouts.

⚠ HAZARD WARNING!
If a pressure cooker's seals, gaskets and valves are in poor condition, it won't work. Or it'll explode. New bits are dirt cheap (check eBay), so make sure yours is in peak order. And read the instructions.

For further information check the manufacturer's website or the slightly dubious-sounding missvickie.com.

■ Measuring cups
The conical type with many different measurements ruled inside can be a lifesaver if you ever have to use an American recipe, as the 'cups' measures they use are otherwise untranslatable. Also good for pre-metric cookbooks.

■ Sweet shop jars
Great for dried stuff like flour, sugar, rice and so on. And look cool too.

■ Big jugs
No jokes, please. Two-litre Pyrex or ceramic jugs are perfect for things like pancake batter or cake mixes; mix, then pour. And the handle's good to hang on to if you're using a hand mixer, to stop your bowl skittering off into disaster.

■ Spong mincers, slicers etc

These are the handle-cranked gadgets that clamp on to the side of a table or worktop. Other makes include National, Harper, and Alpha, and there are plenty more. Verging on the antique now, but if they're in good nick they'll still work well and, crucially, disassemble completely for easy cleaning and maintenance (use olive or sunflower oil, not 3-in-1). That's something many food processor designers still find impossible to get right.

■ The Kenwood Chef

These are the traction engines of the kitchen – old, primitive, and noisy, but also versatile, reliable, and powerful. Extras and spares are still available for even the oldest models, and add-ons like the very handy dough hook or meat mincer can make them invaluable.

■ Enamel stuff

If it's not badly chipped, anything from casseroles to coffee pots can be very usable. Enamel was the non-stick Teflon of its day – it's pretty easy to keep clean.

■ Kitsch spice racks, nutcrackers, butter dishes etc

Whatever. It's your kitchen. Don't bother with anything dirty, rusty, cracked or badly chipped. You probably knew that. Old knives can be more trouble than they're worth, as they may have been badly sharpened for years. Wooden and some plastic utensils can pick up indelible musty odours.

⚠ HAZARD WARNING!

Beware of electrical appliances, particularly if they've got cloth or rubber-covered flex – it'll have perished by now. Funny round-pin plugs, Bakelite switches, and black/red/green wiring (instead of today's brown/blue/green and yellow stripes) are also major warning signs.

Check plugs and wiring thoroughly on electrical appliances before using them.

Motorised mayhem

Food processors are really handy – not utterly essential, as most jobs can be done in other, manual, ways – but the whole idea of a set of razor-sharp blades attached to a powerful motor is somehow attractive anyway. Three things, though, to look out for when buying one:

IS IT HEFTY ENOUGH?

Are the controls chunky, the handles well-attached, and all the plastics thick and dishwasher-proof?

IS THE MOTOR UP TO THE JOB?

Look for a wattage of somewhere approaching 1,000w. Anything over that and you're laughing (or processing, anyway), but get down to much below and it'll struggle with tricky jobs.

IS IT EASY TO CLEAN?

This is crucial, as anyone who's had to pick caked-on glop out of a badly designed device's nooks and crannies will attest. It should be dishwasher-proof and as lacking in complex twiddly bits as possible.

You don't need it, but...

Once you get into kitchen gadgetry, it's difficult to stop acquiring exciting but highly specialist bits of kit. It's like a drug addiction, and often just as expensive. So to feed your habit, here are a few items which are hardly essential, but can be very satisfying.

■ **Mortar and pestle** – A really hefty granite or marble one is superb for crushing spices, making pesto sauce, and is apparently the only proper way to make Thai curry paste. Yes, you can do all the above in a food processor, but it's not as satisfyingly physical.

■ **Baker's peel** – Like a flat shovel, either metal with a wooden handle or all-wood. You may have seen one in your local pizza place – they're for moving pizza or bread in and out of the oven. Useful if you bake a lot.

■ **Pizza stone** – Again, great if you bake a lot. It produces an even, radiant heat that bakes fine bread. You can also use an unglazed quarry tile, which works just as well, though some get brittle after a few uses.

■ **Pasta machine** – If you enjoyed Play-Doh as a child, you'll love this. It's a geared double-roller mechanism for producing thin sheets of pasta out of dough, and has add-ons to cut it into spaghetti, tagliatelle, or whatever. Usually chrome, in a superbly cool retro Italian design.

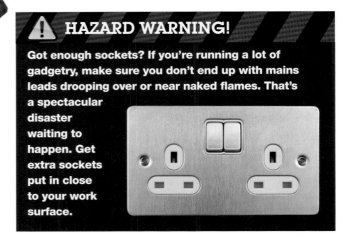

⚠ **HAZARD WARNING!**

Got enough sockets? If you're running a lot of gadgetry, make sure you don't end up with mains leads drooping over or near naked flames. That's a spectacular disaster waiting to happen. Get extra sockets put in close to your work surface.

■ **Iconic toaster** – Maybe. The solidly-built Dualit ones are rebuildable and good-looking, but many older ones will only take one thickness of bread, so crumpet-lovers are out of luck.

■ **Mandolins, mezzalunas, oyster knives etc** – If you like. They don't take up much room. But many of these specialist tools require a lot of getting used to, otherwise they're just collecting dust and very occasionally skinning your knuckles.

■ **Wand mixer** – Braun and others make hand-held mixers that you can plop into a pan or jug to quickly whizz something into a pulp. Can be useful, but can also over-purée stuff into mush.

■ **Oven thermometers, meat probes, and heat sensing guns** – Fun, but unless your oven runs much hotter or colder than it says, a bit irrelevant. A meat probe is one way of finding out if a joint is perfectly cooked, though. Some chefs swear by them.

sticky business: the wand or stick mixer

Chop shops:
Where to buy your kit

Once you've put together your wishlist of essential culinary gubbins, it's time to go shopping. Here's where, and how, to splash your cash.

- Knowledgeable, specialist cookware shops are the best option. You can handle, compare, and sometimes even try out tools, and they'll advise you if you're buying the right thing for your style, use, and budget. But the problem is that they are, firstly, few and far between (mostly in posh towns), and, secondly, often expensive. If you can afford it, though, or you decide it's worth splashing out on a few select bits, definitely give them your custom.
- Department stores – John Lewis are jolly fine, and most of the regional variations like Jarrolds in East Anglia or Fenwicks in the North carry a fair selection of good-quality kitchen stuff.
- If there's a branch near you, Lakeland carry a vast range of unusual merchandise such as single egg poachers and banana ripening bags; but more importantly, their basics aren't bad.
- Supermarkets often have a small but worthwhile range, and some are surprisingly decent. A big Sainsbury's or Tesco will usually have some usable kit at good prices, Waitrose have a cut-down version of the John Lewis range (not cheap, but very good), and even the super-cheap ones can surprise. Lidl, for instance, often have weird one-off sales of everything from motorcycling kit to shower curtains, but it's very cheap and often decently made in Eastern Europe, and kitchen gear sometimes pops up there at embarrassingly low prices.
- Car boot sales and charity shops can be fertile sources of stuff like bread knives, chopping boards, and so on. Give everything a proper eyeballing to make sure it's in good, clean condition, and be prepared to scrub it thoroughly, but someone's great-granny's 1923 kitchen scales will still work just fine today.
- Local shops can come up trumps; an old-fashioned ironmongers, if you're lucky enough to have one nearby, can be a treasure trove.
- The Internet. You can buy absolutely anything you need, and a lot of stuff you don't. Unfortunately, you often can't take a close look at the details or get a good idea of sizes, so be very careful. Amazon's the giant, eBay can produce some bargains, particularly on used stuff, and a quick Google search will produce almost any item you can imagine ('kitchen tools' – 57,600,000 results). But buying on the net is always a lottery. It's good for small machinery like coffee makers or pasta makers, but factor in the cost of delivery, plus customs duty if you buy from outside the EU, and it might not be such a bargain.

Travel toolkit: the bare minimum

If you're going away and think you'll end up cooking, you'll need some reliable basics. You'll definitely need:

- A good chef's knife.
- A small sharp knife.

Wrap them carefully in a tea towel, then put them in a side pocket of your bag (but not in your hand luggage, if you're flying. Unless you enjoy cavity searches.

Most self-catering places will have some form of chopping board, spoons, and some pans of highly variable quality.

But if you're going right off the beaten track, and don't know what will be available, if anything, the next level up adds:

- A serrated knife or bread knife.
- A biggish frying pan, ideally with a lid.
- A medium-sized steel casserole or deep saucepan with a short handle so it'll fit in the oven as well as on the stove.
- A decent chopping board.
- A large metal spoon or ladle.
- A spatula or wooden spoon.
- Salt and pepper plus a few of your favourite herbs and spices (see page 26).

Obviously that lot will be heavy. Fine if you're driving, but if not, pack it in a bag with strong handles and preferably wheels, and prepare for some heaving.

Keep your edge – knife work if you can get it

Decent knives are the most essential things you can have. Buy flimsy, blunt ones and you'll be hacking big lumps out of yourself while making your food into random mush. Buy good ones, keep them sharp, and you'll immediately start to feel like a proper cook.

The main type you'll need is a chef's knife. They usually have a blade about 20cm long, shaped like a long triangle, sometimes with a slight curve to the edge. They'll do most things, like slicing, chopping, and carving. Names worth looking out for are Sabatier (confusingly, several marques share this label), Wüsthof, Henckels, Victorinox, and the very stylish Global. Or even FA Porsche, if you really must.

Go somewhere that has a decent selection (see 'Chop shops' on page 16) and handle a few. Does it fit your hand comfortably? How's the weight? If you can, find a flat surface and try a few trial cuts. And be prepared to spend slightly more than you'd expect. £20 and up is reasonable. Of course, if you want a hand-made ceramic Japanese chef's knife that can split a single hair into quarters, you can pay thousands. And it'll shatter if you drop it. Oops.

OTHER KNIVES YOU'LL NEED (DON'T SKIMP)

- Small (6–10cm blade) sharp-pointed knife for vegetables, and fiddly things like boning fish. Sometimes called a paring knife.
- Smallish serrated knife (8–12cm) for cutting tomatoes and other tricky, slippery things.
- Bread knife, with a long (20cm or so) serrated blade.

stay sharp: the one on the left is a classic chef's knife

OTHER KNIVES YOU MAY JUST WANT

- **Cleaver:** Huge, heavy, dangerous. Excellent. Rectangular bladed, usually, and good for big bits of meat.
- **Oyster knife:** Short, pointed, and heavy-bladed, for cracking the little sods open.
- **Boning knife:** This has a thin, flexible 10–15cm blade for sliding round ribs and so on. Tricky to use well. Can also work for filleting fish.
- **Mezzaluna:** A weird crescent-shaped thing with a top-mounted handle, used for chopping herbs. Again, quite difficult to master but some swear by them.
- **Soft cheese knife:** Has holes in the blade to stop it sticking. Also used by some sushi chefs for fish.
- **Grapefruit knife, ham slicer, prawn-deveiner:** Really?

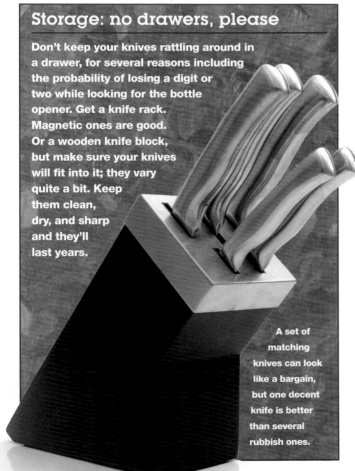

Storage: no drawers, please

Don't keep your knives rattling around in a drawer, for several reasons including the probability of losing a digit or two while looking for the bottle opener. Get a knife rack. Magnetic ones are good. Or a wooden knife block, but make sure your knives will fit into it; they vary quite a bit. Keep them clean, dry, and sharp and they'll last years.

A set of matching knives can look like a bargain, but one decent knife is better than several rubbish ones.

STEEL YOURSELF – HOW TO STAY SHARP

You might well have one of those criss-cross plastic-handled 'knife sharpener' gadgets in a kitchen drawer somewhere. If so, open a window and hurl it out. It's rubbish. If you have a good knife, you need a good sharpener, which almost always means a steel. Some, mainly Japanese, cooks swear by oilstones; others spend fortunes on improbably complex grinding machinery. But a steel's simple, easy, and quick. First, buy a good one. Spend at least half what you spent on your best knife. Look for a sturdy handle, a point on the end to hold it steady when using it vertically, and ridges that are crisp and well-defined. And here's what to do with it:

1 Hold the steel in one hand, the knife in the other. Keep your thumb and fingers behind the guard – it's there to prevent nasty accidents. The knife should meet the steel at an angle of around 20°.

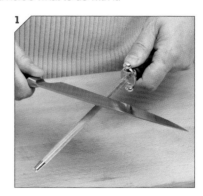

2 Run the knife down the steel away from you, sharpening the knife from heel to tip. Do this three or four times, briskly but not too fast. Then swap hands and repeat for the other side.

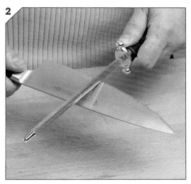

3 Alternatively, stick the point of the steel in a hefty chopping board, hold it steady and run the knife vertically down it, using the same 20° angle and swiping action. Then do the other side.

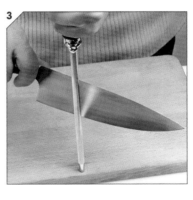

Do this every time you use your knife and it'll stay pretty sharp for a long while. After a lot of use, though, it'll start to lose its edge, which is when you need to get it professionally sharpened. Look for 'knife sharpening' in your local directory, or ask your local butcher, who may well know someone or even do it himself for a small fee.

Heavy equipment: the big stuff

Of all the bits of kit you need, there are only two you can't do without – a good knife (see page 16) and a source of heat. Which usually means a hob and an oven. Unless, of course, you have room for a huge bonfire in your kitchen. If so, excellent.

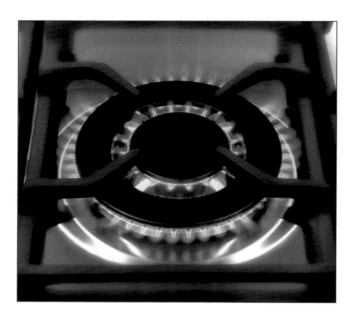

Most people, though, have the standard set-up: either an all-in-one cooker or a separate oven and a hob set into a worktop. And that's just fine. Provided they work properly, there's nothing wrong with that; it's predictable and unfussy. But there are certain things to bear in mind when choosing one.

THE HOB

Gas is the standard for cooking. Chefs rarely use anything else, because it's fast, controllable, and produces a decent amount of heat.

Electric rings are slow to heat up and, worse, slow to cool down – when something's about to boil over, it's a nuisance to have to take it off the hob rather than just turn the knob.

Induction hobs are fussy about which pans you use – Pyrex or ceramic won't work, and only magnetic metal pans will work, which rules out many aluminium or copper ones – but they run relatively cool and clean (they work by magnetically oscillating the pan, so don't waste much heat).

AGAs, Rayburns and the like are a whole different animal, and demand a change of technique to make use of their steady always-on heat. Many owners also have a gas hob or grill to cover the bits that the big stove can't do.

THE OVEN AND/OR GRILL

This is usually electric today. However, many keen cooks still swear by gas ovens, because they give a 'wetter' heat, which is good for baking.

Fan ovens give a more even heat and some claim to cook faster than the non-fan equivalents. Check your oven's manual and adapt recipes to suit.

The combined oven and grill, while common, is a bit of a bodge. If you can get a separate grill, go for it – if you can find a gas one, now highly uncommon, even more so.

Professional gas grills, if you've got a lot of money, are known as 'salamanders' and will go high enough to roast your eyebrows clean off.

THE PRO STOVE

If you fancy getting serious and putting in a big range cooker, try looking for a make that also serves the professional market, like British marque Falcon or the pricey French Lacanche stoves.

They come in home decor-friendly colours and are available from many decent department stores.

Or if you don't mind the industrial look, get a used ex-restaurant stove. They're heftily built and, more importantly, relatively easy to maintain yourself if necessary, with spare parts easily available. Try to get one that's been recently professionally serviced. Names to look out for include Falcon (again), Lincat, Hobart, Parry, or Moorwood. Look for catering equipment suppliers in your local directory, or try eBay. Again, check your local directory for installers – or ask a local restaurant who they use.

If you're able to specify options on a new range, useful things to have include a wok burner (a big, powerful – 5,000W or so – burner), a charcoal grill, which can be fantastic for a barbecue-style food but can also be a swine to clean, and ovens with self-cleaning linings.

MORE GEAR

Fridges aren't that interesting, but you need one. The bigger the better, and ideally with the fridge at eye level and the freezer below, to the side, or separate rather than on top. Look for a self-defrosting one, and newer ones should have a decent energy rating – A or A+. Tall American-style fridges are cool, and have lots of room for the floor space they take up, but can be surprisingly noisy because they've got a big compressor.

Do you need a **microwave**? Probably. They don't really cook food so much as make it hot, but they're invaluable for certain things like defrosting stuff or steaming vegetables quickly – and they cook a mean sponge pudding.

Get a **dishwasher**. They're a superb invention and will make even your messiest, most pan-intensive cooking guilt-free.

Protection: Keep clean, stay safe

You don't need a full set of chef's whites to cook. But it's annoying when your best shirt ends up looking like a Jackson Pollock painting and all your arm hairs are smouldering. If you're the messy type, try these tips:

- Always take your watch off. It might be waterproof to 100 metres, but is it boiling oil-proof?
- Roll your sleeves up. Cuffs are a nuisance and will get filthy.
- Consider an apron. Pros: you'll stay clean. Cons: you look a bit of a berk. Your choice.
- Oven gloves are better than a tea towel. The separate ones give you more freedom than the joined-up type, but will get separated when you most need the pair. Try to get some that cover your wrists at least, if not your forearms.
- Keep plenty of tea towels handy and wash them often. Plain, heavy cotton is classiest and toughest. Souvenirs from long-shut tourist attractions are deeply rubbish, but will still work.
- Tea towels, oven gloves, and aprons should be hung near – but not within flammable range – of the stove. Not in a drawer: that's too much fumbling.
- If you're doing posh dinner for guests, change after the messy, sweaty stuff's over. They'll understand.
- Always wash your hands, knife, chopping board and any other utensils or crockery thoroughly and quickly after you've been dealing with raw meat or fish. Salmonella might sound like an exotic seafood dish but it's decidedly not funny. Very few good dinners feature a life-threatening disease as a final course.

Your workshop: perfect kitchen layout

If you're about to plan a kitchen from scratch – lucky you. The rest of us have to put up with some long-dead tenant's idea of where to shove the sink. But even if you're stuck with a tiny or odd-shaped space, there are things you can do to make it more practical.

FROM SCRATCH: THE MAJOR REBUILD

You'll probably run across 'the magic triangle' – the supposedly perfect arrangement of cooker, sink, and fridge that allows you to access all of them with minimum reaching. Take this with a pinch of salt. It was thought up in the '50s when every housewife spent half her life elbow-deep in washing up. You'll probably spend most of your cooking time at a chopping board, ideally close to the hob. The fridge might be useful close by – you never know when you'll need another cold beer – but the sink, not so much. Which leads on to:

- Get a dishwasher, dude. They keep dirty dishes out of the way, and they needn't take up too much room.
- Plan for plenty of worktop space. A good area close to the hob is crucial. Try to allow an area for a heatproof surface, or a decent-sized trivet, to stop hot pans scorching their way clean through expensive wooden worktops.
- Where's the bin? This is important. Under-counter waste receptacles that you can slide peelings and general crud into are excellent. Something 20ft away that you have to carry a wobbly pile of leftovers to, much less so.
- Put some decent lighting right over where you're going to work. If you've got ceiling lights, make sure they aren't behind you, so when you bend over you're working in your own shadow. If you've got spotlights make sure they aren't too strongly directional, so you're working in a pool of light and everything else is in total darkness.

- Consider open doors. Can you still get around when the dishwasher, oven, or cupboards are open? Or will you bark your shins on a red-hot oven shelf twice a week? Not fun.
- While it's nice to look out of a window, be careful where you place the hob. Strong breezes can blow out gas jets, while flapping curtains can catch alight, thereby burning down your entire house. Which is always irritating.
- Try not to place anything that you can't wipe down within a few feet of the hob. Sizzling oil spatters, bubbling soup spits, and a good session using a red-hot griddle will cover everything with a layer of smoky, superheated particles. Talking of which...
- If you're putting in a cooker hood, make sure it's extremely powerful. Many are barely worth bothering with, particularly after the filters get slightly clogged. Recirculating ones are useless – get one that extracts smells to the open air. Look for a power rating above 200W, though watch the noise level. 70dB is quite loud enough unless you're a Motörhead fan.
- Lastly, entertainment. A TV? Dangerous. That crucial goal/ murder/car chase will always happen when you're juggling a pan of scalding fat. A computer? Dodgy, unless it's a knackered old laptop you just use to check recipes, and you don't mind if it eventually cops a caseful of pasta sauce and dies. A stereo? Perfect. Big speakers at ear height, a choice of radio, CD, or (safely tucked away) iPod, and you're off. There's something about cooking and loud music that works well, which is why many chefs are closet metalheads.

MINOR MODS: MAKE THE MOST OF IT

If you're renting, sharing, or otherwise stuck with your kitchen as it is, don't despair. You can still try a few tweaks that will make it a much better place to lash some dinner together.

- Store your tools properly. The kitchen drawer where everything rattles around in a giant mess of corkscrews and cocktail sticks is, frankly, rubbish. You wouldn't treat your workshop tools like that.

- If you've got any wall space, try putting up a rack or some rails, buying a load of those S-shaped hooks, and hanging as much as possible up there. Most utensils have a hole in the end of the handle. This is what it's for.

- Most of the long-handled stuff like wooden spoons, ladles and spatulas can be stuffed into a tallish bucket-shaped jar or can. Make sure it's heavy enough not to tip over when you grab for a spoon.

- Use all available wall space for shelving. Even thin shelves (80–100mm) will be fine for herbs, spices, oil, jars and tins, glasses, booze, condiments and so on. They don't stick out any further than a radiator; just make sure you space them far enough apart if you're storing tall things on them.

- If your shelves are above a radiator, try not to use them for anything that will be affected by heat – a few examples are sauce, ketchup, canned fish, or beer. Boiled lager? Lovely.

- Add hooks to the bottom or front of shelves for mugs, jugs, tea towels, oven gloves (if they're close to the oven) and so on.

- Free-standing steel workshop shelving units are amazingly cheap and will take a load of weight – just fine for crockery, tins, machinery, bottles, bowls, saucepans, and other hefty, bulky items. If you don't like their grungy industrial look, slap a bit of paint on or even run a bit of net curtain wire across the top and hang suitably decorative material over the front.

- Kitchen trolleys on wheels (often sold as 'butchers' blocks') are handy if you're desperately short of worktop space. Try to get a solidly built one with brakes on the wheels. You don't want it wobbling or shifting when you're using a sharp knife.

Work smart: clean as you go

It might not sound like huge fun, but unless you have a housemaid, or don't mind everybody around you wanting to kill you, it's a good idea to be tidy when you cook. It's also safer and more efficient. This is why chefs keep their workstations spotless. Being surrounded by piles of slippery peelings and wobbly piles of used pans when you're trying to do something delicate and dangerous is really not a good idea.

If you're close to a bin, use it often. If not, allocate a bit of worktop for waste – peelings, eggshells, chicken skin etc – and empty it between operations.

Swapping between cooking, say, main course and pudding? Or fish and salad? Wash your hands, knife, chopping board – anything else you're going to re-use. Good hygiene and good sense.

Keep a tea towel handy – over your shoulder if you like that casual cheffy look. They're good for handling hot pans, opening stiff jars, wiping up small spillages and many more jobs (including annoying the cat with if you're bored).

If you've got a dishwasher, excellent – bang pans, utensils and bowls in it as you've finished with them.

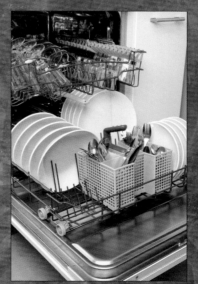

Out of sight, out of trouble. If not, stack stuff in the sink. But not so much that you can't get to the taps any more, or have to empty it again to put the plug in.

Once a dish is safely simmering or roasting, give your cooking area a swift wipe down. But beware – hobs stay hot for quite a while.

8 THS **1**   **2**   **3**   **4**   **5**   **6**   **7**   8

1 millimetre (mm)   0.04 inch   1 inch   25 mm
1 metre (m)   3.28 feet   LENGTH   1 foot   0.3 m
mm   1 kilometre (km)   0.62 mile   1 mile   1.6 km

1 0   2 0   3 0   4 0   5 0   6 0   7 0   8 0   9 0   10 0   11 0   12 0   13 0   14 0   15 0   16 0   17 0   18 0   19 0   20 0

CHAPTER 2
COMPONENTS

Input equals output. You only get out what you put in. Garbage in, garbage out. You get the idea – and it's even more important when you're cooking, as you eat the end result. Hopefully.

So choosing decent ingredients is crucial. But that doesn't mean spending a fortune on single-variety hand-knitted balsamic vinegar or rare-breed beef from beer-fed, daily-massaged cows with their own suite at the Kyoto Hilton. It means knowing a bit about what's good and what isn't, being a bit clever about shopping, and keeping a few vital bits in stock so you can throw together a last-minute meal without running to the nearest inconvenience store and coming back with a lucky dip of frozen rubbish.

A well-stocked store cupboard, a decent selection of herbs and spices and a few intelligently-chosen ingredients in the freezer can be the foundation of thousands of different dishes. If you also get the hang of when to buy what, from in-season veg to surfing sell-by dates, you can eat cheaply, reliably, and very well any day of the year. Plus you get to lash round the shops in record time, meaning you get to the pub quicker. Isn't that the point?

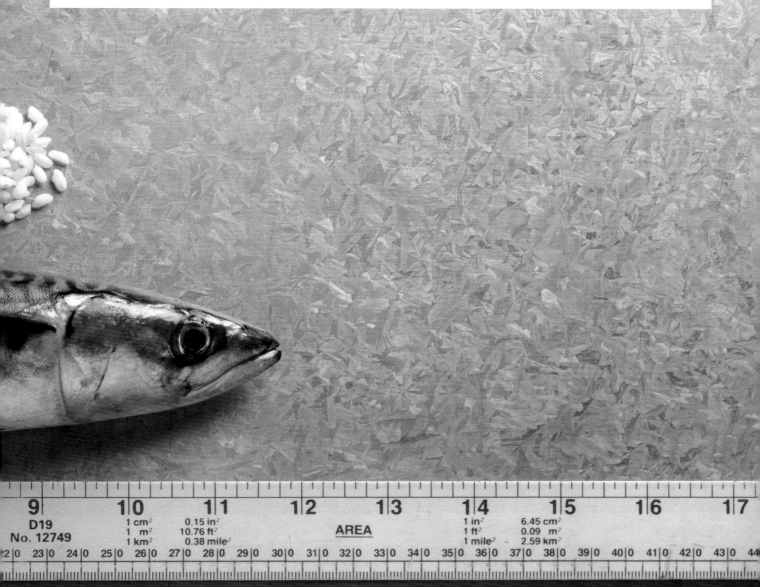

9 10 11 12 13 14 15 16 17

D19
No. 12749

1 cm²	0.15 in²
1 m²	10.76 ft²
1 km²	0.38 mile²

AREA

1 in²	6.45 cm²
1 ft²	0.09 m²
1 mile²	2.59 km²

2|0 23|0 24|0 25|0 26|0 27|0 28|0 29|0 30|0 31|0 32|0 33|0 34|0 35|0 36|0 37|0 38|0 39|0 40|0 41|0 42|0 43|0 44

Cupboard lovelies: stuff you must have

Very few people have the time or energy to go shopping for food every day. So on those days when you just want to make a meal without hassle, a well-stocked cupboard is your best friend.

You need a good store of general ingredients that you can use to make a range of meals – varied enough not to be boring, but reliable enough so that you don't need to rack your brains every time. Here's how to build up your own stock of invaluable basics.

JARS

In the cupboard's fine until they're opened, when in most cases you need to keep them in the fridge.

- **Anchovies**
- **Olives**
- **Jam, marmalade, lemon curd, Marmite, etc** – for toast and snacks. Also see 'emergency pud' below.

CANS

Keep these in a dry, coolish cupboard. Don't forget to keep them restocked when you run low.

- **Tomatoes** – chopped, preferably. You don't need the ones with garlic, herbs or whatever.
- **Beans** – baked beans if you like them; haricot, cannellini and/or red kidney beans too. Chick peas can also be useful.
- **Fish** – Tuna, salmon, herring or whichever fish you prefer.
- **Coconut milk** – the secret ingredient in most Thai curries, also good in many other dishes.
- **Sponge puddings** – excellent emergency pud.
- **Custard** – goes well with the sponge pud.

BOTTLES

Keep oil out of bright light, but if it gets cold and turns cloudy, don't worry – just put it on a radiator and it'll clear.

- **Olive oil** – you don't need extra virgin for cooking. Buy a big can of no-frills olive oil from a local corner shop or cash'n'carry, then if you want to look classy use a funnel to decant it into a nice bottle.
- **Sesame oil** – brilliant for Chinese or Thai cooking. Good for salad dressing too. Buy it from a Chinese shop if you can, as it's much cheaper.
- **Hazelnut, walnut, super-duper extra virgin single estate organic olive or other posh oil** – if you insist and can afford it. Nut oils are good in salad dressing.
- **Groundnut, sunflower, safflower, rapeseed, corn oil and so on** – all these 'light' oils are OK for frying, particularly deep frying, because they'll get very hot before starting to pong. But they don't taste particularly special.
- **Plonk** – it's always useful to keep a splash of wine handy, for you or the dish, so unfinished bottles are good. But remember, if you wouldn't drink it, don't cook with it. The only place for fortnight-old stale party leftovers is down the sink.

PACKETS

Again, keep somewhere cool, dry, and out of the sun.

- **Rice** – long grain's the classic, but risotto or paella rice is good too.
- **Pasta and/or noodles** – fresh pasta can be great occasionally, but dried is just fine, and dirt cheap. Straight-to-wok noodles are a huge timesaver.
- **Couscous** – excellent for salads (as is bulgar wheat) as well as main meals.
- **Lentils** – preferably the green French ones, sometimes called 'Lentilles de Puy'. They're tastier than the orange or brown ones.
- **Flour** – self-raising if you fancy cakes, plain anyway, and bread flour if you want to have a crack at baking your own. Bread flour is sometimes called 'strong' flour.
- **Sugar** – for baking, tea, and occasional other use.
- **Butter** – you don't have to keep this in the fridge unless it's hot. Get a decent, airtight butter dish, keep it out, and it'll be spreadable instantly.
- **Stock** – many supermarkets do packets or tubs of chicken, beef, veg or fish stock. Great as a basis for soups, stews and so on.

FRIDGE STUFF

These are the long-life essentials you should usually have lurking on a shelf:

- **Bacon** – bacon bits or 'lardons' are handy, but it doesn't take long to chop up a few rashers. Try to buy from a butcher, as the packet stuff is usually watery.
- **Smoked mackerel** – peppered or not, whichever you prefer. Lasts ages and can be used in all sorts of ways.
- **Eggs** – free-range are nicer, but watch out for weasely packaging that says 'barn eggs', 'barn fresh', 'farmyard laid' or anything similar. Unless it actually says 'free range' it isn't.
- **A ham** – if you've got a lot of people to cook for, shrink-wrapped gammon is good. It lasts a long time, will do several meals, and can be surprisingly tasty (see page 88).

VEG

You can keep these in the fridge, but potatoes, garlic, onions, and many root veg will be fine in a basket, string bag or other cool, airy spot.

- Potatoes
- Onions
- Chilli peppers
- Red pepper
- Tomatoes
- Carrots

FREEZER FOOD

Again, stock up once and you'll never have a 'Cripes, there's nothing to eat' moment.

- **Peas, beans or other green veg** – cook fast from frozen, instant healthiness.
- **Sausages, lamb or pork chops, chicken portions, or any other small (hence swiftly defrostable) bits of meat.**
- **Stewing beef or lamb, and/or mince.**
- **Some fish** – whole trout, salmon steaks, white fish fillets, smoked fish (good for the kedgeree recipe). Peeled prawns are particularly easy and quick.
- **Leftovers** – though some things, like cooked rice, don't freeze well. Never hurts to stick some spare food in a bag or a plastic, lidded, takeaway carton.
- **Ice cream** – it's what the freezer's for.

PERFECT 10: CUPBOARD ESSENTIALS

Here are the ten things you must keep in the kitchen at all times. Given all of these you can lash together an edible meal with almost any other ingredients, or, at a pinch, none. Run out at your peril.

1. Olive oil
2. Onions
3. Tinned tomatoes
4. Pasta (or rice if you prefer it)
5. Salt and pepper
6. Potatoes
7. Herb(s) (see page 26)
8. Tinned tuna
9. Garlic
10. Eggs

Tasty bits: herbs, spices, sauces and so on

Almost everything needs a bit of seasoning. From a sprinkle of salt and pepper to a handful of herbs or a giant dollop of ketchup, it can make the difference between bland human fodder and lip-smackingly tasty dishes. So you need to get your seasoning selection sorted.

SEASONINGS

- **Salt** – Some people insist on crystal, rock or sea salt, others don't care. The bigger crystals taste somehow saltier, which is something to do with their shape and the way your taste buds work. Whichever you choose, just don't overdo it.
- **Pepper** – Buy black peppercorns and a grinder. They're not expensive, and a half-decent grinder should last years. Those tubs of ground white pepper are pointless and tasteless, the pre-ground black stuff nearly as bad. Pink peppercorns (not really peppercorns at all, but who cares) are a staple of proper Chinese cooking, but it's a subtle difference in flavour.

HERBS

- **Sage, rosemary, thyme, oregano, and bay** – Essential, and nearly as good dried as fresh. Fennel seeds have an interesting aniseedy flavour too. There's a good all-purpose mixture called Herbes de Provence which contains most of them, but don't confuse it with the useless 'mixed herbs' which seems to be sweepings from the factory floor.
- **Basil** – This doesn't dry too well, but most supermarkets sell plants that will last long enough for you to strip them of their foliage and eat it, provided you keep them watered and somewhere with daylight.

- **Coriander** – Not the same as the dried seeds or ground spice, its peppery, spicy flavour is good for Indian, Thai, and Mexican food, and is often available in bunches from Indian shops. Easily mistaken for...
- **Parsley** – This comes in two varieties: curly parsley – a bit of a British cliché – and flat-leaved, which looks rather like coriander but has a milder, fresher flavour. Good with fish, potatoes, and in salads.
- **Mint** – Best bought fresh, it's great on potatoes and makes a mean cup of digestion-soothing tea. Also fine in cocktails like Pimm's, mojitos and more.
- **Chives** – Oniony, but milder and fresher-tasting. Salads, spuds, fish, all work well with this.
- **Fennel and dill** – Both feathery, aniseedy herbs that work a treat with fish.
- **Tarragon, fenugreek, hyssop, sorrel, savory etc** – Mild-flavoured herbs; tarragon can work well with chicken, fenugreek is mildly curryish. Experiment by all means.

If you've got space for a windowsill plant pot, why not produce your own fresh herbs? Supermarkets or garden centres sell small thyme, rosemary, parsley, oregano (or the almost identical marjoram) and sage plants, among others. A small bay plant, for instance, can grow new leaves just as quickly as you can use them.

SPICES

- **Ground cumin and coriander** – Chili con carne (see page 66) wouldn't be the same without these two. Likewise curries and couscous.
- **Nutmeg, cinnamon, allspice, cloves** – Mostly used for cakes and pies, though cinnamon also pops up in North African cooking, and a dash of nutmeg can be excellent with mashed potatoes or parsnips. Cloves can be a bit much, so go easy – one or two's plenty for most things.
- **Cayenne pepper, paprika, and pimentón** – All vaguely similar reddish, warm-to-hot powders. Pimentón, sometimes called smoked paprika, is what gives much Spanish food its distinctive smoky flavour – it's the red stuff in that Spanish sausage, chorizo.
- **Five-spice or seven-spice** – A handy mix of common Chinese or Thai spices; a good shortcut to authentic-ish flavour.
- **Seeds and berries** – Cumin, coriander, and cardamom seeds are handy for curries and so on. Fennel seeds are excellent in small quantities with almost anything. Mustard seeds can add a bit of zip to dishes, and Juniper berries – one of the main ingredients in gin – are superb with game or rich stews.

SAUCES

- **Mustard, ketchup, brown sauce, pickle, BBQ sauce etc** – Very much up to you. But get decent stuff – it lasts ages (unless you drown everything in ketchup, in which case stop it now) and the better brands are less acid and sugary. Mustard can be good for making salad dressing too (see page 102),

- **Vinegar** – Good vinegar – cider or wine vinegar – is useful around the kitchen. Malt vinegar (or 'non-brewed condiment' if you're really cheaping out) is good on chips. Don't confuse them.
- **Balsamic vinegar** – Not actually the same stuff. Also stonkingly costly and annoyingly middle-class, but can work wonders on salads and roast veg, among many other things. Buy the best you can; some cheap ones are fairly poor. Look for 'Aceto Balsamico di Modena' on the label. Made in the same place as Ferraris, and nearly as expensive.
- **Soy sauce** – A Chinese staple – they often use it instead of salt – and also good to add a bit of tangy richness to some meat or veg dishes.
- **Fish sauce** – This smells worse than you can imagine. A few drops, though, will add salty goodness to Thai food. Usually Vietnamese, it's also known as Nam Pla or Nuoc Mam.
- **Worcestershire sauce** – An English institution and, like most of them, a bit of a mixed blessing. A splash will spice up a gravy or soup, though. And a Bloody Mary.

STOCK

- **Cubes** – Fairly convenient but pretty artificial-tasting; don't rely on them to make your food taste of anything other than stock cube. They're salty, too, so watch how much extra salt you add.
- **Liquid** – A bit more convenient still, and somehow less plastic-tasting than the cubes. Still salty, though. Easy to add too much and drown the flavour, so glug lightly.
- **Powder** – Marigold vegetable stock is pretty but make sure it dissolves properly. Lumpy bits are horrid.
- **Real stock** – If you've got a leftover chicken carcass, fish trimmings or meat bones it's a simple job to make yourself some real stock (see page 57). Incredibly useful stuff. Many shops also sell pots of stock that are a decent alternative if you can't be bothered to make your own.

Speed shopping: supercharge the supermarket

Learn to shop like a pro and it'll make you into the Schumacher of the supermarket. Because, let's face it, nobody really wants to spend more time than necessary in one of those clangy, over-bright, people-fleecing sheds.

So here's how you can get in, get some good stuff, and get out without wanting to bludgeon somebody to death with a bag of frozen broccoli.

Remember, supermarkets are designed for a very specific reason – to get as much money out of your wallet as possible, by keeping you there as long as they can, and making sure you pass as many aisles as possible on your way from one necessity to the next. So subvert their system. Refuse to be steered, and go your own way.

■ Try not to go shopping when you're starving – you'll come out with a huge pile of snacks and no proper food. The opposite is true, too. Go in just after a big meal and you won't buy anything.

■ If you use the supermarket fairly often, get one of those trolley tokens that fake a pound coin, and stick it on your key ring. It'll save that annoying dash to Customer Service when you find you haven't got a quid.

Basket case: get organised, get essentials, get out

- The fresh fruit and vegetable section is almost always by the entrance, to give an impression of freshness and wholesome natural produce. But you don't want to buy veg first. Go straight past it.
- First stop ought to be the meat or fish counters. After all, that's the mainstay of the meal. Unless you're veggie of course, in which case by all means ignore this.
- Once at the relevant counter, check out what looks fresh, seasonal, and in good condition – see page 32.
- Particularly if it's getting near the end of the day, check out what's being marked down. If there's an assistant hovering with a price gun, sneak off for a minute or two and watch what they're up to. They may be about to cut the price of just what you were about to buy.
- The meat or fish should have given you a few ideas about what to cook, and what goes with it. So once you've chosen your main ingredients, head back to the veg counter and buy whatever you fancy to go with it (see pages 82–83 for a few ideas).
- In the same style, now's also a good time to buy pasta, rice, couscous and so on, plus tins, bottles, and jars of stuff.
- Then, still with the number of meals in mind, head towards drinks and desserts.
- Once you're quite sure all of your meals are accounted for, that's the time to race up and down all the other aisles collecting the dull everyday stuff like loo paper, cat litter, and washing powder.
- Get frozen stuff last, or your ice cream will be soup by the time you get home.
- Once you hit the checkout, put the heavy, bulky stuff on the belt first. That'll be a firm foundation to put softer stuff on top of. You really don't want a jumbo-sized bag of barbecue charcoal on top of your eggs or tomatoes.
- Keep a couple of trays or boxes in your boot to stop stuff sliding about, unless your supermarket offers boxes, which is very handy. Or unless your route home is via a drag strip and therefore has no corners.
- Go home. Put it away. Get on with your life.

LISTMANIA: GET IT ORGANISED

- First, work out how many meals you'll have to shop for, and whether you're catering for 15 or just yourself. Splitting your list up by Monday/Tuesday/etc is a reasonable way to go.
- Keep it loose – there's no harm in just writing 'meat x 5' or 'green veg x 3'. That'll give you enough flexibility to pick the best, or best value, ingredients when you get to the shop (see the supermarket shopping tips opposite).
- Then list the staples you've run out of, and anything you've noticed is getting dangerously low in your store cupboard. It's a good idea to roam around the kitchen while you're making your list, opening the fridge, freezer, and cupboards and checking what's there.
- If you're very organised, clip your list to the fridge or hang it on the wall and fill it in throughout the week as you run out of, or short of, things. But don't forget to cross them off if you've made a sudden dash to the local shop and bought some of the items that you'd listed.
- Only when you've got your food and drink list done should you move on to household necessaries like bog rolls, washing powder etc. One thing at a time. Stay focused.
- Take a pen or pencil with you to the shop, to tick things off as you buy them, or you'll forget what the first things you bought were and go round in endless circles.
- If you're on a tight budget, compare your list with the final receipt when you get home, and try to spot what was surprisingly expensive, and where you went off-piste and bought pointless but attractive rubbish.

List making might seem like hassle, but once you get used to shopping with a list going without one will feel like bungee jumping without a rope.

The specialists: shops with the right stuff

Supermarkets are convenient, and often (if not always) cheap. But they're not the only option. There are the old classics like the butcher, fishmonger, greengrocer, baker or delicatessen, farmers' markets if you live out of town, and a confusing array of ethnic shops if you don't.

Specialist shops may sell some unfamiliar products, they won't have the comforting, explanatory signs and labels of your local megastore, and they'll sometimes rely on you having a bit of knowledge to buy the right thing. But they're the best way to buy a whole load of food, kit and so on that you won't find in the supermarket aisles. They're also a great source of advice, can save you quite a bit of money, and can be far more fun than the usual trolley dash.

CLASSIC FOOD SHOPS

Not all of these are any good. There are bakers, greengrocers, and butchers in most areas, and some of them are really not worth bothering with. One test is whether they sell everything pre-packed. If they're just buying in vacuum-packed meat, cling-filmed veg, or bagged sliced bread and reselling it, walk away. This doesn't generally apply to fishmongers, because it's not a big enough market to make a pre-packed fish shop profitable. If you run across a shop with a good range of stock, and there's someone there who seems to know what they're doing, treasure it. Go often.

Don't be afraid to ask about their stock. If you don't know what a cut of meat or a particular fish is, they should be able to tell you. And don't be afraid to ask for advice. They should know how to prepare, and often cook, most of the things they sell. If they haven't got something, they ought to be able to suggest an alternative. If they appear clueless or surly (unless you're being a nuisance at a very busy time, or when they're closing), think twice about going back. It's their lookout if they lose customers. A good shop will be happy to help.

Try to explore the outer limits of their stock. Unfamiliar cuts of meat, weird-looking vegetables or scary fish could be a great discovery, given a bit of guidance. If it's horrible, tell them next time you're in; they might knock some money off your bill.

If you've got an ingredient in mind but they haven't got it, ask if they can order it for you. Most will. Alternatively if there's something you think would sell, suggest it. Bakers, for instance, can usually try a small batch of new loaves or rolls without huge outlay.

Expect to pay more than supermarket prices, but also expect better quality, a wider choice, and some expert help with things like jointing and boning meat or cleaning and gutting fish.

DELICATESSENS

These vary wildly – from lovely, knowledgeable shops packed with stunning and rare cheeses, meats, herbs, and wines, right through to grubby little tourist traps with a food section comprising two dusty boxes of pasta and a dead wasp.

A good deli often has an area it specialises in – cheese, for instance, or Spanish food, or smoked fish, or virtually anything else you can imagine. That's a good place to start when sampling their goods.

Delis can be expensive. Sometimes that's because their stuff is exclusive, unusual, and valuable. Sometimes it's because it's a rip-off. Be wary, and apply the same tests as anywhere else. Is their stock all pre-packed? Do they know much about what they're selling? Can they give useful advice?

FARMERS' MARKETS

The farmers' market, though it's modelled after the age-old local market, is a relatively new thing, and many have strict rules about how far away their produce comes from (stretched a bit wider in central London) and what sort of things are sold there. But not all, so be aware.

If you're an organic eater, watch your step. Not all of the produce will meet official organic standards. With some things, like wild fish or game, that doesn't matter. But some stallholders will fudge the issue. Just because the carrots are dirty that doesn't make them organic.

This is a great chance to meet the people who actually make your food. Don't waste it. Be adventurous and inquisitive. Make friends with the person who makes your favourite cheese, or grows amazing garlic, or bakes the best loaf you've ever tasted. They'll often have tips and even recipes for you.

FARM SHOPS

Farm shops can be full of wholesome, fresh local produce. But not all are – there's a lot of frozen food and it's comparatively rare to find organic veg.

Their stock is usually designed for long shelf-life, as they have a smallish and rather irregular stream of customers. But that might mean you get great local hams and smoked fish, preserves, pickles, and things like good bread flour.

They do have a real link to seasonal produce, so when fruit or vegetables come into season (see page 32), they'll often have piles of them at good prices.

ETHNIC SHOPS

The first trick is spotting which ethnic group runs a particular local shop. If it's got the word *souk* in the name it's probably North African; *dükkân* is Turkish; *sklep* is Polish; the distinctive characters of Chinese or the languages of the Indian subcontinent should be a clue too.

Each will have a particular specialisation, which has a lot to do with their national cuisine. Many will sell basics like rice, oil and so on in huge quantities at remarkably low prices.

- Turkish-run shops often have a great selection of fruit, vegetables and fresh herbs. The long, mild green peppers are excellent.
- Polish or Eastern European shops will, of course, have some excellent sausage, and beer strong enough to run your Skoda on.
- North African shops will sell couscous (see page 55) and all the kit to go with it, such as the superb but viciously hot sauce, harissa (see page 71), and the special pan you can use to cook it in, called a couscousière. It's just a metal pot with a steamer on top, but it's huge, cheap, and versatile.
- Chinese, Thai, and Vietnamese shops will sell sesame oil, soy sauce, fish sauce, coconut milk and so on – usually far cheaper than supermarkets.
- Bangladeshi shops will often have a freezer section full of fish, including some terrifyingly large tilapia (a sort of giant carp), but also good value shellfish.

Beware of chilli peppers. Many cuisines use hot chillies, some in mouth-puckering quantities. But it's very difficult to tell which are mild and which are thermonuclear. Ask, or be very careful using them. Test a tiny bite before adding them to a dish, and keep a glass of beer or milk handy just in case.

Meat counters, whether Muslim-approved, religiously-certified halal or otherwise, can look random and, frankly, grubby if you're used to squeaky-clean packaged supermarket food. Are you going to cook something for long enough or hot enough to kill any bugs? If yes, you're fine. Stewing lamb is a good cheap bet. Lightly grilled chicken, though, might not be quite so clever. If you have any doubts, avoid.

Season's eatings: what's best when

Thanks to air travel and high-tech greenhouses, you can get almost any food at any time of the year. But it's often either insanely pricy, in dodgy condition, or has been flown in on a dirty great cargo jet from some of the world's furthest-away and politically dodgiest regimes.

So here's a guide to what's in season in the UK (and the closer bits of Europe for some fruit) and when. It's not exact, because many of these vary a bit every year, but do look for in-season food in the shops – it'll be fresh, therefore tasty.

This sort of thing is why they invented the Internet – for a detailed, user-friendly and regularly updated list try www.eattheseasons.co.uk, and there's a handy table at www.bbcgoodfood.com/content/local/seasonal/table/.

JANUARY

Vegetables	Fruit	Meat	Fish
beetroot	apples	duck	clams
brussels	lemons	guinea fowl	cockles
cauliflower	oranges	hare	haddock
celery	pears	partridge	hake
leeks	walnuts	venison	halibut
parsnips			lemon sole
potatoes			monkfish
rhubarb			mussels
swedes			oysters
turnips			plaice
			turbot

FEBRUARY

Vegetables	Fruit	Meat	Fish
brussels	bananas	guinea fowl	clams
cauliflower	lemons	hare	cockles
leeks	oranges	venison	haddock, hake
parsnips	pears		halibut, lemon
potatoes	pineapples		sole, mussels
rhubarb			oysters
swedes			salmon
			turbot

MARCH

Vegetables	Fruit	Meat	Fish
cauliflower	bananas		cockles, cod
leeks	kiwi fruit		hake
purple sprouting	lemons		lemon sole
broccoli	oranges		mussels
rhubarb	pineapples		oysters
spring onions			salmon

APRIL

Vegetables	Fruit	Meat	Fish
asparagus	bananas	wood pigeon	cockles
broccoli			cod
radishes			salmon
rhubarb			sea trout
rocket			
spinach			
spring onions			
watercress			

MAY

Vegetables	Fruit	Meat	Fish
asparagus	cherries	lamb	cod
broccoli		wood pigeon	crabs
carrots			Dover sole
new potatoes			halibut
radishes			lemon sole
rhubarb			plaice
rocket			salmon
spinach			sea bass
spring onions			sea trout
watercress			

JUNE

Vegetables	Fruit	Meat	Fish
artichokes	cherries	lamb	cod
asparagus	strawberries	wood pigeon	crab
aubergines			Dover sole
broad beans			haddock
broccoli			halibut
carrots,			herring
courgettes			lemon sole
fennel			lobster
mangetout			mackerel
new potatoes			plaice
peas			salmon
radishes			sardines
rocket			sea bass
runner beans			sea trout
spring onions			
turnips			
watercress			

SEPTEMBER

Vegetables	Fruit	Meat	Fish
artichokes	blackberries	duck	clams
aubergines	grapes	grouse	cod
beetroot	melons	guinea fowl	crab
broccoli	peaches	lamb	Dover sole
carrots	pears	rabbit	grey mullet
courgettes	plums	venison	haddock
cucumber	tomatoes	wood pigeon	halibut
fennel			herring
garlic, leeks			lemon sole
mangetout			lobster
onions			mackerel
parsnips			monkfish
peas, peppers			plaice
potatoes			salmon
radishes, rocket			sardines
runner beans			scallops
sweetcorn			sea bass
turnips			squid
watercress			turbot

JULY

Vegetables	Fruit	Meat	Fish
artichokes	apricots	lamb	cod
aubergines	blackberries	rabbit	crab
beetroot	blueberries	wood pigeon	Dover sole
broad beans	melons		haddock
broccoli	peaches		halibut
carrots	raspberries		herring
courgettes	strawberries		lemon sole
cucumber	tomatoes		lobster
fennel			mackerel
French beans			plaice
garlic			salmon
mangetout			sardines
new potatoes			scallops
onions			sea bass
peas			sea trout
potatoes			
radishes			
rocket			
runner beans			
turnips			
watercress			

OCTOBER

Vegetables	Fruit	Meat	Fish
artichokes	apples	duck	clams, crab,
beetroot	chestnuts	goose	grey mullet
broccoli	grapes	grouse	haddock, hake,
carrots	pears	guinea fowl	halibut, lemon
celery	tomatoes	hare	sole, lobster
fennel	walnuts	partridge	mackerel
leeks		rabbit	monkfish
onions		venison	mussels
parsnips		wood pigeon	oysters, plaice
potatoes			scallops, sea
swedes, turnips			bass, squid
watercress			turbot

NOVEMBER

Vegetables	Fruit	Meat	Fish
artichokes	apples	duck	clams
beetroot	chestnuts	goose	haddock, hake
celery	cranberries	grouse	halibut, lemon
leeks	pears	guinea fowl	sole, lobster
parsnips	walnuts	hare	monkfish
potatoes		partridge	mussels
swedes		pheasant	oysters, plaice
turnips		rabbit	scallops, sea
		venison	bass, squid
		wood pigeon	turbot

AUGUST

Vegetables	Fruit	Meat	Fish
artichokes	apricots	lamb	cod
aubergines	blackberries	rabbit	crab
beetroot	blueberries	wood pigeon	Dover sole
broad beans	melons		grey mullet
broccoli	peaches		haddock
carrots	plums		halibut
courgettes	raspberries		herring
cucumber	redcurrants		lemon sole
fennel	tomatoes		lobster
French beans			mackerel
garlic			monkfish
mangetout			plaice
onions			salmon
peas			sardines
peppers			scallops
potatoes			sea bass
radishes			
rocket			
runner beans			
watercress			

DECEMBER

Vegetables	Fruit	Meat	Fish
beetroot	apples	duck, goose	clams
brussels	chestnuts	grouse, guinea	haddock, hake
cauliflower	cranberries	fowl, hare	halibut, lemon
celery	pears	partridge	sole, monkfish
leeks	tangerines	pheasant	mussels
parsnips	walnuts	rabbit	oysters, plaice
potatoes		venison	scallops, sea
swedes, turnips		wood pigeon	bass, turbot

Rotten or ripe?
Spot if it's off

Freshness is vital to how anything tastes. Make dinner with a pile of fresh ingredients and you can't go wrong. But use a bit of rancid fish and it's immediately dustbin material. Make sure that what you're buying is in good nick. Here's how.

- Sell-by dates are a guide, but only that. They don't tell you how stuff's been stored, or whether it's any good. Check them but don't rely entirely on them. Here's a trick: If you look at the back of a supermarket shelf you might find something a few days younger – of course, they try to get rid of the older stuff first. Break the system.
- Fish should look like they could swim away at any moment. Bright, clear eyes, shiny skin, pink gills, bright colours if it's something like mullet, trout, or mackerel. Not dull, grey, and exhausted. Smell it if you can; you should get a briny sea tang, not a noseful of overpowering fishiness.
- Meat ought to be a healthy pink colour, not grey or an artificial brownish-red (cheap mince or sausage meat can be dyed). Pork is lighter, beef darker, and lamb between the two. Again, smell it if you can – if it's strong, it's getting on a bit.
- Vegetables should be firm, crisp, and lacking in brown bits, bruises, and soggy patches. Some, like onions or potatoes, may sprout if they're badly kept. Others will just go soft. If you've seen old biddies squeezing fruit and veg, this is why. It irritates greengrocers no end, but largely because they're worried about the Old Lady Mafia spreading the word about their dodgy produce.

Cheesy choice: stinky can be good. Sometimes

- Fruit is similar to vegetables. Apples and pears should be solid; oranges, lemons and the like will give a little, but if they squish like a half-deflated tennis ball run away. Bananas give off a gas that will ripen other fruit faster if they're next to it in a bowl, so keep them separate unless you need things to get ripe quickly.
- Dairy produce like milk, butter, cheese and so on will spoil easily if kept too warm, so make sure you buy it from the fridge. Watch out for milk that looks bitty, or butter that smells. Cheese is supposed to smell, though, so if you like yours ripe choose the stuff nearest its sell-by date. Supermarkets often sell perfectly good brie or camembert cheap because it's a bit too ripe for them; check the bargain shelf.
- Eggs are almost impossible to test in the shop, but they do last several weeks (longer in the fridge) so check the date on the box carefully (and also check that none are cracked).
- Dried goods like rice, dried pasta and so on are unlikely to be off, but you never know. Aged pasta, for instance, will refuse to soften properly. This is a case for checking the date.
- Tins which are bulgy, rusty or deformed are a definite no. A minor dent is up to you, but anything that causes a hole, even a pinprick, will spoil the contents.
- Jars, like tins, ought to be almost everlasting, but check that the lid hasn't gone rusty round the bottom rim and let air in.
- Vacuum-packed food is usually a good thing, but again, check that the pack's intact. Meat will last ages in the fridge if it's been vac-packed, and steaks are sometimes matured this way.

Put it away: how to store food

You don't have to refrigerate everything to death. Cupboards are perfectly fine for dried goods like rice, pasta, flour, sugar and so on. Herbs, spices, and oils generally like being kept out of direct sunlight, but are otherwise fine on a shelf or in a cupboard.

Bread will stay fresh in a bread bin or cupboard away from anything smelly. Most condiments like mustard, brown sauce, and ketchup don't have to be in the fridge; the label might warn you to keep some refrigerated, but any cool, dark place will be OK – except for anything that's mayo-based, which should always be kept in the fridge.

Even many vegetables – potatoes, onions, garlic, carrots and most root veg, cabbages – are fine in a string bag, well-ventilated shelf, or basket. Just don't let them get moist or clammy.

Tins? Anywhere dryish. It's also worth investing in a few plastic storage containers, Tupperware style. This might seem deeply sad and mumsy, but they're handy for random odds and sods like half-used packets of stuff. Think of them as the kitchen equivalent of the Old Holborn tins your granddad kept in his shed, full of wood screws and 3/8in dibble grommets.

STAY COOL: FRIDGE WISDOM

Try to keep things that have to be refrigerated, like meat, fish, and salad, in the right spot – fish and meat near the bottom where it's coldest, dairy and eggs in the middle, salad veg in the drawers where it won't get frozen, and things that only need light cooling – like beer – in the door shelves. Don't cram the fridge too full, don't put hot food in (it'll warm everything else up), keep food covered or sealed to stop smells mingling, defrost it regularly, and if you've got a thermometer handy, check your temperature – a domestic fridge should be between 2 and 4°C.

SELL-BY DATES: OBEY OR IGNORE?

These are more for the shop's convenience than yours. And even if your food's past its 'use by' date, it may still be edible. Milk and eggs, for instance, will still be usable, if refrigerated, for quite a while past their sell-by dates. The key is to smell it, taste it, inspect it for mould and soft bits and, above all, use your common sense. Things like spices and condiments will usually be fine for ages, but may just lose their strength. You can always compensate by using a bit more.

But don't take absurd risks with meat, fish (particularly shellfish) and anything defrosted. Projectile vomiting is not a good way to find out that something's past its best. Here's an annoying slogan for you: If in doubt, chuck it out.

LESS THAN ZERO: FREEZER TIPS

Despite what most people think, food doesn't go bad if it's frozen for a long time. Given an uninterrupted power supply, you could freeze something today and your great-grandchildren could eat it safely in a century's time.

But they wouldn't enjoy it much. Over time, food suffers from freezer burn – where it gets dehydrated and greyish-brown dry spots appear – and the likelihood is that it'll become dry, the texture will change, and it'll taste much less appetising. Yum. But the colder you store stuff, the longer it'll stay decent. So check your freezer's star rating, which means the following:

★	-6°C
★★	-12°C
★★★	-18°C
★★★★	-18°C with -26°C fast freeze setting

And here's a rough guide to how long you can store food in a 3- or 4-star rated freezer, in months:

Vegetables	12–15	White fish	8–10
Meat joints or mince	10–12	Prawns, shellfish	6
Poultry	12	Oily fish	4
Bacon, sausages	4–6	Ice cream	6

Portion control, we have a problem

Do you know how much to buy? Do you come back from the shops with a random collection of ingredients, then have to juggle quantities and portions? Here's a quick guide to how much of everything you need per meal, per person. It varies according to how much you burn, so be flexible. But don't overdo it and get porky. See page 140 for more on that.

- Meat and fish: 150g (raw)
- Pasta: 100g (dry)
- Rice: 75g (dry)
- Veg: 80–120g
- Cheese: 100g

CHAPTER 3
GET GOING

If you give a man a fish, as the saying goes, you feed him for a day. But if you teach him how to fish, you feed him for life. It doesn't mention what happens if you teach a man how to fillet a fish, but that's what this bit is all about – basic cooking skills, to use for all manner of things.

It's all very well following recipes, but when somebody's just invited themselves round and you've got 20 minutes and a totally random fridgeful of food, the latest glossy celebrity chef's book is going to be as much use as a semolina kayak. What you need is enough culinary suss to look at a heap of ingredients and go 'That goes with that, I could use some of that on the side, I've got a bit of something else in the cupboard, and I'll prepare it like this.'

And that's what, hopefully, you can pick up here and over the next couple of chapters. If this is a workshop manual, here's the bit where you find out which way to turn the screwdriver. And no, you don't get pork chops with a left-hand thread.

Top chopping: knife skills

Basically, a knife is a simple device for separating one thing into several bits. A high-powered laser beam would also work, or a chainsaw, or a Jedi lightsabre, but they're more difficult to fit on the knife rack. So a knife will do.

Unfortunately many of the things that you need to cut, until they invent the cubic cow, are slippery, come in tricky shapes, or have fiddly bits. This is where knowing how to handle a knife comes in useful.

What you're trying to achieve is maximum speed and efficiency, with minimum danger and damage to yourself and your food. And there are certain things you need to master to get this right.

THE GRIP

Most people hold a knife with all four fingers and thumb wrapped round the handle. This is fine; it feels natural and it's pretty secure. But chefs, who use knives a lot, tend to vary that. Some hold it further towards the blade, with the forefinger along the top of the blade. Others go even further forward, with the thumb along the side of the blade and the forefinger along the top, or curled opposite the thumb. Try them all while chopping something; you may find that one feels more natural or gives you more control, depending on the size of your hand and the shape of your knife.

THE ACTION

One useful tip is to keep the blade close to your chopping board. Never lift it high in the style of a medieval broadsword, fun though that may be. Keeping your strokes neat and small economises on energy, maximises accuracy, and minimises the chance of disembowelling a passer-by. Keep strokes neat and controlled; if your knife is properly sharp (see page 16) there should be no need to use huge amounts of force.

THE BLADE

Which part you use will vary according to what you're cutting. If you're chopping something finely, like herbs, use the centre of the blade and rock it backwards and forwards, barely lifting it off the board. Using the flat of your other hand on the blade can steady it, but keep fingers well clear. If you need more force, use the heel of the blade (the bit nearest the handle) and cut with a short, tidy stroke. The area near the point of the blade is best for slicing accurately – vegetables like onions and cabbage are best tackled this way.

THE OTHER HAND

Cutting things isn't just a one-handed operation; use your other hand to guide, steady, and support the knife, or to keep whatever you're cutting still and in the right position. The classic style is to use your spare hand to hold the food on the board with your fingers in a rough arch-shape, knuckles towards the blade, guiding the blade with the backs of your fingers. **But keep your fingertips tucked in at all times.** There are finger guards available for the easily scared, but once you've nicked yourself a couple of times you'll definitely remember to do it right anyway.

SKILLED SLICING

Here's how to cut something without adding diced fingertip to the recipe. In this case, a potato, but the technique applies across the board. As it were.

1 Hold your prey down firmly with the fingertips. Arch your fingers so the knife slides down the back of your knuckles and keep your fingertips well back.

2 If you're chopping something round (like a spud) take one slice off the edge, then lay it on the flat side for stability.

3 Repeat, slice by slice, until it's done. Go at your own pace. Slow and safe is better than fast, flashy and mildly maimed.

⚠ HAZARD WARNING!

Always keep your fingers out of the way. This can't be stressed too highly. There's a first aid panel opposite in case it all goes whoops-shaped, but just remember that a sharp knife can cause some pretty major damage if you're stupid or clumsy – or inebriated: chopping with a sharp knife is not a task to tackle after a few bevvies. That's why God invented kebabs.

What to do if it all goes wrong

■ THE FIRST AID KIT

Keep some simple stuff handy – plasters, paracetamol, antiseptic, bandage, tweezers, sharp scissors, aloe vera ointment or other soothing cream. No need for ribcage shears, defibrillators or oxygen tents. Sorry.

■ MINOR CUTS

Raise the wound above the heart until the bleeding stops, make sure it's clean and dry, then put a plaster on it. Stick the plaster across the cut so it holds the edges together. If you're going to carry on cooking, just make sure the plaster doesn't come off and fall in the food. That's why chefs' plasters are bright blue – so they can be spotted easily in the soup.

■ SEVERE BLEEDING

Check there's nothing (glass etc) still in there. But if it's in deep, leave it there – you could make things worse. Press on the wound with a clean tea towel or cloth, and raise it above the level of the heart. Then bandage it firmly. Take paracetamol or ibuprofen if you're in pain – aspirin slows blood clotting.

■ BURNS AND SCALDS

Run them under cold water as quickly as possible, and for at least ten minutes. If it's a nasty one, put a clean, non-fluffy cloth over it to keep it sterile. Cling film will work too. Raise the limb to stop it swelling.

■ CHOKING

Try a sharp wallop between the shoulder blades. If no luck, shove a clenched fist under their breastbone and push in and up, quickly. Check the mouth for obstructions. Repeat until normal service is resumed. If still no luck, call for help.

■ IF IT'S SERIOUS

Call 999 (or 112 – this works in Europe too) if you're in any doubt at all. Some seemingly minor stuff, like small but deep burns, can be nastier than you initially think.

Cutting it: meat is (not) murder

Cavemen must have wasted a lot of time hacking away at half a mammoth with a bit of flint and some deer antlers. These days we have sharp knives and helpful butchers, but it still helps to know a few things.

If you need to cut up a bit of meat, you really only need to know a few simple things.

- Butchers are good at this stuff. It's what they do. Tell them what you're going to use your meat for and they should sort it out for you. If they refuse or mess it up, find a new butcher.
- You need an extremely sharp knife (see page 16). Or preferably two – a biggish one, plus a small pointy one for fiddly bits. A cleaver is fun too but, disappointingly, very rarely useful.
- Meat has a grain, like wood, and it's usually best to cut along it because it's easier, and because you're less likely to hack your lovely bit of prime cut into fibrous dog food.
- A bit of fat doesn't matter. Meat's dry without it. There's no need to winkle out every tiny molecule.
- Bones, too, are often best left in. Cook them with the meat and dispose of them later. They'll add their flavour to a stew or casserole, then they'll be easy to fish out when it's cooked. Can you imagine boneless lamb shanks or oxtail stew? Boring.

FOWL PLAY: JOINTING A CHICKEN
The classic puzzle, but straightforward enough. Keep the shapes of chicken portions in your head, then you know what you're aiming for.

1 Cut the wings off. Hold them out from the body, then chop through the 'armpit' joint. As a rule, the joints are just a little further in than you think.
2 Cut the legs off. Same principle. Then cut through the 'knee' joint, if you need smallish bits.
3 Now the tricky(ish) bit. Holding the body of the chicken firmly, stick the knife in at the top of the breastbone, at about a 30° angle, and run it down the breastbone to separate one breast portion. It helps to use either a knife with a bit of bendiness or a small one here. Then turn the thing round and repeat. It's actually easier to do than it is to describe: just imagine the shape of a chicken breast portion and cut under and round it.
4 That leaves you with a few odds and sods that, if you're making something with full chicken portions, you can leave on the carcass and boil up for stock (see page 57).
5 If you're going the whole way and de-boning it for a pie (page 136), a curry (pages 90–93) or whatever, use a small sharp knife to winkle out the bits underneath, either side of the tail end, and the odd scrap you'll no doubt have left at the front when you cut the breast portions away.
6 To go totally boneless, cut along the bones of the two leg portions and peel the meat away, using a small knife to loosen the more reluctant bits. There's very little worth digging out of the wings, so throw them in with the stock or save them for roasting and nibbling.
7 The skin should peel off fairly easily, with only a little persuasion. But do it before you start chopping up the meat into smaller bits. Skin can go in the stockpot too.
8 If you're after smallish chunks, hold the meat flat on the chopping board, cut along the grain until it's in strips, then cut crosswise, firmly keeping it steady. Your knife *is* extremely sharp, isn't it?
9 Do a final check before throwing it into whatever you're cooking – if you've just missed when cutting the joints, a small bit of bone could have escaped. It's always embarrassing when your dinner guests choke to death.

WILD ONES: RABBIT, PHEASANT, PIGEON, ETC
Don't. Just don't. Joint them by all means, but if you try to debone them, after three hours you'll end up with a million tiny bones and four grams of tattered meat. Cook them on the bone and deal with it on the plate.

BIG BEASTS: BEEF, PORK, LAMB

Usefully, most cuts of meat you'll run across are pretty simple, or pre-prepared – unless you've just shot a wild boar and need a few pointers on cutting it up, in which case, well done, and there's an American book called *The Wild Butcher* (Creative Publishing International, 2007) which is full of tips for hairy-chested kill it/chop it/cook it/eat it types. For the rest of us, who do our hunting at the local supermarket, it's rare that you need to do serious butchery. The few things you might need to do are:

- **Scoring** – pork, particularly cuts like belly or leg (page 81), will usually have a thick layer of skin. This will turn into crispy crackling if you score it by cutting lines or a criss-cross grid pattern into it, about 10mm deep. Use a frighteningly sharp knife for this – a Stanley knife is actually perfect.
- **Cubing** – if you've bought a bit of cheapish steak for a chilli (page 66) or a bolognaise-style pasta sauce (page 67), cut it into strips along the grain first, then hold it steady against the chopping board and cut crosswise.
- **Mincing** – same as above, but more finely. Make sure your knife is sharp – you're trying to cut it, not crush it.
- **Boning** – if you really do need to take the bone out of a big lump of meat, use a small sharp knife and work your way along the bone, loosening it as you go. Then turn it over and do the other side. Slow and steady is good, otherwise you'll end up with lots left on the bone. Good for stock, though (page 57).

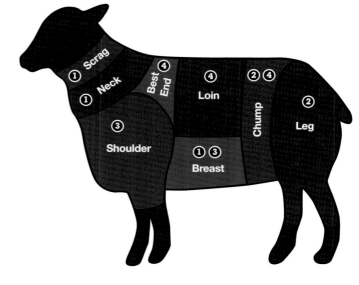

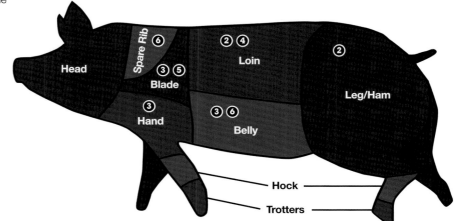

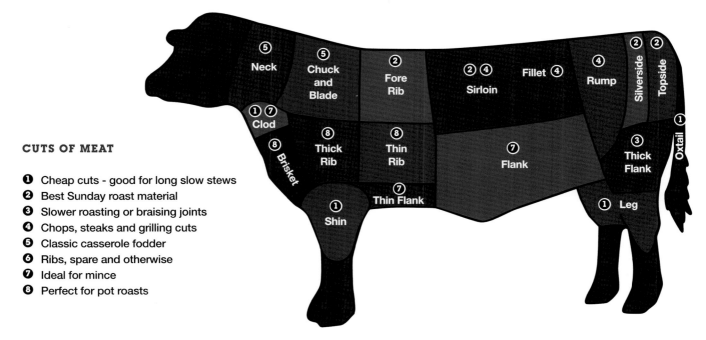

CUTS OF MEAT

❶ Cheap cuts - good for long slow stews
❷ Best Sunday roast material
❸ Slower roasting or braising joints
❹ Chops, steaks and grilling cuts
❺ Classic casserole fodder
❻ Ribs, spare and otherwise
❼ Ideal for mince
❽ Perfect for pot roasts

Scaly tales: how to prepare fish

Most fish comes pre-scaled and gutted, so it's not something you need to worry about. However, occasionally you'll forget to ask the fishmonger to do it, or you'll have caught one and, unless it's from one of our more chemically dodgy waterways, you fancy eating it.

1 **Descaling** – if you've got a scaly fish like a mackerel, mullet, salmon and so on (flatfish don't count) you'll need to descale it. You can buy fish scalers, which have metal prongs or ridges, but the back of a smallish, stiff-bladed knife works. Run a finger along the fish from tail to head, and you'll feel the scales, and which way they run. Holding it firmly, and preferably over the sink or a big bowl, run your knife down the length of the fish umpteen times, until it feels smooth. Rinse it occasionally to remove the debris. Now fish the scales out of your plughole and bin them.

2 **Gutting** – use a small, sharp knife. Stick it in under the head, just behind your fish's chin, then cut back towards the tail. About 5cm should be enough. Now stick your fingers in and, wincing slightly at the cold, slimy things inside, yank the lot out. You may have to cut a few bits free at one end or the other. Rinse it under the tap, and peer in to check it's all clean and innards-free, including the dark line down the backbone.

3 **De-gilling** – the gills are the frilly bits that stick out from the two slots behind its head, in case you didn't know. Get in there with a pair of scissors and cut them out as neatly as you can.

4 **De-pinboning** – quite a few fish, particularly oily fish like mackerel and salmon, have needle-sharp bones known as pin bones. They're actually its ribs. Get inside the cavity with a pair of pliers and yank them out. If you really hate bones, try skate – it's got soft, comb-like cartilage instead.

5 **Fin-trimming** – you don't have to do this bit, but it makes it look neater. Grab the fins that stick up from the backbone and under the belly, pull them up and whip them off with scissors. Tidy the tail into a v-shape if you want to be flash.

6 **Filleting** – hold the fish steady on your board, then, starting at the head end, cut down to the backbone, then along it. A series of short cuts, working along the bones, will work best. Then turn it over and do the other side. If it's a flatfish, much the same applies, but it's easier to cut the top and bottom sides into two fillets each.

7 **Total deboning** – now we're getting serious. If it's a round fish, cut all the way along the belly of the fish. Lay it flat, opened out and belly down, on the board and give it a quick ninja-style thump all along its backbone. Not too hard – you're not trying to mash it, just loosen the spine. Then turn it over, cut the backbone just behind the head, grab it and pull. It should come away whole and fairly easily. Use a small knife to ease it out if not. Cut it at the tail end, and there you go – a floppy fish. Check for pinbones (see above) and it's ready to cook.

8 **Skinning** – do you really have to? Leaving the skin on helps keep fish stay moist during cooking, and it's far easier to remove when it's cooked. But if you need to do it, start at the tail end and make a cut round one side of the tail. Get your fingers in and loosen it a bit, then hold the skin tight and pull hard. Hopefully it'll peel off in one piece. You may need to persuade it here and there with a small knife. Then do the other side.

Note: Flatfish are just normal-shaped fish that have been steamrollered, so everything is sideways on but otherwise very similar.

Nice plaice: a fish, feeling a bit flat

Slippery when wet

Fish are slippery. Put a bit of salt on your fingers and rub it in so you can get a better grip.

Mussel power: moules and more

Much like their namesake Jean-Claude van Damme, mussels have a reputation for being tricky to defeat and not really worth the hype. Nonsense. While neither have made many great action films lately, the shellfish have at least got the advantage in taste.

You usually buy live ones in a net bag. They'll keep for a couple of days in the fridge, but if you're worried about the odd bit of grit and sand, take them home and dump them into a big bowl of cold water, changing the water every few hours, until you're ready to cook them.

When it's mussel-munching time, give the shells a quick scrub with a stiff brush and, using a small stiff-bladed knife, pull off the 'beards' – the stringy bit they attach themselves to rocks with. They should be tightly closed; if any are already open or cracked, bin them. Then cook – see moules marinière (page 73). If any don't open when they're cooked, *don't eat them!*

BE SHELLFISH: PRAWNS AND SO ON

Like most fish, prawns are far easier to deal with once they're cooked; stick your thumbs in between their legs and pull the shell apart, then whip the heads off. If you need to do it while they're raw the same principle applies, but you'll probably need to use a small knife to cut down the belly before peeling back the shell and beheading them. You get extra points if you peel away the black vein that runs down its back, which can be gritty and bitter.

Lobsters can be truly scary, but if you really must tackle a live one, put it in the freezer for at least two hours. If it's cold enough, it'll hibernate then painlessly snuff it. Just to be sure, stick the point of a knife into the centre of the cross on its back, at the back of the head. That'll finish it off. Then, if you're just using the meat, slice it in half down the backbone and fish out the squelchy bits – stomach, liver, intestines, roe and so on. If you want to cook it whole, hurl it into a very large pan of violently boiling, salty water for about 20 minutes per kilo. If in doubt, overcook a little – nobody ever orders lobster medium-rare. Then get stuck in with pliers, pincers, tiny forks, a full metric socket set, and anything else you can think of to get the shell and claws cracked and all the meat out.

For crab, follow much the same routine, but stick a stout skewer into the nerve centres behind the eyes and boil for 30 minutes per kilo. Once it's done, and cooled a bit, you can dress it – turn it on to its back, twist off the claws and legs, and stick a strong knife in the line between the pale undershell and the darker upper one. Work the undershell loose and get rid of it. Then pull out and bin the stomach (a little squidgy bag) and the greyish gills, charmingly known as 'dead men's fingers'. To dress a crab properly, crack the claws and legs, dig into the shell and get all the meat out. Wash the shell and dry it. Then mix the meat with mayonnaise, lemon juice, salt, and plenty of black pepper; fresh chopped parsley, mustard or a chopped hard-boiled egg too if you fancy. Stick it back into the shell and eat.

The crying game: onions and other veg

Vegetables come in all shapes and sizes, but only a few are tricky to prepare. And even those are easily conquered when you know the right method. But this category does contain one of the few foods to use chemical warfare in its defence. We are talking, of course, about...

ONIONS

If you're sensitive to onions' weeping gas, don't fall for any of that nonsense about wearing goggles or cutting them underwater. Just be fast and decisive and use a sharp knife.

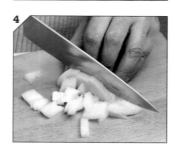

1 Cut the two ends off.

2 Cut the onion in half from top to bottom and peel the papery outer skin off.

3 Cut it into slices lengthways. Hold it steady with a claw-like grip, using your knuckles to guide the knife and keeping your fingertips tucked in out of the way.

4 Then cut it the other way, again using the same grip. Done.

5 Now wash your hands and don't touch your eyes for a few minutes.

ASPARAGUS
- Break off the thick, woody bit at the base of the stem. It should snap easily.
- Wash briefly – they're often grown in sand.

BROCCOLI, CAULIFLOWER
- Cut across the stem, about two-thirds of the way up, to separate the florets (the little tree-shaped bits).
- You can eat the stem of broccoli, but split it vertically so it cooks as quickly as the rest.

CARROTS
- Easy. Cut the top and tail off, slice and dice.
- There's no need to peel unless they're very old and crusty – just wash.

CABBAGE
- Cut in half lengthways, then put each half cut-side down and slice thinly from top to bottom.
- The stalk can be dense and woody, so cut it out in a V shape, or don't bother with the bottom 3cm.

CHILLI PEPPERS
- Read the hazard warning on page 91. Go on, scare yourself.
- Cut the top off, then slice down the middle.
- Holding each half skin-side down, run your knife along the chilli to scrape off the seeds. Throw them away very carefully.
- You can use these whole for a milder flavour – unless they burst, when you'll get napalmed. Check them over for splits or soft bits before use.

COURGETTES, SQUASH, PUMPKIN, AUBERGINE
- Take the top and tail off, then halve (or slice if it's a courgette).
- If you need to de-seed a big pumpkin, use a sturdy spoon and just scoop them out. Wipe it out with kitchen towel afterwards.

FENNEL
- Much like onions, but not toxic. Cut the bottom and any brown bits off, then chop as above.

GARLIC

- Break up the bulb into individual cloves by pressing down on it firmly with the heel of your hand.
- Loosen the papery skin by crushing each clove very gently with the flat of your knife.
- Chop one end off, then peel the skin off and do the other end.
- To chop finely, cut lengthways then crossways. If you need it crushed, smash it with the flat of your knife. Garlic presses are for pussies.
- Extra points for cutting it with a razor blade, in the style of *Goodfellas*.

LEEKS

- Cut the root end and the green end off.
- Make a shallow cut down its length and peel the first few layers of skin off.
- Wash it – leeks collect grit and mud between their layers.
- Slice crossways or, for finer bits, halve lengthways, then cut into 5–8cm lengths. Slice those finely lengthways.

MUSHROOMS

- Don't wash them – just brush the dirt off.
- Cut the end of the stem off if it's grubby, then slice as you like.

PARSNIPS

- Like carrots, except you will need to peel them. If they're not very fresh the skins go soft, so you'll have to use a sharp knife rather than a peeler.

PEAS AND BROAD BEANS

- Pop the pods apart with your thumbs, then run a finger or thumb down the inside to ping the peas/beans into a bowl.
- Check them over carefully for duff ones or wriggly things before cooking.

PEPPERS

- Cut the tip off.
- Cut the whole top off. Then reach in with two fingers and pull out the core and its seeds.
- If you're slicing it, get rid of any spare bits of seedy flesh as you go.
- If you want to roast it, just stick it on a gas burner, turning it with tongs or a fork once in a while. No gas? Bung it under the grill.
- If you want to skin it, put it in the oven for ten minutes at 180°C, then shove it in a bag – paper's best, but plastic will do – for five minutes. The skin should then peel off nicely.

POTATOES

- As above – whether you peel is up to you, but in general they're tastier, if less slick, with the peel on.

RUNNER, FRENCH OR STRING BEANS

- Using a small, sharp knife, cut at an angle across one end, then peel off the 'string' that runs down the edge. Turn over and repeat.
- If they're very young and fresh don't bother. Bite one to find out if they're stringy or tender.

TURNIPS, SWEDES, CELERIAC, BEETROOT ETC

- Like parsnips but football-shaped. Here's a trick – once they're peeled, take a slice off one side, so there's a flat surface for it to rest stably on while you chop it up.

TOMATOES

- Use a serrated knife.
- Pick off the green bit at the top.
- Cut them in half lengthways, lay them flat, then keep going until they're as finely chopped as you need.
- If you need to de-skin them, put the kettle on.
- Now get two bowls ready. Put some cold water in one – add ice if it's not very chilly.
- Make a shallow cut down the length of each tomato – just through the skin.
- Fill the second bowl with boiling water. Put the tomatoes in it for ten minutes.
- Take them out and put them in the cold water for five minutes.
- The skins should have loosened nicely. Grab the edge with your thumb and peel.
- Leave them in a colander over the sink to drain for 20 minutes, as they'll be a bit watery.
- Or live with a bit of tomato skin. It won't kill you.

Pipped at the post: fruit prep

APPLES AND PEARS

- Cut in quarters, then cut a v-shaped slice out of the middle, where the pips live.
- Cut off the stalk and the tough skin at the end. Slice at will.

APRICOTS, PEACHES, NECTARINES ETC

- Stone them by cutting right round the circumference, right down to the stone in the middle. Then grab the fruit and twist; it'll split in half and you can winkle out the stone.

LEMONS AND LIMES

- To juice a lemon or lime, cut it in half, then squeeze hard. But place your other hand under it, fingers slightly apart, to catch the pips. Don't try this if you have any paper cuts.

And there's more: eggs, beans etc

The egg is one of nature's most cunning bits of packaging – shockproof, compact and surprisingly tough. Here's how to crack the skill of opening it – plus perfect pulse prep.

CRACKING! EGG PREP

You might think that it's easy getting the usable bit out of nature's second most successful bit of packaging (after the banana). But there's a knack to cracking it without getting bits of shell everywhere.

1 If you're cracking eggs into a bowl or cup, use one with a thin rim. A fat one will smash the egg rather than neatly bisect it.

2 Keeping your wrist stiff, firmly and decisively tap the middle of the shell against the rim. Then stick your thumbs into the crack and separate the shell, letting the contents slide out.

■ If you're a TV chef, you'll be able to do this with one hand by using the first and third fingers to separate the shell once it's cracked.
■ An alternative method is to tap it medium-hard on the worktop, then split the shell with your thumbs: less chance of getting shell in the bowl, more chance of an eggy worktop.
■ Use a separate bowl or cup, rather than throwing the egg directly into the other ingredients. Then if you get a dodgy one, or a bit of shell, it won't ruin the lot.
■ Use the point of a teaspoon to fish out any stray bits.
■ If you just want the white or yolk, separate it by holding the split shell over the bowl and tilting it until it's vertical. The bottom half will act like a cup, keeping the yolk intact while the white goes in the bowl. Hopefully.

PULSE-RAISING: BEANS, LENTILS AND SO ON

These are why the tin was invented; tinned chick peas, kidney beans, haricot beans and so on are dead easy. But dried ones are stupidly cheap and don't contain the salt and, often, sugar of their canned brethren, so if you've got the time they're better. But they do usually need soaking.

■ Lentils and split peas don't need soaking.
■ Most of the others need soaking for several hours before you cook them. They're tough as old boots otherwise.
■ The best bet is to soak them overnight. Just put them in a bowl with some cold water and leave them. A teaspoonful of bicarbonate of soda can make it faster. Don't add salt.
■ Alternatively, bring them to the boil, then leave them in the pan with a lid on for at least an hour.
■ When they're soaked, throw the water away, then cook them by boiling them in fresh water for ten minutes.
■ They'll double in size when soaked and boiled, so allow plenty of water and use a decent-sized pan.
■ Don't add salt to the cooking water – it makes their skins tougher.
■ Kidney beans must be boiled for at least ten minutes, or they have horrible effects on your insides (see hazard warning).
■ A pressure cooker is a good, quick way of cooking beans. Add a splash of oil to the cooking water to stop it foaming.

⚠ HAZARD WARNING!

Beware the curse of the kidney bean. If you're using uncooked red kidney beans, they have to be boiled for at least 10 minutes otherwise the toxins they contain in their outer skins will have terrible effects. As few as four dodgy beans can cause nausea, vomiting, abdominal pain and violent diarrhoea. Not nice.

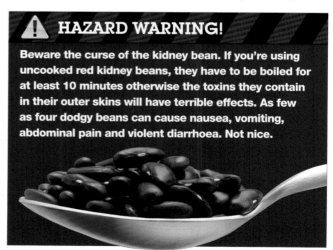

Pre-cooking cooking: marinades and rubs

Sometimes the flavour's best added beforehand – and that's where marinades and rubs come in. The principle's simple; take a wet mixture of oil, juice or booze (that's a marinade), or a dry mix of spices and herbs (that's a rub), and apply liberally to whatever you fancy.

The flavours soak into the food, then you can cook it as simply as you like, or in some cases not at all (see the gravlax recipe on page 104), and it'll still zing with tasty loveliness.

It's best to marinade things overnight, ideally in the fridge, so that it's got plenty of time to work, but a shorter time will still give you the effect – just not as strongly, as you'd imagine.

Here are three examples, but once you get the idea you can experiment with umpteen combinations of your own:

ALL-PURPOSE RED MEAT RUB
Mix together a teaspoonful each of:

- Dried sage
- Dried oregano
- Dried thyme
- Ground coriander
- Mustard powder
- Paprika
- Black pepper
- Sea salt

plus
- 2 crushed cloves of garlic
- A quarter of an onion, finely chopped
- 1 tablespoon of olive oil

When it's well mixed into a dryish paste, smear it all over steaks, chops, or whatever meat you've got handy. Grilling or griddling works well with this; barbecuing is even better.

STEW MARINADE
Put your chunks of meat (around 500g – increase the amounts below for bigger dishes) in a glass or ceramic bowl, then add:

- Half a bottle of dry red wine
- 2 sprigs of fresh rosemary
- 2 bay leaves
- 5 juniper berries (if you have them)
- 3 cloves of garlic, peeled but not chopped
- 1 onion, peeled and halved
- A pinch of salt
- A twist of pepper

Cover the dish and stick it in the fridge overnight, if not longer. The marinade can be saved to add to your casserole later on if you like.

FISH MARINADE
This works for pretty much any fish. Again, use a glass or ceramic bowl, as metal ones can react with the lemon juice. Mix this up and pour it over your fish:

- Juice of one lemon
- A splash of cider vinegar
- 2 glasses of white wine
- A handful of fennel seeds (if you have them) or 2 sprigs of fresh dill (or 2 pinches of dried)
- 2 cloves of garlic, peeled but not chopped
- Half an onion, peeled
- A pinch of salt
- A twist of pepper

Leave in the fridge, covered, for about two hours. Being quite acidic, this will actually partly cook your fish, so you won't need to cook it for quite as long. Works brilliantly on kebabs of meaty fish like tuna or monkfish – just throw the lot in, skewers and all.

Seasoned, sorted: now go and fire up the griddle

CHAPTER 4
FIRING IT UP

Here comes the bit where it gets properly dangerous. And useful. This is the part where you get to apply heat, which is what makes the difference between raw ingredients and proper food. When that first caveman put a nice bit of mammoth on the cave fire, they discovered that something very fine happened to it, and that's what we've been trying to improve on ever since. So now we do roasting, barbecuing, grilling, griddling, boiling, steaming, baking, microwaving and simmering, to name but a few. However, while it's still difficult to beat a big bit of meat and a fire, nowadays most of us have got a stove in our kitchen, which saves all that hauling sticks about and rubbing two rocks together. So this is the bit where you get to turn the heat up to 11 and play with fire. Or in the case of a microwave, turn the dial to a random number of seconds, and wait while it does something indescribably complex at a molecular level, then goes 'ping'. What's that all about? It's fascinating in a Star Trek way, but the real fun's in big naked flames and skin-peeling temperatures. Gentlemen, start your burners...

What's cooking?
A stove style guide

Just like any skill, there are some specialist terms involved in cooking. So here's our guide to all the basic terminology you'll need, how it works and what it does.

GRILLING

The classic fire-on-food technique, usually done these days under an electric or gas grill. It's also what you do when you barbecue something. Americans call it 'broiling', confusingly.

GRIDDLING

This is nearly as brutal and simple, but there's a pan – ideally iron and ridged – between flame and food. A great way to cook things like steaks or chicken portions, as the fat runs off into the grooves and you also get professional-looking brown lines on your meat. Also works for sliced vegetables, prawns etc.

SHALLOW FRYING (OR PAN-FRYING, OR SAUTÉING)

Many, many dishes start this way – a light splash of oil over a medium heat, in a flat-bottomed pan. Quick, healthy (if you use olive oil rather than lard) and easy.

DEEP FRYING

Think chip shop – just dunk something into a lot of very hot oil until it's cooked. Covering it in batter first can help too (yes, a Mars bar if you like). Messy and tricky at home, though – even purpose-built domestic deep fat fryers don't have the volume you need to make sure that the oil stays hot when you put the food in, which is the secret to crisp results rather than soggy failures. Best left to the pros unless you're willing to spend money on a serious fryer and an awful lot of oil. But see our chips recipe on page 85 if you're really keen.

BOILING

It's just throwing something into hot liquid, usually water, at 100°C (unless you're on top of Everest, when it's just 69°C thanks to lower atmospheric pressure). As long as your liquid is bubbling, it's boiling. Simmering counts too.

STEAMING

Suspending your food over a pan of boiling water so the steam cooks it. Good for vegetables, as they stay crisp, and also good for saving energy by cooking one dish over the top of another.

ROASTING/BAKING

Two words, one basic technique. For some reason, roasting is usual for meat and veg, baking for fish and bread or cakes. Why? No idea. However, it's just a process of putting food into an oven, which produces dry heat, and letting it cook.

MICROWAVING

A different thing entirely. The physics are beyond everybody except Stephen Hawking, but basically it excites particles within the food, thereby heating them. Not 'cooking' as we know it, but occasionally useful and good for reheating and defrosting stuff.

OVEN TEMPERATURE

We're using Celsius (aka Centigrade) for oven temperatures, because it's simple. And Fahrenheit starts at 32° below zero, which is just silly. But here's a chart if your oven's got a different set of digits on its knob. Ahem.

Celsius	Fahrenheit	Gas Mark	Description	Useful for
110°	225°	¼	Tepid	Warming plates
125°	250°	½	Barely warm	Not much
140°	275°	1	Still cool	Still not a lot
150°	300°	2	Warmish	Long, slow stews
165°	325°	3	Moderate	More of the same
180°	350°	4	Fairly hot	Longer-cooked meat dishes
190°	375°	5	Quite hot	Loads of stuff – roasts, pies etc
200°	400°	6	Hotter	Baking bread
220°	425°	7	Hot	Faster meat
230°	450°	8	Really hot	Roasting veg
240°	475°	9	Scorching	Pizza, crisping things quickly
250°	500°	10	Blazing	If yours does this you're lucky
550°	1,000°	11	Fictional	Members of Spinal Tap only

Measuring it up

All the recipes in this book are metric – grams, litres, and so on. Not that there's anything wrong with good old pounds and ounces, but it's much simpler to stick to one type of measurement, and the sums are easier in metric. Hang on, what's three-quarters of two pounds thirteen and half ounces again?

Some recipe books use both. But they often don't warn you that you can't mix them, because the two don't match exactly. To avoid that trap, we're sticking to metric. But here's a quick, rough conversion guide for diehard avoirdupois enthusiasts.

450g = 1lb
28g = 1oz
570ml = 1 pint
4.55 litres = 1 gallon

If you're using an ancient set of scales (nothing wrong with that) with imperial weights, buy some metric ones too. They're cheap and useful. Info about where to buy that sort of thing is on page 15.

Teaspoons, tablespoons and so on will always be a standard measure. It's worth getting hold of a set of measuring spoons and always using those, rather than guesstimating with a wildly varying set of mismatched cutlery. A 'pinch' is a fairly generous two-fingers-and-thumb pickup, while a 'glug' or a 'splash' of liquid is just what it says; one swift upturning of the bottle, not a long pour. Unless it's for your own consumption, of course.

The Internet is full of conversion widgets like convert-me.com, but beware of American ones, as their weights and measures are subtly different. And they often use 'cups', which is the most confusing system of measurements known to humankind.

The roast with the most: Sunday special

There's nothing like a big, juicy bit of meat, oozing juices and accompanied by rich gravy. Sorry, vegetarians. And though it takes a little while to cook, it's really no hassle once you know what you're doing.

BUYING IT

Look for decent, fresh meat (see page 34). But you knew that. Allow about 150g per person for a boneless joint, and double that for bone-in. But be generous – leftovers are a good thing.

COOKING IT

Follow the guide to times and temperatures opposite. Use a roasting tin with a grid if you have one. If not, put the meat on an oven shelf with the tin underneath. Messy, but it works. Or you can perch it on top of a pile of roast veg, but make sure you move them around regularly to stop them getting soggy under the meat and too crispy round the edges.

SERVING IT

Those old-style roast meat platters with spikes to hold the joint still and a non-slip rubbery bit underneath aren't a bad idea, but how often would you actually use one? The best thing to do is use a big plate – with tall enough sides to hold any juices – a very sharp knife, and a stout fork. A carving fork's good, but any solid, heavy-duty one will do.

CARVING IT

The traditional idea that carving meat is one of the things that all real men should know how to do is, frankly, cobblers. Provided you come away with reasonably manageable portions and don't end up with a pile of shredded debris, it'll be good enough. Did we mention that the knife should be extremely sharp? See our roast chicken recipe (page 78) for how to carve a bird; rolled boneless joints (the ones tied up with string) are easy; more complex bone-in ones are best tackled by sliding the knife along the bone to loosen it, then cutting along the grain of the meat.

Some fin quick: fish cooking

Fish don't take long to cook at all. Put them in for as long as a bit of meat and you'll end up with cremated cod, smoking haddock or plaice à la carbonised. You can tell if a fish is cooked by sliding a sharp knife in, right to the bone. If it's white all the way in, it's done. Stop.

- Boiling – 3–4 minutes is fine for all but dense fish like monkfish and halibut, which will take 5–6.
- Pan-frying – 5–6 minutes per side. Wait until one side just starts to change colour, then flip it.
- Baking – 15 minutes at 180°C is plenty for fillets; whole fish could take another 10–15 minutes. Check regularly, and cover them with foil if they look dry; alternatively splash in a glass of wine and add some fresh herbs to your baking tray first and make a tent out of foil, then bake. Mmmm, fragrant.

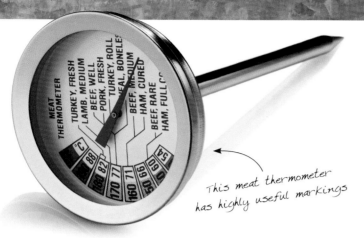

This meat thermometer has highly useful markings

TIMING GEAR: HOW LONG TO ROAST FOR

Roasting meat's easy, if you follow this guide, and a few simple rules.

- Take the meat out of the fridge half an hour or so before you cook it.
- Make sure the oven's up to temperature before you use it (put it on when you get the meat out of the fridge).
- Leave your meat to rest for at least 15 minutes after cooking, either in a switched-off oven with the door ajar, or on the worktop covered loosely in kitchen foil. This helps the muscle fibres relax and lets the juices circulate. A bit longer won't hurt at all, but don't let it get cold.
- Rare pork and chicken are a very bad idea unless you like food poisoning. Stick a skewer in them at the end to make sure the juices run clear. If they're pink, put it back in the oven for another 15 minutes, then test again.

Beef and lamb	20 minutes at 220°C
	then 30 minutes per kilo at 160°C
Pork	30 minutes at 220°C
	then 50 minutes per kilo at 160°C
Chicken	20 minutes at 210°C
	then 45 minutes per kilo at 180°C
Turkey	20 minutes at 220°C
	then 40 minutes per kilo at 180°C

TEMPERATURE GAUGE: THE THERMOMETER METHOD

If you're a keen meat-roaster and/or a gadget freak, you'll have a food thermometer. These are a fiendishly accurate guide to the doneness of a bit of meat, provided you stab their probe far enough in and leave it for 10–15 seconds. Meat is done when it reaches the following internal temperature:

Beef and lamb	65°C (-10°C for rare,
	+10°C for well done).
Pork	70°C (no lower, please).
Chicken	75°C (breast), 80°C (thigh).
Turkey	75°C (breast), 80°C (thigh).

Treat your greens: cooking veg

If you ever had school dinners, you'll know exactly how not to cook vegetables: boil them into a mush of tasteless, greenish slop. There are far better ways to do it, and the basic principles are simple – cook them for the bare minimum of time, leaving them crisp, tasty, and still full of all their nutrients and minerals.

The classic method is boiling – use a biggish pan of lightly salted water – but steaming is just as quick, and you can steam one lot of veg over the pan that another is boiling in, thus saving space, energy, and hassle.

Other methods include roasting, which works brilliantly for almost any root vegetable, tomatoes, aubergines, and courgettes; baking 'au gratin', or as normal people call it 'in a creamy, cheesy sauce'; stir-frying or shallow-frying; and even grilling and griddling for smoky barbecue-style results. And one surprise is that green vegetables are excellent in a microwave. Put them in a non-metallic bowl with a very small amount of water – a couple of tablespoonfuls will do – cover with cling film, and ping them. One thing, though – don't put salt on until afterwards.

THE TIMES TABLE

Time is in minutes. Microwave times are for 250g – and add two minutes standing time.

	Boil	Steam	Nuke
Green beans (frozen)	5 (4)	4	6 (7)
Broccoli	4	5	6
Brussels	7	7	7
Carrots	8	8	6
Cauliflower	5	5	7
Leeks	4	3	4
Parsnips	8	8	5
Peas (frozen)	4		6
Potatoes	18	18	5

Everything you always wanted to know about eggs

First fact: they come out of a chicken's bum. If you're still not put off, then you need to know how to cook them. The subject's full of old wives' tales and folklore, but apart from being a miracle of packaging, eggs are pretty straightforward to deal with.

BOILED EGGS

Take your eggs out of the fridge a few minutes before you use them – if they're freezing cold they'll crack. Put them in a good-sized pan of cold water, then bring to the boil. When the water boils, turn it down and start the clock. Three minutes' boiling will give you soft-boiled eggs, five minutes fully set ones. For hard-boiled, seven to eight is about right. Don't forget to run hard-boiled eggs under the cold tap if you want to peel them immediately, otherwise you'll burn your fingers.

FRIED EGGS

Heat a splash of cooking oil, lard or butter in a frying pan over a medium heat. When it's starting to sizzle, crack your eggs into it (see page 46). Use a spoon to splash a bit of oil over them every so often so that the top cooks, or turn them over carefully with a spatula for American-style 'over easy'.

POACHED EGGS

Forget all those poaching cups – just boil some water in a large frying pan, add in a slug of vinegar if you like, then gently tip in an egg (cracking it into a cup first helps). Let it cook for about 3-5 minutes (you can 'fllick' the water over the top of the egg to help it cook). Lift out carefully with a slotted spoon. You know when your eggs are fresh as it will stay in a nice compact shape. Old eggs will spread out.

SCRAMBLED EGGS

Crack your eggs into a bowl and whisk them around a bit with a fork or whisk. Don't go mad, you're not making a soufflé. Meanwhile, heat a lump of butter in a saucepan, preferably a non-stick one, over a medium heat. Pour in the eggs and stir with a spoon for a couple of minutes, adding a splash of milk or cream if they look a bit dry.

OMELETTES

Put a thumb-sized lump of butter and a splash of olive oil into a smallish frying pan and put it on a medium heat. Crack two eggs into a bowl and beat them with a fork. Add a tablespoonful of milk and a pinch of salt and pepper and stir in. Pour the mixture into the pan. Cook it until it starts to set, pushing the edges in with a spatula occasionally so they don't stick. Fold it in half with the spatula, then tip it on to a plate and eat. (See page 151 for more ideas)

MORE EGGY GOODNESS

Eggs are a vital part of tortilla (page 107), pasta (page 134), most desserts and cakes (chapter 7), and even burgers (page 65). Is there anything they can't do? Well, they make a pretty rubbish cricket ball substitute...

> ## Pickled silly
>
> **Not exactly cooking – but they had to go in somewhere. Hard boil some eggs, peel them and pack them into a sterilised jar. Pour in enough malt or white vinegar to cover them and seal the jar. Leave them to pickle for 5-6 week – then open a bag of crisps and pop one in.**

Cool carbohydrate: Pasta, rice and couscous

You can't have chips with everything, you know. Well, probably. Pasta, rice and more exotic grains are quick, easy and the foundation of loads of meals.

BASTA! BE A PASTA MASTER

The Italians have a saying: 'You can't drown pasta'. That's rule one for cooking pasta, then – use a big pan and loads of water. Get it to the boil, then bung in a splash of olive oil and a pinch of salt, followed by your pasta – roughly 125g per person. Then boil briskly on a medium heat.

If you're using dried pasta, check the packet for cooking times. A rough guide is that small, very thin stuff like 'angel hair' capellini will take 5–6 minutes; spaghetti 8–10; tagliatelle, fusilli or penne 10–11; and really chunky stuff like thick farfalle 13–15. Add five minutes for whole-wheat.

Test it towards the end of the cooking time. It should be cooked, but still have a bit of bite to it – 'al dente', as it's called. When it's done, drain the pan into a decent-sized, stable colander, preferably in the sink. Don't try wobbly arrangements with lids, sieves or the like. That's a big pan full of a lot of scalding water.

For truly excellent pasta, put the empty pan back on a low heat with a thumb-sized lump of butter in it. When it starts to melt, add the pasta and stir until all the butter's coated the pasta.

SECRET OF THE ORIENT: GET YOUR RICE RIGHT

According to some people, cooking light, fluffy rice is as tricky as fighting off 500 crazed ninjas. Don't believe them. This is a pretty foolproof method. But you will need to measure it carefully, time it right, and use the correct size and type of pan – with a heavy base to distribute the heat evenly, plenty of room for expansion, and a tight-fitting lid.

First, measure out your rice. We're talking about basmati or long grain rice here – see page 74 for risotto or paella. This is one of the few examples when it's best to adopt that horrible American method and use cups. Or, more likely, a mug. About half a mug of rice per person is plenty. Tip it into your pan. Then measure out one and a half times the amount of water, again using the mug. Into the pan with it, plus a pinch of salt.

Bring it to the boil, then put the lid on and turn it down to a low simmer. Simmer it for 15 minutes without lifting the lid. Then test it – if it's pretty much done, fluff it up with a fork then put the lid back and leave it for anything between 5 and 15 minutes more; the steam will make it lighter. Done.

With the grain

These two look roughly the same, and crop up in roughly the same areas – the Middle East, Greece, Turkey, and India. However, they're not identical. Couscous is made out of semolina wheat, rolled and coated with flour, while bulgar wheat is made of boiled and cracked durum wheat. You don't really need to know that, but the end result is that couscous is softer, and doesn't need cooking as long; bulgar is nuttier and more toothsome. Both, though, make a fine base for pretty much anything where you'd otherwise use rice, and are very fine as salads too (see page 101).

COUSCOUS

1 **Put the kettle on.**
2 **Put about 100–125g per person into a biggish bowl.**
3 **Add a glug of olive oil per helping. Stir it in with a fork. You can use butter (about half a thumb-sized lump per serving), but that makes it more stodgy.**
4 **Pour in boiling water – about double the volume of the couscous. Stir.**
5 **Wait two or three minutes. Stir again.**
6 **After another three minutes it should have swelled until it's absorbed all the water. You're good to go. Add salt if you like.**

BULGAR WHEAT

1 **Put 100–125g per person into a medium saucepan.**
2 **Add roughly double the volume of water. Add a pinch of salt if you like.**
3 **Bring to the boil, then simmer for about 15 minutes until the water is absorbed. Keep a close eye towards the end so it doesn't dry out and burn.**

ALTERNATIVES AND IDEAS

■ **Couscous is the foundation of a bigger, stew-like dish of the same name – see page 71.**
■ **You can use stock (see page 57) instead of water to boil bulgar wheat, giving it a heartier flavour.**

Combinations unlocked: more complex cooking

Sometimes you'll end up using more than one cooking style to get a dish to work. Sounds complicated, but it isn't – because there are some very simple techniques involved. Here they are.

Seal the deal: put meat into a very hot pan

SEALING (USE BEFORE ROASTING)

Nothing to do with clubbing cute marine mammals, this is usually used for big bits of meat, and what you're trying to do is get the outside to form a crust, locking moisture in so it doesn't go dry while it's cooked. Get some oil very hot in a large pan and bung in your meat, turning it regularly so it goes brown and very slightly burnt-looking all over. Then continue to oven-cook it according to your recipe (like the one on page 70).

BROWNING (USE BEFORE STEWING)

This works on the same principle, called the Maillard reaction. It turns starch to sugar, and gives cooked – particularly grilled or roasted – food that delicious tang. Just throw lumps of meat into a pan with a little hot oil in it and stir about until browned. A great start to a stew, a pasta sauce, or a chilli con carne (page 66). When you've browned your meat, you'll usually end up with a crust on the bottom of the pan, so go on to...

DE-GLAZING (USE AFTER THE ABOVE TWO)

Once your browned meat has left a layer of delicious burnt bits in the pan, pour in a glug of wine or stock, then scrape away with a metal spoon (or a plastic/wooden one, if you're using a non-stick pan) until the bits have been absorbed and the pan looks vaguely clean again. Then add the other ingredients for an extra-tasty dish.

DRY FRYING (USE BEFORE CURRYING)

This is great for curries (page 90) and other spicy dishes. Make up a spice mix of dry spices and seeds like coriander, cumin, cinnamon and so on, then bang them in a very hot pan and stand well back. They'll smoke and sizzle, but after a minute or so the flavours will have intensified and mingled, and you can add the rest of the ingredients. This one can smell out your entire house, so keep the extractor fan on high or a window open.

FLAMBÉEING

Spectacular and mostly pointless, but huge fun. Fill a ladle or a large metal spoon with wine, brandy, or any other flammable, drinkable liquid. Hold it over a gas burner to warm it up and let the alcohol start to boil off as gas. Then tip it slightly so the flame catches the edge of the liquid and it should start to burn. Now tip it over your sizzling dish or into your pan. Mind your eyebrows, there can be a pretty big 'whoomf' as it all goes up. And be accurate; a splash of blazing liquid on a flip-flop-clad foot will be painful and embarrassing.

Leftovers into essentials: making stock

What do you do with all those spare bits of meat or fish?
Meat bones, post-roast chicken carcasses, fish heads
and so on – straight in the bin, right?

Stock up: make sure there's enough water to cover your carcass

Wrong. Hurl them into a pot with a few vegetables
and herbs, boil them for a few hours while you do
something more interesting, and you've got an
invaluable and dirt-cheap source of rich, flavourful
stock which you can use as a great basis for umpteen
recipes like gravy (page 77), pasta sauces (page 67),
risotto or paella (page 74), and curries (page 90). You can
also buy pre-made stock, which is fine, but it's not cheap at
all, and if you think too hard about where industrial leftovers
come from you may want to reconsider.

1 Put your leftovers in a big pan or stewpot. Stick to one
 type at a time – fish, chicken, beef, lamb, whatever.
2 Add a few vegetables (see below), herbs (ditto) and plenty
 of water – about a litre would be fine for a whole chicken.
3 Bring it to the boil. If a scum forms on the top, skim it off
 with a big spoon.

4 Turn it down to a very low, barely-bubbling simmer and
 leave it for a few hours – at least two, but more's fine.
 Don't let it boil dry or let the gas go out.
5 The traditional vegetables are an onion, a carrot, a stick of
 celery, and a potato, but leeks, parsnips, garlic, turnips, and
 many others will work too. You don't need much, though
 – it's a flavouring, not a main ingredient.
6 Herbs usually include a bay leaf or two and a sprig each of
 thyme and parsley, but rosemary, oregano, sage (particularly
 with chicken), and dill or fennel (with fish) will work just as well.
 A tablespoonful of peppercorns will add heat.
7 Add a pinch of salt if you're using uncooked bones, but
 cooked stuff like a roast chicken carcass may not need it.
 Taste it near the end to check.
8 Sieve it into a large jug or bowl. If you're feeling really
 pernickety, you can sieve it through muslin or cheesecloth.
 It should be clearish, but a bit of sediment won't hurt.
9 Let it cool, covered, for an hour or so. Then, unless you're
 intending to use it very soon, put it in smallish plastic boxes,
 freezer bags and so on and bung it in the freezer. Ice cube
 trays or bags will work too. It'll keep for ages. To defrost
 quickly, put it in a pan with an inch of water and put on
 a lowish heat. It'll take a few minutes at most.

Fire! Essential barbecue knowhow

Even if a man has never so much as reheated some Ready Brek, they're somehow supposed to be able to barbecue. It's in our genes, apparently. This is cobblers. Barbecuing is better if you think about it a bit.

Doing a decent barbie is no less difficult than cooking anything else, and needs just as much forethought and planning. But there are a few simple rules that can make life much easier and the results more reliable if you're forced to put on a comedy apron and light some charcoal.

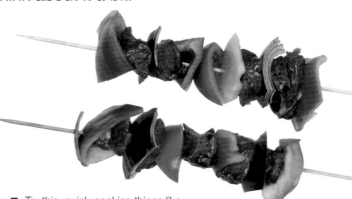

- First, make sure your barbecue is good and hot. The charcoal should be whitish-grey and pretty much smokeless. This will take a good 20 minutes, if not longer, so start it going well before you need to cook on it.
- Put the rack or shelf on top well beforehand. Heat from the bars is an important part of the cooking process.
- The classic barbecue dishes – chunky burgers, chicken drumsticks, T-bone steaks and so on – are actually the most difficult to get right, because they need to be well cooked right through to the middle. But often the outside will be black and crusty before the inside's done. So cheat by pre-cooking that tricky stuff. Stick it in a low oven or microwave it to cook the centre, then use the barbecue to crisp the outside and give it that smoky flavour. Just be careful not to leave part-cooked meat hanging around for ages.

- Try thin, quick-cooking things like flattened chicken breasts or rump steaks (use a rolling pin or mallet to pummel them), fish fillets, or skewered kebabs of seafood and/or veg.
- Marinade fish beforehand in oil and herbs plus lemon or lime juice – the acid will part-cook them so they'll be done faster.
- If you want to barbecue bigger meat joints, put a double layer of foil under them and a loose dome of foil over the top to create a mini-oven. Allow plenty of time, and make sure there's enough charcoal to keep it hot.
- Whole corn on the cob in its leaves can be good – soak them in water first to stop them catching fire.
- Make a jug of oil, garlic, herbs, salt, and pepper, and maybe a dash of chilli or lemon, and brush it on to the food to keep it moist. Don't use too much, though, because it'll catch light.
- If you've got bushes of any herb growing in your garden – rosemary, bay, sage, thyme and so on – or have a neighbour, or even a local public garden with some (ask the gardeners), save the prunings. They're good stuffed on top of the charcoal to give a herby, smoky flavour.

⚠ HAZARD WARNING!

Obvious, but it needs saying: you're dealing with naked flames, real fire, and a lot of heat. Make sure your barbecue is on solid, flat ground, away from anything flammable. Keep fire-lighting fluid or matches well clear, and don't be tempted to squirt lighting fluid or, worse, petrol or other flammable liquids on to hot charcoal. Unless you don't like your eyebrows.

Danger! Fire! Explosions! Extreme cooking

In any activity, no matter how dangerous or scary, there's always somebody who has to go a step further. When tightrope walking's not frightening enough, they have to try tightrope walking without a net. Over a pool full of killer whales. Naked. In stiletto heels. And so on.

Well, cooking's no different. Somebody always asks the question 'Yes, but what if...?' Well, here are a few examples which start to answer that question.

- **Car cookery** – it's quite possible to cook a bit of fish or chicken on your car's exhaust manifold or turbo. Select a spot that gets good and hot, wrap your food in foil and tie it on well, away from moving parts. Downside: a lingering taste of oil and exhaust on your food, and a very lingering smell of old fish in your car.
- **Chicken a la lava** – one Hawaiian recipe involves wrapping a chicken in banana leaves, placing it on a shovelful of fresh molten lava, then putting another shovelful on top. When the lava's set, the chicken will be done. Hit it hard with a shovel to crack the lava open, and eat. Downside: you need a live volcano handy, and a large amount of luck not to fall in and die.

- **Dishwasher delight** – you certainly can poach salmon or similar in the hot steamy inside of your dishwasher. But as this is almost certainly very close to a perfectly functional oven, why would you? Ditto toasted sandwiches made with a steam iron. Downsides: Utter pointlessness, mess.
- **240v sausage** – some Scandinavian lunatics decided to cook a frankfurter by sticking a metal fork in each end, then wiring them up to opposite terminals of a mains plug. Smoke, sparks, and mayhem ensued. Unfortunately, the sausage ended up scorched at the live end and raw at the neutral one. Downside: High electricity bills. Also, high chance of death.
- **Death from the deep** – every year, several people in Japan die from eating fugu fish. This is a highly prized and costly delicacy; the only minor disadvantage is that if the chef is very slightly sloppy when taking out the fish's poison glands, it will kill you quickly and unpleasantly. Upside: You won't have to pick up the bill.

Deep-fried whole turkey

This is a Deep South dish, from the parts where everybody drives a muscle car, moonshine liquor is the number one industry, and beer is for breakfast. Couldn't come from anywhere else, could it?

Difficulty 🥄🥄🥄🥄🥄 | **Actual work** 30 mins | **Total time** 2 hrs | **Serves** 6 - 8 hillbillies

TOOLBOX

- A clean oil drum or giant cooking pot of at least 25 litres capacity
- A plank or sturdy stick, at least 1.5m long
- At least 2m of rope (not nylon)
- Large butane (Calor) gas burner, around 180,000BTUs output
- Frying thermometer
- A very large plate or tray
- At least two currently sober people

COMPONENTS

- 6–7kg turkey
- At least 15 litres of high-temperature oil, eg corn, sunflower or groundnut
- Salt and pepper

METHOD

1 Making sure the pan is stable on the burner, pour in the oil and heat it to 180°C. Clip the thermometer to the side of the pan if possible, so you don't have to keep leaning over to check it.

2 While that's heating up, clean the turkey, dry it with kitchen towel to make sure it's absolutely dry inside and out, and season it with salt and pepper.

3 Tie the rope round it like a mountain-climbing harness, round the wings and behind the legs, so it dangles head-end down. Make sure it's absolutely solid and won't slip.

4 Tie the other end of the rope to the middle of your plank. The length is crucial here – the turkey must be the same distance away from the plank as the top of the oil is from the top of the pot, plus about 5cm. In other words, when you rest the plank on top of the pot, the turkey should hang just submerged.

5 When the oil's at the right temperature, one person needs to pick up each end of the plank, stand either side of the pot and lower the turkey gently in. It will hiss, bubble, spit, and threaten to overflow, so mind your feet and keep your face well clear. If your rope's the right length, the plank should rest on the sides of the pot, with the turkey frying in the oil.

6 Stand well back, and keep an eye on the temperature. Don't let it get above 190°C. Between 165–180°C is fine.

7 After 55 minutes, grab the plank, take the turkey out and lay it somewhere large and greaseproof to rest for at least 30 minutes. It'll continue cooking, and should end up wonderfully juicy with a crispy skin. Turn off the burner.

8 Eat, accompanied with rice and beans, Cajun-style. Now's the time to crack open the beer and shout 'yeeee-haw'.

9 Remember, that oil's going to be very hot for a very long time. Leave it until the next morning to dismantle everything. If you can pour the oil back in its container(s), it'll keep for three or four frying sessions.

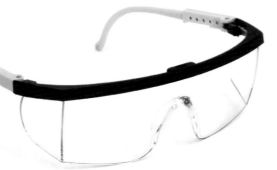

Protection racket: Goggles are handy. Also a fireproof suit

⚠ HAZARD WARNING!

Don't be stupid. Try this only if you're exactly sure what you're doing, you've got all the right gear – and you're sober. Also do it outside, in the open. Things could get messy, y'all.

Blazing mussels, Batman!
Brazucade or L'éclade

This recipe, from the South of France, is cunningly designed to include the possibility of an enormous forest fire. After cooking it, you can sit with a glass of chilled white wine and some tasty seafood and watch the entire region burn to ashes.

Difficulty | **Actual work** 20 mins | **Total time** 30 mins | **Serves** Whole fire crew

TOOLBOX
- A large board, at least 50cm square
- 4 25–50mm nails
- A hammer
- A bucket
- A good couple of bucketfuls of dry pine needles or straw
- Matches

COMPONENTS
- 3kg of mussels
- A few bucketfuls of salt water
- 500g of butter
- 3 cloves of garlic
- 1 sprig of fresh thyme or rosemary
- Salt and pepper

However, given a good supply of mussels and a pyromaniac, it's spectacular, impressive, and quick. Best cooked on a beach backed by pine woods, where most of the ingredients fall neatly to hand. Plus it's more difficult to set fire to the sea.

METHOD
1 Scrub the mussels and pull off their 'beards' (see page 43).
2 Peel and crush the garlic.
3 Chop the herbs finely.
4 Add them, and a pinch or two of salt and pepper, to the butter. Mix in well.
5 Go and get a bucket of clean seawater.
6 Hammer your nails into the centre of the board in a square measuring about 2.5cm on a side. Then pour water over it to soak the board.
7 Stand four mussels, hinge side up, in between the nails so that they form a cross. Then, using this as a prop, arrange the rest of the mussels, all hinge side down, in a rough spiral round them until the board is full.
8 Go and get another bucketful of seawater.
9 Cover the mussels with a 25cm layer of pine needles or straw. They must be very dry.
10 Light the corners (windward side last) and stand back a bit. It should smoulder for a few seconds then go whooomf!
11 When all the straw or needles have gone out, the mussels should nearly all have opened. They'll be cooked, and have a lovely smoky flavour. And some annoying bits of ash, so give them a quick splash in the seawater, then dunk them in the garlic butter.
12 Now check there aren't any bits of the undergrowth still smouldering. Nothing ruins a good meal more than being beaten up by angry firemen.

CHAPTER 5

MAIN FEATURE

If you went to see a band, you'd be a bit disappointed if they didn't play any of their hits, wouldn't you? Well, this is the bit where the guitars get turned up a notch, the drummer hits a familiar groove, and the best-selling singles get an airing.

These are the classic dishes that everybody should know how to make – and usually they're also the foundations for a whole set of other dishes. If you know how to make a pasta sauce, you know how to make chilli con carne. And when you master that, any other meat-based stew is only a couple of ingredients away. The same goes for roasts, fish dishes, and even the many variations of curry, from Indian to Vietnamese and Thai.

Here are the building blocks for umpteen main meals. Follow, learn, experiment, and before you know it you'll be turning out impressively slick dishes from memory – no recipe books required. Learn your own sure-fire classics and off you go.

Now put your hands in the air, here comes the sing-along chorus...

It's all legs and breasts with you: sizzled chicken

Griddled chicken makes a midweek meal that will sizzle with flavour, and works as well with a summery salad as some warming veg. It's low in fat, easy to prepare, incredibly quick and very tasty. What's not to like? Unless you're a chicken, that is.

Difficulty | **Actual work** 10 mins | **Total time** 20 mins | **Serves** Up to you

TOOLBOX
- Griddle pan, frying pan or grill
- Spatula

COMPONENTS
- Chicken breasts, skin-on
- Salt and pepper
- 1 teaspoonful of dried sage
- A splash of olive oil

METHOD

1 Heat up your griddle pan or grill, full blast.
2 Dribble a splash of olive oil on to the skin side of your chicken, then sprinkle with a pinch of salt, pepper, and dried sage.
3 When the pan's really hot, wallop the chicken in. If you're using a griddle or frying pan, press it down a little.
4 After two minutes, turn the heat down to medium. Leave them for ten minutes. Don't flip, prod or fiddle.
5 Turn them over. The front should be nice and crispy. Leave them for another seven to eight minutes.
6 Done. Put on a warm plate, dribble the pan juices over them, and serve with salad and chunks of bread or mash (page 89) and any other veg you like (page 53).

Cheap chicken!

Chicken can be bought very cheaply. Most corner shops or bottom-end supermarkets will offer pale, frightened-looking lumps of poultry cowering under clingfilm in a polystyrene tray. And in many cases it's bizarrely inexpensive. But if you possibly can, give the low-rent stuff a swerve. It'll taste of nothing, have the texture of a squash ball, and will have been hacked up in some giant, messy slaughtering shed in the Far East with all the hygiene regulations of a Tarantino film. Go for free-range, British, and/or organic – it should actually taste of chicken and it won't play Russian roulette with your immune system.

ALTERNATIVES AND IDEAS

- Leg portions are just as good, and can be cooked exactly the same way, but will take about five minutes longer per side.
- Skinless portions are healthier, and again can be cooked the same way, but use plenty of oil to make sure they don't dry out or stick, and give them less heat to start with.
- Try marinading chicken first – see page 47 for a few ideas.
- The classic combination of sage and onion is hard to beat, but thyme, rosemary, oregano, and tarragon also work well with chicken. Chilli flakes, paprika or pimentón (see page 27) will spice it up a bit.
- Try cutting a deep slot in the end of a chicken breast – or down the bone for a leg – and pushing in a peeled, crushed garlic clove, a lump of butter, a pinch of herbs, and a little salt and pepper before cooking. It's a sort of cheat's chicken Kiev.

Extra strong mince: burgers and meatballs

If you can whip up a decent burger or some meatballs, you can feed yourself and any number of other people easily and expertly. Plus the ingredients are cheap and it's quick and easy. And you get to squelch around wrist-deep in minced meat. Lovely.

Difficulty | **Actual work** 15 mins | **Total time** 25 mins | **Serves** 4

TOOLBOX

- 2 mixing bowls, one medium-sized, one small
- A biggish plate or tray
- Spatula
- A griddle pan, frying pan or grill

COMPONENTS

- 500g of decent quality minced beef
- 1 egg
- 1 medium onion
- Salt and pepper

METHOD

1 Break the egg into the small bowl. Add a pinch of salt and pepper and mix with a fork.
2 Chop the onion finely.
3 Put the mince and onion into the large bowl
4 Add the egg and mix thoroughly. It should be a sticky, lumpy paste.
5 Get in with your hands and squish the mince together into the right sized and shaped lumps – burgers, meatballs, or a scale model of the Millennium Falcon, if you're feeling adventurous. Pat them firmly into shape and put on the plate as they're finished.
6 Now wash your hands.
7 For burgers, warm up a griddle pan, a frying pan with a very small amount of oil in it, or a grill (make them quite flat if you're barbying, to make sure they cook all the way through). Put the burgers in on a medium heat, and cook for 15 minutes – longer for big ones – flipping them occasionally. For meatballs, put in a frying pan with a decent coating of oil over a medium heat. Keep turning gently so they don't disintegrate. They should take about 15 minutes too, depending on size.

ALTERNATIVES AND IDEAS

- This works with any minced meat – pork, lamb, chicken, venison, kangaroo, you name it – provided it's reasonable quality: very cheap mince will be too fatty and your burgers will fall apart. Some meat, like venison and kangaroo, has very little fat, so adding 50g (a couple of rashers) of chopped bacon will stop them being too dry.
- Experiment with seasonings. Keep it to a teaspoonful or so, and don't go mad, but you could try Worcestershire sauce, mustard, horseradish, dried or chopped fresh sage, rosemary, thyme or parsley, chopped garlic, anchovy essence (yes, it really works and doesn't taste fishy), chilli sauce, chilli flakes, redcurrant jelly (brilliant for lamb burgers), or anything else that takes your fancy. One add-on at a time though, and stay subtle or it'll be a palate-scaring mess.
- This also works for salmon – buy flakes, or get boneless fillets and crumble them into bits. You'll definitely need to add breadcrumbs to keep it together, and quite possibly a second egg; but wait until your mixture's in the bowl, and if it's still a bit loose add it then.

Italy's other ball game!

For the classic Italian spaghetti sauce with meatballs, cook an onion and two chopped cloves of garlic in a frying pan over a medium heat. When they're starting to soften (about five minutes), put in the meatballs and cook for five minutes, until they're going brown. Then add a glass of red wine and a bay leaf, cook for two minutes, and throw in a 400g can of chopped tomatoes. Now put your pasta pan on (see page 55). Fifteen minutes later it'll be perfect for that Lady and the Tramp scene.

The Texas tornado: chilli con carne

This is a classic Texas dish (hence the beef), so best enjoyed while sitting round a campfire, listening to some down-home country and western, and randomly shooting things with your granpappy's Colt .45. Failing hunks of bread and vast amounts of cold beer.

Difficulty | **Actual work** 25 mins | **Total time** 2 hrs + | **Serves** 6+

TOOLBOX
- Large metal stewpan or casserole

COMPONENTS
- 3 rashers of bacon or 1 packet of lardons (bacon bits)
- 500g of beef (cheap stewing steak to best sirloin – your choice)
- 2 250ml bottles of lager-style beer
- 2 onions
- 2 cloves of garlic
- A glug of olive or corn oil
- 2 400g tins of red kidney beans
- 1 400g tin of chopped tomatoes
- 1 red pepper
- 1–3 red chilli peppers, depending on taste
- 3 teaspoonfuls of ground cumin
- 1 teaspoonful of ground coriander
- 1 teaspoonful of dried oregano
- Salt and pepper
- 1 bunch of fresh coriander

METHOD
1 Open the beer. Pour one bottle into a glass. Have a slurp. Lovely. Put your pan on the hob, on a medium-low heat.
2 Slice the bacon into roughly 1cm squares, then put in the pan. Stir occasionally.
3 If you're using steak or any other big lump of meat, cut it into roughly 2cm lumps.
4 Chop the onion reasonably finely. Same with the garlic. Chop the red pepper into 1–2cm bits, and slice your pepper(s) into 2mm rings. De-seed them (see page 44) if you want it milder. If this is your first time, go for caution rather than bravery (and read the hazard warning on page 91).
5 The bacon should have produced a fair amount of fat by now. Add a glug of oil, turn the heat up to full, then throw in the meat, bit by bit so that the temperature doesn't drop too much. Stir it about until it's going brown.
6 Throw in the onions and garlic. Stir them for two minutes.
7 Pour in the other bottle of beer. Stir it. Keep the heat high. Give it two minutes to stop foaming and spitting.
8 Add the tomatoes, kidney beans, red pepper, chillies, and spices – except the coriander. Stir it about a bit. Have another slurp of beer and wait for it to come back to the boil.
9 When it's boiling, turn it right down as low as your hob will go, until it's barely bubbling. Go away and do something else for at least an hour and a half (usefully, the length of the average football match or F1 race). Don't forget your beer.
10 The longer you leave it the better it will be, provided you don't let it evaporate and go dry. Add water if that looks likely. Letting it cool overnight, with a lid on, then reheating it gently the next day gets you bonus points.
11 About ten minutes before you want to eat, wash the coriander (it can be weirdly gritty) then cut the stalks off, chop the leaves finely, and add it to the chilli.
12 Check the seasoning – the bacon may have added its own salt, so you may not need much – and eat. Yeee-haaaar.

ALTERNATIVES AND IDEAS
- Ideas you could try include using wine instead of beer; adding a dollop of Worcestershire sauce, brown sauce, ketchup, mustard, Tabasco, or other hot sauce; adding a tablespoonful of tomato purée; using stock, either in a cube, bottled or fresh (see page 57); using chopped fresh tomatoes; roasting the red pepper first; adding pimentón, paprika, fennel seeds, chilli flakes or a cinnamon stick (see page 27); using black beans or haricots instead of kidney beans; leaving the beans out entirely; cooking it while standing on one leg... Use your imagination and raid your cupboard.
- To get closer to the Mexican original, use pork instead of beef, leave out the bacon, and use black beans.

Beware: manky mince!

Yes, you can use mince if you absolutely must. Do you know what goes into that stuff? Eyeballs, gonads, and nipples, that's what. However, buy the best you can and it'll be just fine. Cheap mince will be full of fat, so cut down on the oil, and you may need to drain it before you add the veg.

Ragu? Sugo? Bolognaise? Pasta sauce explained

The basic meat-and-tomatoes sauce that comes with pasta is called many different things, depending largely on whether you come from Pisa or Peterborough. But it's very simple and very, very tasty. Even in Peterborough.

Difficulty | **Actual work** 20 mins | **Total time** 1 hr 15 mins | **Serves** 4 - 6

TOOLBOX
- A large pan
- A food processor (optional)

COMPONENTS
- A large glug of olive oil
- 500g of lean beef – steak or similar if possible
- 2 medium onions
- 1 carrot
- 1 stick of celery
- 1 400g tin of chopped tomatoes
- 300ml of chicken stock (see page 57) or a cube plus 300ml water if you must
- 2 bay leaves
- 2 sprigs of fresh rosemary
- Salt and pepper

METHOD
1. Put the oil in your pan and put it on a medium heat.
2. Chop the meat into roughly 2cm chunks.
3. When the oil's hot, throw in the meat and stir for a minute or two.
4. Chop the onions (see page 44), carrot, and celery roughly. Chop the rosemary finely – the leaves, not the stalks.
5. Throw the veg into the pot, along with the bay leaves, rosemary, and a pinch of salt and pepper. Stir it for ten minutes, keeping the heat moderate.
6. Add the tomatoes and stock, stir to mix, and bring back to the boil.
7. If you want fine-textured sauce, fish out the bay leaves and bin them. Put it all into a food processor (warning – hot sauce splashes well) and whizz briefly until it's smoothish, but not soup. Put it back in the pan, bring to the boil, then simmer for an hour. If you don't mind a few lumps, just leave it simmering for about an hour. Longer won't hurt, provided it doesn't start to get too thick. Add water if it looks like it's starting to.

One warning, though...

Never serve an Italian 'Spaghetti Bolognaise'. It doesn't exist, as the meat sauce comes from Bologna (where it's served with tagliatelle), but the long, thin noodles from Naples, where they have them with a much less meaty sauce. Confusing chaps, those Continental johnnies.

ALTERNATIVES AND IDEAS
- Stir in a large glug of cream or milk a few minutes before serving to make it richer and smoother.
- Start it off by frying some chopped bacon bits.
- Add chopped parsley towards the end for a fresher taste.
- Use a teaspoonful of tomato purée along with the tomatoes for a more concentrated tomatoey flavour.
- This sauce makes a fine filling for ravioli.
- This is also the same sauce you use for lasagne. Which is made as follows...

Meat between sheets: lovely lasagne

Utterly stodgetastic but gorgeous, this is really a remix of meaty sauce plus pasta, with a bit of added creamy sauce. Undo that top button and get stuck in.

Difficulty | **Actual work** 25 mins | **Total time** 1 hour | **Serves** 4 - 6

TOOLBOX

- An ovenproof dish, roughly 6–8cm deep and 25cm by 20cm
- A large pan or saucepan
- A medium-sized saucepan
- Spatula, drainer, or large slotted spoon
- A bowl
- A large plate
- A cheese grater

COMPONENTS

- Meaty pasta sauce (see above)
- 1 packet of lasagne pasta sheets
- 60g of butter
- 120g of flour
- 700ml of milk
- Salt and pepper
- A splash of olive oil
- A pinch of ground nutmeg
- 100g of parmesan cheese

METHOD

1 Fill the large pan with water and put on to boil.

2 Melt the butter gently in the medium-sized pan. Don't let it burn.

3 When it's melted, take it off the heat and mix in the flour. Do it gradually and keep stirring (use a wooden spoon) until it looks like thick wallpaper paste.

4 Start adding the milk, bit by bit. When it looks smooth, put the pan back on the heat and gradually add the rest of the milk, stirring all the time.

5 When it looks smooth, add a pinch of salt and the same of ground nutmeg. Congratulations. You have created béchamel sauce.

6 Put the oven on at 190°C.

7 By this time, the water should have boiled in the big pan. Add a pinch of salt, a splash of olive oil, and the lasagne sheets. Boil for the time it says on the packet – they vary between makes. (You can also buy lasagne sheets that you don't have to boil first – they just go straight into the layering process in point 10 – check the cooking details on the packets).

8 Fill the bowl with cold water.

9 When the lasagne's cooked, take it out gently with a spatula or slotted spoon, dunk it in the cold water to stop it cooking, and lay it flat on the plate to dry.

10 Assembly time. Put a thin layer of meat sauce on the bottom of the dish, then a layer of pasta. More meat sauce, béchamel, then a grating of cheese and a little black pepper. Then repeat – pasta, meat, sauce, cheese, etc – until you've finished it all or the dish is full. It's best if you end up with béchamel, then a bit of grated cheese on top. Don't leave too much pasta uncovered or it'll burn.

11 Bake in the oven for 30 minutes, or until it's starting to look brown on top. Eat with a nice Chianti, fava beans, and somebody's liver (optional).

More frog, anyone?
Toad in the hole

This is more of an assembly-line job than a make-it-from-scratch recipe. But the end result is truly more than the sum of its parts – stodgy, meaty, and delicious. It's still got a funny name, though.

Difficulty | **Actual work** 15 mins | **Total time** 35 mins | **Serves** 4 - 6

TOOLBOX
- Mixing bowl
- Whisk or hand mixer
- A large, deep roasting tin

COMPONENTS
- 100g of plain flour
- 2 eggs
- Pinch of salt
- 200ml of milk
- 6–8 sausages
- A glug of olive oil or 50g of goose fat or lard

METHOD
1 Stir the flour, salt and eggs together in a bowl.
2 Gradually whisk or mix in the milk until it's a smooth batter. Put it in the fridge to rest (ideally for an hour).
3 Put the oven on at 200°C.
4 Put the oil or fat into the bottom of the roasting tin and put it in the oven.
5 After five minutes, put the sausages into the roasting tin, roll them about to coat in the hot oil, and stick them back in the oven for ten minutes.
6 Take the tin out, push the sausages about a bit to make sure they haven't stuck, then pour in the batter.

7 Put it back in the oven for at least 20 minutes, until the batter's fluffy and brown on top. Try not to open the door or it'll flop.
8 Serve with gravy (page 77) and a lukewarm pint of Old Throgmorton's Yorkshire Wallop. Or similar.

Cheap sheep: lamb shanks

This takes a couple of hours or so, but is well worth it for the big hunks of rich, meaty and tender lamb in lip-smacking gravy that you'll end up with. The perfect antidote to a chilly, damp day. What's more, it's a very cheap cut of meat. Winter stodge heaven.

Difficulty   **Actual work** 20 mins   **Total time** 2 hours +   **Serves** Variable

TOOLBOX

- Large pan or metal casserole with a lid
- Metal spoon
- Slotted spoon or strainer
- Roasting tin

COMPONENTS

- Lamb shanks – one per person
- 500ml of chicken, lamb or vegetable stock – your own (page 57) or shop-bought
- Half-bottle of red wine
- 1 jar of redcurrant sauce or jelly
- A glug of olive oil
- 1 onion
- 1 carrot
- 1 stick of celery
- 6 cloves of garlic
- 2 sprigs of fresh rosemary or 1 teaspoonful of dried
- 2 bay leaves
- Salt and pepper

METHOD

1 Open the wine. Have a glass to check it's OK.
2 Cover the bottom of your pan with oil, then put it on a high heat.
3 When it's very hot, stick in your lamb shanks to brown. If you've got a lot, do them in batches of two or three so the oil doesn't cool too much, and put the done ones on one side. It will sizzle, spit, and smoke. This is normal. Make sure all sides are well browned.
4 While that's happening, chop your veg into 3cm chunks, peel the garlic cloves and squash them a little with the flat of your knife.
5 Take the shanks out of your pan and put to one side, on a plate or similar. Put in the vegetables and give them five minutes' browning, until they start to soften. Keep stirring so they don't burn and stick.
6 Put the shanks back, then pour in the wine. Keep it on a high heat so the alcohol burns off. Add the herbs and a twist of salt and pepper.
7 Put in the stock and stir. If there's not enough to cover at least three-quarters of the shanks, top it up with water.

8 When it's come to the boil, turn it down as low as you can and put the lid on. Leave it for about two hours. Longer won't hurt, provided the liquid doesn't evaporate too much. If it's looking dry, add boiling water.
9 Fifteen minutes before you want to eat, put the oven on at 160°C.
10 Pull the lamb shanks out of the liquid and put them in the roasting tin. Stick it in the oven.
11 With a slotted spoon or drainer, fish out the veg and put them in a bowl at the bottom of the oven.
12 Turn the pan up to full blast, with the lid off, so the liquid starts to reduce and thicken.
13 Add about half a jar of redcurrant sauce or jelly. More will make it sweeter, less more savoury. Go easy if it's your first time, darling. Stir well.
14 When the liquid's nice and thick and gloopy, put it into a jug. Sieve it if you're fussy. Get the lamb out of the oven and serve it with the veg and gravy. Mash (page 89) is brilliant with this. Also couscous (opposite).

Paris-Dakar Rally, via Tunisia: couscous

This comes from North Africa – Tunisia, Algeria, and Morocco. But you're more likely to run across it in France, where they have a couscous restaurant in every middling town or above, exactly like curry houses in the UK.

Difficulty | **Actual work** 25 mins | **Total time** 1.5 hrs | **Serves** 4 - infinity

TOOLBOX

- A big stewpot (a couscousière is ideal)
- A steamer – optional
- Two biggish bowls and a small one
- Ladle
- Slotted spoon /strainer

COMPONENTS

- 500g of stewing lamb
- 1 sml white cabbage
- 2 onions
- A splash of olive oil
- 1 500ml tin tomatoes
- 1 400g tin chick peas
- 200g each of any five of the following: aubergine, broccoli, carrots, celery, courgette, French, broad or runner beans, leeks, parsnips, peppers, potatoes, squash, sweet potato
- 2 teaspoons of turmeric
- A pinch of ground cumin, coriander, cinnamon, cayenne pepper, and paprika or pimentón; DON'T use curry powder
- Fresh coriander
- Salt and pepper
- 500g of couscous
- 1 tin or tube of harissa

METHOD

1 Dice the lamb into roughly 3cm cubes.
2 Chop the cabbage and onion finely.
3 Put the oil, meat, cabbage, and half the onion into your pot and add about 1 litre of water. Bring to the boil.
4 Reduce the heat, then simmer for 30 minutes.
5 Prepare your veg. Dice chunky ones into 2cm or so cubes, slice carrots, dismember broccoli, etc.
6 Add the tomatoes, spices, chick peas, veg, and half a teaspoonful of harissa. Give it a good stir. Bring back to the boil, then simmer for another 30 minutes.
7 Chop the coriander finely.

Harissa: atomic ketchup

This hot, spicy, garlicky red sauce is dangerous but very addictive. You can get it in quite a few supermarkets, or try any North African, or sometimes Turkish, shop. Look for makes like Le Cabanon or Le Phare de Cap Bon, which come in red-and-yellow tiny tins or tubes. Mil is another one, or there are posher makes like Barts and Belazu.

8 Everything should be soft and well-cooked by now. Taste it, and add salt and pepper if necessary. Add the coriander, and a bit more water if it's a bit thick and lumpy.
9 Make couscous as on page 55. Or you can steam it over the stew for about ten minutes in a steamer, so it soaks up the flavours.
10 Make the hot sauce by putting a tablespoonful of harissa into a small bowl, then add a spoonful or two of the liquid from the stew and stir until it's fairly liquid.
11 Put the couscous grains in a bowl. Using a slotted spoon, fish out the meat and veg, and plonk them on top. Decant the liquid into another bowl (or serve it from the pot if you're not fussy). Have a bit of everything, and stir in hot sauce to taste.

Fishy business: superlative soup

If you've ever had that almost unpronounceable South of France speciality bouillabaisse (bwee-a-bays, if you insist), you'll know what a proper fish soup is like. Orangey-red, smooth but not watery, and full of fishy flavour.

Difficulty **Actual work** 10 mins **Total time** 15 mins **Serves** 6 +

TOOLBOX

- Big pan/stewpot
- Wooden spoon or spatula
- Slotted spoon or strainer
- Serving plate or big shallow bowl

COMPONENTS

- 2kg of fish in total – at least six types, with plenty of variety from oily to white fish, firm-fleshed ones to gristle-boned flatfish, the more the better; smoked fish can work too
- 2 litres of water
- A large onion
- A leek
- 4 tomatoes
- 2 cloves of garlic
- A large splash of olive oil
- A piece of orange peel
- A pinch of thyme and parsley
- A bay leaf
- A pinch of saffron (a stupidly expensive spice; use pimentòn or turmeric – see page 27 – if you haven't got any)
- Salt and pepper

The proper Marseille version is made from umpteen varieties of local fish, including several obscure and scary-looking types covered with lumps, spikes and spines. There's very little chance of finding those in your nearest shop, but we can do a pretty reasonable imitation with our own species. This makes a large amount of soup, and the more types of fish you have the better, so make it for lots of people or be prepared to freeze a lot of leftovers.

METHOD

1 Fill the kettle up and put it on.
2 Chop the onion, leek, garlic, and tomatoes.
3 Pour enough olive oil into your pot to cover the bottom. Put it on a medium heat.
4 When the oil's hot (test it by dropping a small piece of onion in – if it sizzles, you're good to go), add the veg.
5 Cook it, stirring occasionally, for about five minutes, until it starts to change colour but before it goes really brown.
6 Throw in the firmer fish and cook for a minute.

Rouille

There are loads of variations, but this one is easy, quick, and powerful. It's like atomic bread sauce. A mortar and pestle is the best thing to make this in, but a food processor will work too.

1 Soak a slice of bread per person in water, then squeeze it out. Put it in your mortar or processor bowl.
2 Add two de-seeded red chillies and a clove of garlic per person. Mix well.
3 Add a good splash of olive oil and mix it in.
4 Using long tongs and wearing an anti-radiation suit, serve to unsuspecting friends. Watch their heads explode.
5 Actually, a small dollop will add a bit of welcome punch to your soup. It's hot and garlicky, but highly addictive.

7 Pour in about two litres of boiling water.
8 Turn up the heat so it's boiling fast (you want the oil and water to stay mixed, not separate) and boil for five minutes.
9 Then put in the softer fish, the herbs, and orange peel and boil for another five minutes.
10 Take it off the heat, taste it, and add salt and pepper if you think it's needed.
11 Using a slotted spoon or strainer, lift out the fish and put them on a serving plate or bowl. Put the fish and the soup on the table, and eat with slices of French bread, warmed in the oven for ten minutes – real headbangers smear raw garlic on it – grated cheese (gruyere is good), and rouille. What's that? Only the best thing to come out of Marseille since Eric Cantona. See above.

Love mussels: moules marinière

Sounds posh, French, and complicated. Isn't. Try 'mussels in plonk' – that sounds less poncy. And it's ridiculously fast. And amazingly messy, if you eat it in the approved get-stuck-in-with-your-fingers style. But all the better for it.

Difficulty | **Actual work** 15 mins | **Total time** 20 mins | **Serves** 2 - 4

TOOLBOX

- A large pan with a lid
- Slotted spoon or drainer
- A large bowl
- Colander or large sieve

COMPONENTS

- 1.5kg of fresh (live) mussels
- A large glug of olive oil
- 1 onion
- 1 stick of celery or 1 leek or half a head of fennel
- 4 cloves of garlic
- 1 large sprig of fresh parsley
- 1 bay leaf
- Half-bottle of white wine
- 300ml of water
- Pepper

METHOD

1 Clean your mussels (see page 43).
2 Put a good splash of olive oil into the pan and put it on a high heat.
3 Peel the vegetables and garlic, then cut them into very small pieces (roughly 5mm).
4 Put them into the pan and stir well for five minutes, until they soften. Don't let them burn.
5 Add the wine and water, the bay leaf, and a good couple of twists of pepper, slap the lid on and bring it to a fast boil.
6 Put the mussels in the pan, and give it a shake to make sure they're all submerged or nearly so. Put the lid back on and leave it boiling hard for three minutes.
7 Chop the parsley finely. Also, put some soup bowls somewhere to warm.
8 Check the mussels. They should all (or at least 90 per cent) have opened. If not, put the lid back and give them another minute. When they're ready, fish them out with a slotted spoon and put them in a colander over a big bowl, to catch the spare juice. Put the pan lid on top to keep them warm.

9 Boil the juice left in the pan hard, with the lid off, to reduce it. After a couple of minutes, add the juice that's dripped from the mussels into the bowl.
10 After another couple of minutes, throw the chopped parsley into the pan, stir, and turn it off.
11 Put the mussels into the bowl, pour the liquid from the pan over the top, and stick it on the table with the warm soup bowls. You'll need a spare bowl for shells, and plenty of napkins if you use the shells as pincers or scoops, like the French do. Crusty French bread and cold white wine are the only other things you'll want with this. Oh, and if you find a mussel that isn't open, *don't eat it.*

Open wide: if they don't do this when cooked, avoid

Rice, but twice as nice: risotto and paella

This may invite death threats from both Italians and Spaniards, but risotto and paella are basically the same thing. That thing is rice, cooked in stock with other bits added, like seafood, meat or vegetables.

The main difference is that risotto (the Italian one) often has cheese added and is a bit more soupy; paella usually features saffron and is a bit more crunchy. And they're both dead straightforward.

You'll need two pans: a medium saucepan for the stock and a biggish frying pan. Get a paella pan – flat, two-handled, steel – if you intend to make it a lot; otherwise, don't. It's not essential.

The first, and major, ingredient is rice. You'll find bags of rice in most supermarkets these days labelled 'risotto rice' or sometimes 'paella rice'. That'll do. If you want to get more nerdy, risotto varieties include Carnaroli, Vialone Nano and Arborio, while paella uses Calasparra or Bomba. DON'T use pudding rice, or 'short grain'. It won't work.

Use about 125g per person (same as pasta, roughly). So a 500g bag will do a meal for four hungry people.

The stock is also important. Make plenty, and try to stick to the theme of your dish: veg stock for mostly veggie ingredients, chicken for most meaty things, fish for a seafood concoction, and so on. Fresh stock is great, but you can cheat if you like. Cubes if you're desperate, liquid stock if possible, or best of all make your own (see page 57). Add a bay leaf, an onion or shallot, a clove or two of garlic, pepper (careful with the salt if you're using stock cubes), your choice of herbs – oregano's good for paella, thyme or basil for

Easy cheesy: parmesan is a risotto secret

risotto – and if it's paella, something to give it its distinctive orangey colour, like pimentón (smoked paprika), saffron, or maybe turmeric.

If you're on the Continent, look out for something called Spigol – it's a small yellow box full of sachets of ready-mixed paella spice. Brilliant.

METHOD

1 Make stock (at least 250ml per person). Leave it simmering.
2 Heat a little oil in your pan. Sauté a sliced onion, plus leek, celery, fennel, tomato, and garlic if you fancy. Add lardons (bacon bits) if you want too. And if you're using big chunks of chicken or chorizo, get them browned too.
3 When the onions etc are soft, add the rice. Cook it for a few moments to absorb the oil. Add a splash of wine now, if you want. Then start adding ladlefuls of the hot stock.
4 It'll take about 25 minutes to cook, so time adding the other ingredients to suit that. Small stuff like prawns or peas can go in near the end; bigger stuff like chunks of carrot or broccoli will need longer to cook.
5 Here's the difference: if you're making risotto, keep stirring, and just before the end, when the rice starts to go soft, add a handful of grated cheese (ideally parmesan) and stir it in. If you're making paella (and are brave), don't stir – just leave it on a very low heat. It's supposed to have a crust underneath, but not a black, charred one, so watch that heat.

Fish + mash + slop = heaven: fish pie

This is too good to save only for those occasions when you're catering for a non meat-eater, but that's certainly one good excuse to make it. It's a tad messy, as it involves several different operations, so make sure you delegate the dishwashing.

Difficulty | **Actual work** 30 mins | **Total time** 1 hr | **Serves** 4 - 6

TOOLBOX

- A biggish saucepan
- A frying pan
- Slotted spoon or drainer
- Colander
- Potato masher or strong fork
- Pie dish

COMPONENTS

- 750g of fish – boneless, skinless white fish fillets like cod, hake, haddock or coley are easy; smoked fish is great; or fillet and bone your own (see page 42); not too much oily fish, though; you can use some shelled prawns, mussels or scallops too
- 750g of potatoes
- A thumb-sized lump of butter
- 1 small onion (or half a big one)
- A glass or two of white wine
- 1 tablespoonful of plain flour
- A bay leaf
- A sprig of fresh parsley or 1 teaspoonful of dried
- Salt and pepper

METHOD

1. Fill the saucepan with water and a pinch of salt, put it on a high heat. Wash your potatoes, chop the fish into roughly 3cm chunks.
2. Chop the onion and garlic finely and put them in the frying pan with the bay leaf and a good pinch of salt and pepper.
3. Pour a glass or two of white wine into the frying pan. Add enough water to bring it up to a good 3cm below the rim. Put it on to boil.
4. The saucepan should be boiling now. Put the potatoes in, wait for it to boil then turn it down (there's a more detailed recipe for mash on page 89).
5. When the liquid in the frying pan's boiling, add the fish, gently. Don't let it slop everywhere.
6. Put the flour in a mug or cup and dribble a tiny amount of cold water in, stirring all the time. It should mix into a smooth paste by the time the cup's half full. Stop at that point.
7. After five minutes the fish will look white and cooked; take it out with a slotted spoon or drainer and put it on a bowl or plate for a bit. The onion and garlic will be fine in the pan, or with the fish. It doesn't matter. Leave the bay leaf in. Don't turn the pan off, though.
8. Put the oven on at 190°C.
9. Leave the frying pan boiling until the fishy, winey liquid has reduced to about 2cm deep. Meanwhile, chop the parsley.
10. Add the flour/water paste to the frying pan, stirring all the time so it gets absorbed and thickens the liquid into a soupy, thickish sauce. Stir in the parsley. Turn it off and fish out the bay leaf (but don't throw it away).

Mash up: fantastic fish pie

11. Your potatoes should be nearly done by now. Test them with the point of a knife.
12. When the potatoes are soft, drain them into a colander, put them back into the saucepan, add the butter, and mash them.
13. Assembly time. Put the fish in the dish (hey, a poem!), then pour the sauce over it, stirring a bit to get it well mixed. Dollop the mash on to the top and smooth it down. It doesn't have to look too professional, but if you want extra style points make a pretty pattern in the top with a fork and put the bay leaf in the centre.
14. Put the pie in the oven for 20 minutes or so, until the top's starting to go slightly brown.
15. Extract, serve, eat. You won't need much with this except maybe a bit of green veg. And possibly the rest of that bottle of white wine (cider's good too, for some West Country chic).

The beast of British: roast beef

It's the classic Sunday dinner, and at its finest it makes you come over all patriotic and stiff-upper-lipped. Jolly good show, tally-ho chaps, etc etc.

Difficulty | **Actual work** 20 mins | **Total time** 1.5 hrs + | **Serves** 4

TOOLBOX
- Roasting tin with grid
- Metal spoon

COMPONENTS
- Joint of beef (sirloin, rump, topside); 800g-1kg
- Salt and pepper
- Olive oil
- 1 tablespoonful of mustard powder (optional)
- 1 tablespoonful of flour (also optional)

METHOD
1 Heat the oven to 220°C.
2 Rub a splash of olive oil into the meat, then season with a pinch of salt and a generous twist of black pepper.
■ Alternatively, mix a tablespoonful of mustard powder with the same of flour and rub it into the skin of the meat. Then add salt and pepper as above. This makes the fat crispier.
3 Put the meat in a roasting tin, on a grid. Or throw in some vegetables to roast (see page 83). Put it in the oven. If you're making Yorkshire puddings (see opposite), start them now.
4 After 20 minutes, take the joint out, spoon some of the fat over it – basting it – and put it back.
5 Turn the oven down to 160°C for the rest of the roasting time (see guide on page 53).
6 Baste it every 20 minutes to half an hour. When it's done, whip it out to rest somewhere warm, loosely covered with foil, and put in your Yorkshire puddings.
7 When the Yorkshires are done it'll be nicely rested and ready to carve. A quick verse of Land of Hope and Glory at this point, and off you go.

Beefy beauty: perfection on a plate

The Yorkshire pudding

Though any Yorkshireman would probably beat you to death with his clogs for saying so, this is exactly the same basic mixture as pancakes (page 152). But you can use beer instead of milk, which is lighter. And far more manly, by 'eck.

METHOD
1 Make the batter a good while beforehand – as soon as the meat's gone in is good.
2 Stir the flour, salt, and eggs together in a bowl.
3 Gradually whisk or mix in the milk or beer until it's a smooth batter. Stick it in the fridge.
4 The second your roast comes out of the oven, slam the temperature up to 220°C.
5 Take a couple of spoonfuls of the fat from the roasting tin, put it into a baking tin (half a tablespoonful per pud, if you're using a proper tin with individual holes) and put it in the oven. If there's not enough fat from the meat – use sunflower oil.
6 When the fat's really hot take the tin out and pour the batter into it. Then put it back carefully into the oven.
7 Don't open the door for at least 20 minutes. After 25 your puds should be big, brown, and crispy. Leave them in for a bit longer if you like burnt bits.
8 If your timing's OK, the meat should be ready to serve at pretty much the same time the puds are ready. Job's a good 'un.

Power your boat: great gravy

Whatever your meal's star – chicken, lamb, beef, pork, whatever – the gravy should play a solid supporting role. It shouldn't overpower the meat, but add juiciness and an interesting savoury element. So don't throw in everything on the spice rack plus random sauces.

Difficulty | **Actual work** 10 mins | **Total time** 10 mins | **Serves** Lots

TOOLBOX
- Roasting tin from the meat
- Stout spoon and/or whisk

COMPONENTS
- 1 tablespoon plain flour
- 500ml boiling water or stock
- Half a glass of wine

METHOD

1 Open a bottle of wine. Try a glass to see if it's OK. This is known as 'chef's perks'.

2 When the meat's finished cooking and is resting on a plate, take the roasting tin and drain off almost all the fat (see warning below). Mix in a tablespoon of plain flour.

3 Put it on the hob and heat on medium-high. Add in about half a glass of wine and stir frantically with a metal spoon or whisk to loosen the crusty bits. Then add some boiling water, or better still, water drained from your boiled/steamed vegetables (you can add a stock cube to the water for a fuller flavour).

4 Keep stirring (to avoid lumps) and add more water if it starts to get too thick. It'll evaporate pretty fast, but that's fine because it intensifies the flavour. It needs to bubble away gently for about 5 minutes to cook the flour and wine.

5 Taste it and add more seasoning if needed (a bit of marmite can do the trick).

6 If you end up with any lumps – just pour it into your gravy jug through a sieve.

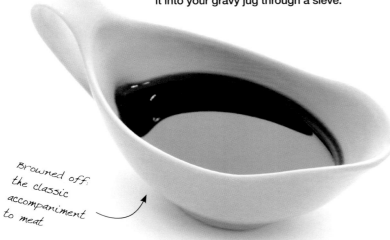

Browned off: the classic accompaniment to meat

⚠ HAZARD WARNING!

Don't tip fat down the drain. It'll clog up the sink and smell deeply horrible. Use a jar or tin, or if you're feeling green, a non-recyclable container such as a takeaway coffee cup, a fast food soft drinks cup, or a juice container with the top cut off. Not a foam cup – they melt. When it's cooled it'll harden, and can then be safely bunged in the bin.

No 'tasty bird' jokes, please: roast chicken

Some people get all twitchy or overcomplicated about roasting a chicken. But it's not difficult, and though you can make it as fussy as you like, simple is usually good. Here goes:

Difficulty	**Actual work** 20 mins	**Total time** 1.5 hrs	**Serves** 4 - 6

TOOLBOX

- A roasting tin, preferably with a rack
- A big metal spoon
- A skewer

COMPONENTS

- 1 chicken, roughly 2kg
- 1 good-sized lemon
- 1 small bunch of thyme, sage or tarragon
- 2 cloves of garlic
- A drizzle of olive oil
- Salt and pepper

METHOD

1 Put the oven on at 230°C.

2 Peel the garlic clove, then wallop it with the flat of your knife to crush it.

3 Stick it inside the chicken (now's a good time to check you haven't got a plastic bag full of giblets up there; if so, pull it out). Incidentally, you want the end furthest from the wings, not the neck end. Just in case you were wondering.

4 Season the inside with a few twists of salt and pepper. Then stuff in the lemon (cut in half) and herbs.

5 Put it in the roasting tin, on a rack if you've got one. Drizzle it with olive oil, spritz with salt and pepper.

6 As soon as the oven's up to temperature, slam it in.

7 After about 15 minutes, take it out and, using a big spoon, splosh the juices from the bottom of the tin all over it. Also known as basting it, if you're feeling expert.

8 Turn the oven down to 190°C and put the bird back.

9 Take it out after 30 minutes and baste it again.

10 After another 20 minutes, check it by sticking a skewer into the fleshy bit between the leg and the body. If the juices are pink, put it back for ten minutes and test again. If not, turn the oven off. If it's not properly cooked, chicken can be deeply dangerous, so make sure the juices are completely clear and always err on the side of safety.

11 You'll need the tin-full of juices to make gravy (see page 77), so put the chicken on a big plate or serving dish and put it back in the turned-off oven, with the door ajar, for 15 minutes. If the oven's otherwise occupied, cover it loosely with kitchen foil and leave it on one side for the same amount of time.

12 Carve. Whip off the wings and save them to put in the gravy, or to nibble later. Slide your knife (nice and sharp of course) between the legs and body, then cut the legs off. You could cut them at about the knee joint to make four bits. Now the fiddly bit – it might help to stick a fork, or even a carving fork, in to hold it steady. Slide the knife down the breastbone, neatly separating the breast portions. No, it won't work perfectly – there'll be bits left over. Use a small sharp knife, or even your fingers, to get all of these off. Don't forget the little tasty bits underneath, and the 'parson's nose' down by the tail has a few morsels worth excavating too. The French call these *sots l'y laissent* – the bits only berks leave.

ALTERNATIVES AND IDEAS

■ Roasted vegetables go well with chicken, so why not save space and do both at once? Quarter an onion plus some sliced parsnip, carrot, sweet potato, squash, fennel, beetroot or whatever. Put it all into the roasting tin, add plenty of salt and olive oil, then put the chicken on top. Roast as above.

■ Roast garlic is very cool too. Take a whole bulb of garlic, trim off any bits of loose papery skin, hack the top off about a quarter of the way down, then add it to the tin. It comes out gooey and surprisingly mild.

■ You could use 100g of butter on the chicken skin instead of olive oil. Use the butter wrapper, foil, greaseproof paper or the back of a spoon to smear it all over, then salt and pepper. This makes it rich and nicely crispy.

■ If you've got lots of fresh herbs (keep an eye open when Council gardeners are trimming the rosemary and bay bushes they often put round properties), put them in the tin under the chicken. The more the better – it'll be smelly and gorgeous.

■ To get really crispy skin, some people stuff butter and seasonings under it. Working from the rear cavity, use your fingers and a small knife to loosen the skin, then shove in lumps of butter with salt, pepper, and possibly herbs.

Stuff it

Traditional stuffing's a good option, but can cause trouble with cooking times, particularly with a small chicken – by the time the chicken's getting dry and overdone, the stuffing's barely warm. It's often better to do it in a separate dish. Here are a few options.

SAGE AND ONION

Put about three slices of bread in a food processor and whizz them into crumbs. Add 100g of butter, a red onion, a mild salad onion or a couple of shallots (nothing too strong) and briefly whizz until they're finely chopped. Tip it into a bowl, then add a teaspoonful of sage, a couple of twists of salt and pepper, and an egg. Mix with a fork until it's about the consistency of lumpy Polyfilla. Put in the oven alongside the chicken for one hour, or stuff the chicken and add 15 minutes to the cooking time (see warning above).

RED PEPPER, WALNUT, AND CELERY

Exactly the same idea, but replace the onions and sage with that lot. For extra smoky flavour roast the pepper first over a gas burner, or under the grill.

CHOCOLATE AND HADDOCK

It's possible, but not recommended. However, the basic principle works for almost any combination of ingredients, with the bread, butter (or oil), and egg binding them together. You may like to try chopped chestnuts, apple, sultanas, fennel, garlic, cranberries, even chorizo and crispy bacon. And flavour with thyme, rosemary, oregano, lemon juice, chillies, a splash of wine... you name it. Experiment away, but don't go too mad in any one direction until you've tried a mild version first.

Slammin' Sunday treat: roast lamb

A decent bit of roast lamb – fragrant with rosemary, juicy and slightly salty – is one of the reasons that Sundays were invented. Make your day with this classic.

Difficulty | **Actual work** 20 mins | **Total time** 1.75 hrs | **Serves** 4

TOOLBOX

- Roasting tin with grid
- Metal spoon
- Small sharp knife

COMPONENTS

- 1 joint of lamb 1.5kg or so – leg is good
- 2 glugs of olive oil
- Sea salt
- Pepper
- 2 sprigs of fresh rosemary
- 6 cloves of garlic

METHOD

1. Put the oven on at 220°C.
2. Peel the garlic, then slice it lengthways into slivers. Cut the rosemary into short sprigs, about 2–3cm long.
3. Using a small, sharp knife make a cut in the lamb's skin. Push in a sliver of garlic and a sprig of rosemary. Then do it again, at about 3–4cm intervals, all over the joint.
4. Put it in the roasting tin, then splash over the olive oil, sprinkle on a teaspoonful of sea salt (normal salt will do if you haven't got the posh variety) and a twist or two of black pepper.
5. Put it in the oven, with roast veg (see page 83) if you're doing them.

Mint sauce

While redcurrant jelly and other fruity sauces are good, the classic lamb accompaniment is mint sauce. It's quick and easy, and here's a very simple version.

METHOD

1. Chop a bunch of fresh mint finely and bung it in a bowl.
2. Pour on 75ml of boiling water. Add 50g of sugar and a pinch of salt. Stir.
3. When it's cooled, add 75ml of wine vinegar. Stir. Done.

6. After 20 minutes take it out, spoon the juices over it and turn the oven down to 160°C. Put it back.
7. Baste every 20–30 minutes. It should take about an hour and a half in total – more for a heavier joint, a little less if you like it pink. Let it rest for 15–20 minutes, either in the oven, turned off and with the door ajar, or take it out and put some kitchen foil loosely over it.
8. Carve and serve with gravy (page 77) and vegetables (pages 82–83).

Cracking crackling: roast pork

While roast beef and lamb are traditional favourites some swear that a sweet, crisp bit of roast pork, with crunchy crackling, is best of all. So here's the pick of the pig.

Difficulty  | **Actual work** 20 mins | **Total time** 1.75 hrs | **Serves** 4 - 6

TOOLBOX
- Very sharp knife – a Stanley knife is good
- Roasting tin

COMPONENTS
- 1.5 - 2kg pork loin or leg
- 1 heaped tablespoonful salt
- A twist of black pepper
- 1 onion
- A splash of olive oil
- 1 bottle or can of cider (more if you're thirsty)

METHOD
1 Heat the oven to 230°C.
2 Score the skin and fat all over your joint. Use a very, very sharp knife – a Stanley knife is excellent for this. Just don't forget to clean the bits of grout or whatever off it, if you've just yanked it out of the toolbox. Cut the skin into a chequerboard pattern of about 3cm squares, or stripes 1.5-2cm apart. This will be easier if the joint's just come out of the fridge.
3 The secret to great crackling is making sure the fat is completely dry. Pat it with kitchen towel all over.
4 Now take a very large tablespoonful of salt and rub it all over the skin, making sure it's well ingrained.
5 Sprinkle on a little black pepper.
6 Chop the onion into fairly thick slices and throw it into the roasting tin.
7 Put the joint on top.
8 Put it into the oven for 20 minutes.
9 Turn the oven down to 190°C, and leave it for another hour.
10 Now turn it back to 230°C for a final 10-minute blast to get the crackling really crispy.
11 Whip the joint out, transfer it to a plate and leave it to rest while you make the gravy.
12 Follow the instructions on p77 for gravy, using the juices in the roasting tin and the remains of the onion, which should have gone really dark brown and very soft, even black and scorched in a few places. Ignore that – it'll make the gravy taste fantastic. Use the cider for your gravy liquid; it goes fantastically well with pork.
13 Eat, again accompanied with cider if you fancy it, and apple sauce (below). Don't forget to be fair when you divvy up the crackling...

Apple sauce

This is the traditional accompaniment to roast pork – it also works well with chops, sausages and almost all other piggy products.

METHOD
1 Peel and core 500g of apples (see page 45). Chop into 1cm chunks.
2 Put into a saucepan with 100ml of water, 50g of sugar, and a squirt of lemon juice (and sage or spices if you fancy), and cook slowly with the lid on, stirring occasionally, until it's gone mushy.
3 Stir in 75g of butter with a fork or whisk. Lovely.

Worth their salt: great roast spuds

Crispy on the outside, slightly fluffy on the inside, scorching hot and slightly salty... that's the perfect roast potato. They're the Holy Grail of dinner – people have gone mad searching for the perfect method. Here are three very tasty variations to save you the trouble.

Difficulty | **Actual work** 10 mins | **Total time** 50 mins - 1.5 hrs | **Serves** 4

TOOLBOX
- Roasting tin
- Biggish pan and colander (for the classic version)

COMPONENTS
- 1kg of potatoes – the classic King Edward, Desirée or Maris Piper are good; look for potatoes described as 'floury'
- Olive or sunflower oil or goose fat (excellent if you can get it)
- Sea salt
- Pepper
- 1 bulb of garlic (optional)
- 2 sprigs of fresh rosemary or 1 teaspoonful of dried (optional)

It's not quite as easy as it looks, this roast potato lark. You need to understand that potatoes can't be hurried – they'll stubbornly refuse to cook any quicker, no matter how hot the oven. They'll take exactly as long as they like, so get over it. There are some short cuts, though, so here are three variations on the greatest spud of all. If you're cooking them alongside a roast they'll stand a bit of variation in temperature, but don't skimp on the time.

VERSION 1: QUICK (50 MINUTES)
METHOD
1 Put the oven on at 200°C.
2 Put two glugs of oil, or two tablespoonfuls of goose fat, into a roasting tin and put it in the oven.
3 Cut your potatoes thinly – slices about 2–3mm thick. No need to peel them.
4 Once the oven's up to temperature and the oil's hot, take the tin out of the oven.

5 Put the potatoes into the hot oil. Sprinkle a big pinch of salt over them. If you want to, you can also add a handful of unpeeled garlic cloves and a sprig or two of fresh rosemary or a pinch of dried.
6 Shake, to coat them with the oil and salt. Put them in the oven.
7 After 20 minutes, take them out and give them a shake or a stir to stop them sticking. Put back into the oven for another 25 minutes.

VERSION 2: EASY (1½ HOURS)
METHOD
1 Put the oven on at 200°C.
2 Put two glugs of oil, or two tablespoonfuls of goose fat, into a roasting tin and put it in the oven.

3 Peel the potatoes (or not – it's your choice)
and cut them into decent-sized chunks; about
5cm on a side, roughly.

4 Once the oven's up to temperature and the
oil's hot, take the tin out of the oven.

5 Put the potatoes into the hot oil. Sprinkle a
big pinch of salt over them. If you want to,
you can also add a handful of unpeeled garlic
cloves and a sprig or two of fresh rosemary or
a pinch of dried.

6 Shake, to coat them with the oil and salt. Put
them in the oven.

7 After 20 minutes, take them out and give them
a shake or a stir to stop them sticking. Keep
doing that until they're done – which should
be about an hour and a quarter. If they're
looking a bit brown, test them with a skewer.
If they're soft and not grainy, they're done.

VERSION 3: PERFECT (1½ HOURS)
METHOD
1 Put the oven on at 200°C.
2 Half-fill a biggish saucepan with water,
add a pinch of salt and put it on to boil.
3 Peel and cut your potatoes into decent-
sized chunks; about 5cm on a side, roughly.
4 When the water's boiling, put them in the pan
and turn it down to a good bubbling simmer.
5 Put two glugs of oil, or two tablespoonfuls
of goose fat, into a roasting tin and put it
in the oven.

6 After 15 minutes, tip the potatoes out into
a colander and drain them. Leave them for
a moment to get properly dry.

7 Take the tin out of the oven. Put the potatoes
into the hot oil. Sprinkle a big pinch of salt
over them. If you want to, you can also add a
handful of unpeeled garlic cloves and a sprig
or two of fresh rosemary or a pinch of dried.

8 Shake, to coat them with the oil and salt and
make the outside fluffy. Put them in the oven.

9 After one hour they should be crispy and
starting to turn brown at the edges, though it
can take up to another 15 minutes. Test with
a skewer – they should be soft and
fluffy on the inside, not
hard and
grainy.

Golden brown: this is a good colour. White with black bits, less so

A tasty trayful: easy roast vegetables

This is a perfect accompaniment to anything you're
likely to cook in the oven, and it's also a fine thing when
you've got a random assortment of veg lurking in the
bottom of the fridge and no idea what to do with them.
Root vegetables are excellent – onions, turnips, carrots,
potatoes, parsnips, beetroots, swedes and so on. Also
good are Mediterranean veg like aubergines, tomatoes,
courgettes, squash/pumpkin, fennel, and garlic. Soft
or leafy veg, less so. Roast peas? Er, no.

METHOD
1 Put the oven on at 180°C.
2 Chop all the veg into chunks 2–3cm on a side.
No need to peel all but the most thick-skinned;
just give them a swift wash.
3 Put them into a roasting tin. Pour over a glug or two
of olive oil and sprinkle on salt and pepper. A sprig
of herbs like rosemary or thyme works well too.

4 Give them a shake or stir to mix it up, then
put in the oven.
5 After 20 minutes, check they're not sticking
and shake/stir them again.
6 Wait another 25 minutes. They should be slightly
crispy on top and gooey in the middle. Perfect.

Raring to go: great steak

It's the most basic dish of all – a big bit of animal roughly griddled until it's edible. But there's more to the perfect steak (or chop) than just heat and meat. Here's how to thrill with your grill.

METHOD

The first rule of steak is: buy the best you can. Thin, cheap bits of low-quality beef fool nobody. Sirloin or rump are best. Fillet's good too, but expensive for what you get.

Second, by far the best way to cook it is on a griddle. Hot and fast are the secrets, so make sure the pan's had a good few minutes over a high heat before putting meat anywhere near it. Put a hand above the griddle – you should feel the waves of heat coming off it.

This will make quite a bit of smoke, so you might want to close any doors and put clean washing out of the way. Then give the steak a quick drizzle of oil, plus a pinch of salt and at least a couple of good twists of black pepper, and bang it on to the pan. If you want it rare, three minutes a side will be fine. Test it by prodding it with a finger or the handle of a wooden spoon. The bouncier it is, the more it's cooked. Well-done steak is the consistency of old plimsolls, so you might want to aim for medium at most.

Leave it to sit for a couple of minutes before tucking in, so the juices can mingle and it can finish cooking.

Seal the deal: get your griddle really hot

Great chops

The less you do to a really good bit of meat, the better. And lamb or pork chops ought to come into that category. Simply grilled or griddled for seven to eight minutes per side, they're delicious with just a splash of oil and some salt and pepper on them.

However, they do take very well to being marinaded (see page 47). The classic herbs are rosemary for lamb and sage for pork. Garlic goes well with either, and so do onions. And if you want to go for a little sauciness, mint sauce or redcurrant jelly work brilliantly with lamb, while apple sauce or mustard are excellent with pork.

No need to get chippy: perfect fried potatoes

Chip shops are perfectly equipped to make, er, chips. And most of us normal humans aren't. Deep fat fryers work best when they're huge, filled with gallons of boiling oil, so that when you bung in the chips the temperature stays high, crisping the outside before they go soggy.

Difficulty 🥄🥄🥄   **Actual work** 20 mins   **Total time** 40 mins   **Serves** 4

TOOLBOX

- Large saucepan
- Deep fat fryer, chip pan with basket, or deep metal pan
- Slotted spoon or drainer
- Plenty of kitchen towel
- Cooking thermometer
- Kitchen fire blanket (see hazard warning)

COMPONENTS

- 1kg of Maris Piper or similar potatoes
- 1 litre of oil (see opposite)
- A good sprinkle of salt

The domestic ones are a bit weedy by comparison. But don't despair – there are ways to get round the problem, and some of them don't involve buying a chippy. There are two simple things you'll need to watch out for, though.

First, use a thermometer if you haven't got a deep fat fryer with one built in. It'll avoid a nasty blaze (see hazard warning) and make sure you get the right results.

Second, try to use the right sort of potatoes. Maris Piper are pretty much the best, but Desirée, King Edward or anything sold for roasting or baking will work.

METHOD

1. Fill the fryer or pan with high-temperature oil like groundnut, corn or sunflower (see hazard warning).You can use half beef dripping if you prefer a heftier taste. Set it for 150°C.
2. Put a pan of salted boiling water on a high heat.
3. Cut up the potatoes; slice along them, turn 90°, then slice again. Try to get the height and width roughly equal – length doesn't matter. Fnarr fnarr.

⚠ HAZARD WARNING!

- Chip pan fires are one of the most common causes of home-destroying, life-threatening conflagrations. To avoid an irritating 'Oh look, the cat's on fire' moment, always use an oil with a high smoke point – sunflower, corn or groundnut. Do *not* use olive oil – it will go up in flames before you get it to a high enough temperature.
- Make sure the pan isn't more than a third full.
- Ideally keep a kitchen fire blanket within grabbing reach (If not a damp, but not dripping, teatowel). Cover the pan with the blanket, which should smother the flames. Turn the stove off but don't lift the blanket for a good few minutes. *Never* attempt to put the fire out with water – it'll cause a fireball.

4. Drop into the boiling water for ten minutes.
5. Fish them out and drain them. Pat them with kitchen towel and put them on a pile of kitchen towel or a cooling tray (or the grill from your grill pan) to dry really well.
6. Bang them in the fryer for ten minutes.
7. Take them out, trying not to drip hot oil everywhere. If you want to, you can stop the process now and bung them in the fridge. They'll be fine for several days, until you need a quick chip fix – in fact some say they're better after a rest.
8. Turn the fryer up to 190°C. When it's hit the right temperature, stick the chips back in for 4–5 minutes. When they go brown, they're done. Bring on the haddock and mushy peas (see page 86).

Sea salt and battery: fantastic fried fish

Perhaps strangely, this is easier to do than chips. Get it right and you'll be well on your way to opening your own branch of The Golden Haddock or whatever your local chippy's called. One particular favourite is The Codfather ('We make you a pollack you can't refuse').

Difficulty   **Actual work** 20 mins   **Total time** 20 mins   **Serves** 4

TOOLBOX

- Deep fat fryer or large pan
- Spatula
- Large bowl
- Whisk

COMPONENTS

- 4 haddock, cod, plaice or whiting fillets, about 300g each
- 250g of self-raising flour
- 1 pinch of salt
- 2 300ml cans of cold lager
- 2 litres groundnut, corn or sunflower oil (see warning on page 85)

METHOD

1 Open one of the cans of lager. Test it carefully and exhaustively to make sure it meets your high standards.

2 Heat the oil to 190°C (See hazard warning). If you're doing the chips on page 85 this can be done before you put them in for their second frying.

3 Put the flour in a bowl, add salt, and dump the fish in it. Take it out and shake it, then put it to one side.

4 Open the other can of lager and pour it into the flour gradually, whisking as you go. It should be fairly thick and not too lumpy when you've finished. If it's like porridge, add more beer. If you just can't get it delumped, push it through a sieve into another bowl. Add a pinch more salt.

5 Coat two of the fillets with batter (just dump them in the bowl), then carefully lower them into the oil by their tails.

6 After 7–8 minutes they should be golden brown, your kitchen will smell like a chippy, and the local cats will be queuing outside your window. Take them out carefully, keep them warm, and do the other two.

7 If you're also doing chips, keep the fish warm and give the chips their final frying. Pause to pin up a couple of posters for the local swimming club and contemplate the strangeness that is saveloys. Marvellous.

Green and squelchy: smushed peas

That weird fluorescent green substance you get at the chip shop is mushy peas. Which is fine, if you like them. This, however, is a whole different thing – and it goes with more than just fish and chips

Difficulty | **Actual work** 10 mins | **Total time** 15 - 20 mins | **Serves** 4

TOOLBOX
- Medium-sized saucepan
- Colander/sieve
- Potato masher

COMPONENTS
- 250–300g of peas, fresh (shelled) or frozen or the same of broad beans
- 3–4 cloves of garlic
- 25ml of oil (about 2 tablespoonfuls)
- 25g of butter (a golf-ball-sized lump)
- About 10 mint leaves or 5 large sage leaves or a large pinch of either, dried
- Salt and pepper

METHOD
1 Fill a pan with water. Add salt and put it on to boil.
2 Peel the garlic cloves, then drop them whole into the water.
3 When the water's boiling, turn it down to a simmer and wait ten minutes for the garlic to infuse and soften.
4 Add the peas and the herbs.
5 When the peas have started to soften – 3–4 minutes for frozen, 5–8 for fresh, 10–12 for really wrinkly old ones, or the same plus 2 minutes for broad beans – drain the contents of the pan into a colander.
6 Return the peas etc to the pan and put it somewhere solid.
7 Add the olive oil and butter, plus a pinch (about three twists of the grinder) of black pepper.
8 Wallop it with the potato masher until it's a lumpy paste and all the oil's been absorbed. Taste it and add salt if necessary, and more pepper if you fancy.
9 Eat it. It also goes well with cooked ham (see page 88). Or on its own with bread, or as a starter.

Tartare sauce

This is a classic fishy accompaniment – and if you make it with home-made mayo (see page 99) you'll never touch the stuff in sachets again.

METHOD
1 Take 250g of mayonnaise and mix in half a small jar of capers.
2 Chop up three or four gherkins into tiny pieces and bung them in too.
3 Chop half a small onion or one spring onion very finely, and mix that in.
4 Chop up a sprig of fresh parsley very finely and mix it in.
5 Add the juice of half a lemon, and a pinch each of salt and pepper.
6 Stir and eat. Or put it in a jar in the fridge and keep it for later. It'll last a good couple of weeks.

Hamming it up: great roast ham

Roasting a ham is one of the easiest, but most impressive, things you can do with meat. Other than the Dance of 1,000 Sausages, but that's another story.

Difficulty | **Actual work** 20 mins | **Total time** 1.5 - 2.5 hrs | **Serves** Variable

TOOLBOX
- Roasting tin
- Foil

COMPONENTS
- A ham
- Something sticky and sweet, eg maple syrup, golden syrup, treacle or honey – even marmalade can work
- Cloves
- Mustard seeds, crushed juniper berries or other spice
- Salt and pepper

First, buy a ham. A full 6kg ham from a good butcher, with the bone in, is great. One of the small, suspiciously round and pink ones vacuum-sealed in plastic from the supermarket will do too. Smoked or unsmoked; your choice. Then cook it, and unless you totally cock it up, it'll look amazing and smell fantastic.

METHOD
1. Heat the oven to 170°C.
2. Stick the ham in for the 40 minutes per kilo, minus 40 minutes. Keep an eye on it, and if it's looking dry and crispy put some foil over it
3. Forty minutes before it's done, pull it out of the oven. Peel off the skin with a sharp knife, leaving a 1cm or so layer of fat.
4. Cut a criss-cross pattern into the fat, and to look totally professional stick a clove into the centre of each square

⚠ HAZARD WARNING!

A big ham fresh out of the oven is sticky, slippery, heavy, and red hot. Exercise extreme caution. When carving it, try to put it on a non-slip surface like a chopping board, rather than a slippery plate. And use a fork to hold it steady when cutting.

5. Pour your sticky, sweet stuff into a mug or bowl – about half a mugful will do, three-quarters if it's a big ham. Add salt and pepper, a small handful of mustard seeds or other spice, and stir.
6. Plaster the mixture – known as the glaze – over the top of the ham. The back of a spoon will do, as will a pastry brush or a small (clean!) paintbrush.
7. Put it back for the final 40 minutes. You can leave it to rest for as long as you like afterwards, or let it go cold and eat it the following day.

ALTERNATIVES AND IDEAS
- Some hams need soaking overnight in cold water before cooking – ask the butcher or read the label. A coolbox or even a bin liner in a large bucket will do for this.
- Another, more complicated, way of doing this is to boil the ham with bay leaves, garlic cloves, and other aromatic stuff for half the cooking time, then roast it for the final half. This can make it juicier, particularly with a smallish ham. In which case, just put the sticky glaze on before you put it in the oven.
- If you're boiling or soaking it, try using cider instead of water. A big two-litre bottle of cheapish but decent cider (not anything with 'Lightning' or 'Ace' on it) will be fine.

Monster mash: perfectly pummelled potato

Some people take this far too seriously. There are recipes that involve pre-cooking, thermometers, ricers, and quite possibly a small thermonuclear reactor. But you don't need all that kerfuffle. Decent mash is easy.

Difficulty | **Actual work** 10 mins | **Total time** 30 mins | **Serves** 4 - 6

TOOLBOX
- Large pan
- Potato masher
- Colander or sieve

COMPONENTS
- 1kg potatoes
- 50-100g butter

METHOD
1 Put a big pan of water on to boil.
2 Peel your potatoes and chop them into medium-sized chunks, about 4cm on the longest side.
3 When the water's boiling, bung them in. Add a pinch of salt.
4 When it comes to the boil again, turn it down to a brisk simmer. Leave them for about 20 minutes (check they're cooked with a sharp knife).
5 Drain through a colander or sieve.
6 Put them back into the pan with a thumb-sized lump of butter per person, then mash with a potato masher until they reach your desired consistency. If they're too thick, add a splash of milk. If you want fluffy mash, use a fork. Don't use a food processor or mixer; it'll be messy and it won't work.

Thoroughly mashed: get a decent masher. One with rivets like this will break

ALTERNATIVES AND IDEAS
- Just lightly crushed is good, with the skin left on (and olive oil instead of butter works well with this).
- Add crushed garlic, a teaspoonful of mustard or a pinch of dried herbs when you're mashing.
- Replace a quarter to a third of the potatoes with swede, parsnip, or that chef's favourite celeriac (a big knobbly root vegetable). Peel them, cut them into chunks, and put them in the water with the potatoes.
- For even more luxury, add double the amount of double cream instead of milk. And wear a crown while eating.

Currying favour: the Indian file

And before anybody objects, that also includes Bangladeshi, Pakistani, Punjabi, Bengali, Peshwari, and any other variation. But when we say 'curry' in Britain we all know pretty much what that means.

Difficulty   **Actual work** 20 mins   **Total time** 30 mins - 1.5 hrs   **Serves** 4

TOOLBOX

- Medium-sized frying pan
- Wooden spoon or spatula
- Slotted spoon or spatula

COMPONENTS

- 500g of lamb, chicken, fish or shelled prawns
- Thumb-sized lump of butter
- 1 tablespoonful of corn, groundnut or sunflower oil
- 1 biggish onion
- 3 cloves of garlic
- 1 cinnamon stick
- 6–8 cardamom pods
- 1 teaspoonful of garam masala
- 1 teaspoonful of ground ginger (or a sugar-cube-sized lump of fresh)
- 1 teaspoonful of ground cumin
- 300ml of water

The basic Indian-style curry (the Thai variation is overleaf) is a slow-cooked, spicy dish in a thick sauce, either oily or creamy. Of course, there are umpteen thousand variations, and that's a drastic oversimplification, but if you really get into cooking Indian food properly, there are plenty of experts willing to teach you the finer details. This is a quick-and-dirty version that you can refine (or roughen) to suit your taste buds.

METHOD

1 Put the butter and oil into your pan and heat it – but don't let the butter go brown or burn.
2 Sort your spices. Crush the cardamom pods with the flat of your knife, break the cinnamon stick into three or four bits, peel and roughly slice the garlic (see page 44), and chop your onion (also on page 44).

Cheat!

If you want to skip the first few steps in the curry recipes, buy pre-prepared curry paste. Patak's are the big name in Indian spices, Bart's and Blue Elephant are two decent makes of Thai paste, and most supermarkets sell their own brands. That'll cut your preparation and cooking time down to mere moments. But it won't taste as fresh, and you'll miss the danger of wrestling with red-hot chillies and the fun of filling your kitchen with napalm-like fumes.

3 If you're using fish or prawns, skip this bit. If you're using meat or fish, chop it into 2–3cm cubes.
4 Throw the meat into the pan and fry until brown, turning regularly. Then take it out with a slotted spoon or spatula and put it on a plate.
5 Fry the onion for three or four minutes.
6 Add the garlic and fry for another couple of minutes.
7 Add the cinnamon and cardamoms. Give them a minute. Keep stirring.
8 Add the other spices. Fry, stirring well so they don't stick or burn.
9 Throw in the browned meat, or fish/prawns, and add the water. Bring to the boil, then lower the heat and let it simmer.
10 After about 20 minutes it should be edible; quicker with prawns and fish. Meat can successfully be simmered for up to an hour longer, until the sauce is rich and thick (no upper-class jokes, please).
11 Serve with rice (see page 55) or Indian bread like chapattis or naan.

ALTERNATIVES AND IDEAS
■ You may notice that this version has no chillies at all. If you want it slightly hot, add 2–3 whole green chillies at the same time as the whole spices. DON'T peel or chop them. But keep an eye out in case you bite one later.
■ If you want it medium hot, de-seed and chop two green chillies and add them at the same time as the garlic.

■ Glutton for punishment? Three chillies, chopped, will produce astonishing, tongue-blasting heat if you leave the seeds in. But don't say you weren't warned.
■ Adding more veg can be a good thing. Try adding diced aubergine, courgette or peppers with the onion, or cauliflower, potato, okra (ladies' fingers), or frozen peas/beans (no need to defrost), at the same time as the water.
■ Replace the water with chicken, lamb or vegetable stock for a richer taste.
■ Add a 500ml tin of tomatoes instead of the water. Just watch it doesn't get too thick. Add water gradually if it starts to look solid.

⚠ HAZARD WARNING!

When preparing chillies, be very careful not to scratch your eyes, nose, or any soft tissues. Which very much includes nipping to the bog halfway through. There are umpteen horror stories about cooks' privates being dangled in pots of yoghurt to ease the crippling pain. Always wash your hands extremely well straight afterwards too – but bear in mind that chilli juice can linger on the skin for some time. And keep your nose away when frying them, too. Tear gas contains capsaicin, the chemical that's in chillies...

Fast and dangerous: Thai curry

Calling Thai and Indian curries the same word is, frankly, silly. While the Indian version is slow-cooked and juicy, the Thai version is quick to lash together and can be as dry as you like. The similarity is the spices and, of course, the heat.

Difficulty   **Actual work** 20 mins   **Total time** 20 mins   **Serves** 4

TOOLBOX

- Food processor or mortar and pestle
- Frying pan or wok
- Spatula

CURRY PASTE COMPONENTS

- 2 medium-sized (approx 8cm) green chillies
- 2 stalks of lemon grass
- 2 shallots
- A thumb-sized lump of fresh ginger
- 3 garlic cloves
- Half a 400ml tin of coconut milk
- 1 lime
- 5 kaffir lime leaves (if not, another lime)
- A 2cm piece of galangal or a bit more ginger
- 1 teaspoonful of coriander seeds
- 1 teaspoonful of cumin seeds
- 1 teaspoonful of black peppercorns
- 1 teaspoonful of sugar
- 1 bunch of fresh coriander
- A splash of soy sauce
- A splash of Vietnamese fish sauce

Here's a medium-spiced, medium-hot version with built-in noodles. But you can miss them out and do rice separately (see page 55) if you prefer.

The start of every Thai curry is curry paste, which is a squidgy, dangerous mixture of spices and other ingredients – but once you've made some, it'll keep for ages, or freeze for the next time. The main difficulty involved is finding the ingredients, but most supermarkets have stuff like lemon grass, lime leaves, and even galangal on the shelves these days. Or try your local Chinese, Vietnamese or Indian-run shop for most of these. Some places even do them prepared and frozen, so you don't have to faff about.

CURRY PASTE METHOD

1 Peel the garlic, ginger, onion or shallots, and galangal if you've got it. Chop roughly into biggish bits and throw in the food processor or mortar.

2 Use a grater to peel the zest (mind your knuckles) from your lime, or limes if you can't find lime leaves. Throw it in. Then halve it/them and squeeze the juice in too.

3 Smash the lemon grass with the blunt end of your knife, or a rolling pin. This stops it being so tough. Slice it into 2cm lengths and lob it in.

4 Top and tail the chillies. If you want it milder, slice them lengthways and scrape out the seeds (see hazard warning on previous page). Put them in too.

5 If you're using a food processor, stick everything else in the bowl and whizz until it's fairly smooth and the seeds have stopped rattling. Add the coconut milk bit by bit until you've got a thick paste.

6 If you've got a mortar and pestle, add stuff roughly in the order of hardness – seeds and lemon grass first, then ginger, and so on, adding the coconut milk last. It'll take a few minutes' worth of grinding, but it'll smell astonishing.

CURRY COMPONENTS

- A good splash of sesame oil (any decent light cooking oil will do, but sesame's best)
- 200g of protein – meat, fish, prawns, tofu etc; if it's meat, make sure it's lean and quick-cooking – pork steaks, frying steak or lamb cutlets, for instance
- Roughly 300g of veg – try picking two or three from: aubergine, baby sweetcorn (or a small tin of sweetcorn), baby tomatoes, bamboo shoots, broccoli, carrots, courgettes French or runner beans, mangetout, red, green or yellow peppers ...but nothing too dense and slow-cooking like potatoes or parsnips
- A 300g packet ready-to-wok noodles, or 250g dried noodles soaked in hot water for 15 minutes or so until soft
- A handful of fresh basil leaves (optional but nice)

7   This makes plenty – one very large curry indeed, but more likely four or so two-person ones or a couple of medium ones. Put the bit you're not using in a jar or plastic container and stick it in the fridge. It'll last three or four weeks.

CURRY METHOD

1   Prepare all the veg and meat/fish – if necessary, cut it into chunks, slices or whatever that are no bigger than a 3cm cube or equivalent.
2   Splash the oil into your pan. Put it on a high heat.
3   If you're using meat, wait until the pan's really hot and bang it in for five minutes to brown.
4   Throw in the curry paste. Keep your head back – it'll give off a fierce burst of pungent, hot gas for a moment as the spices heat up.
5   Add the veg and prawns/tofu/fish. Keep the heat high, and keep stirring.
6   After about five minutes, test the meat and tougher veg with the point of a sharp knife. When they give a little, add the noodles. Keep stirring.
7   Three minutes later, you should have liftoff. Bung in a handful of basil leaves, stir once quickly, then hurl into bowls and serve.

Curry, Chinese, & beyond

Curry often goes in the box marked 'hot, filling slop, good after a few pints'. And the same goes for Chinese, minus a few chillies and plus a cashew nut or two.

   And some of it's really that bad. Some cheap takeaways serve the sort of slop you wouldn't be able to face sober. But decent home-made curries or stir-fries, whether Indian, Chinese or Thai, are a totally different thing. Plus they're dead easy, and give you a real alternative for those days when you want to eat something out of the ordinary. And you won't have to be slaughtered to enjoy them. Your liver will thank you.

Vegging out: no meat, no fish, no problem

If you don't eat meat you already know how to pick your way through the food maze. But what if you suddenly have to cater for a hardline vegetarian or vegan? Here's your answer.

83) can be a hearty meal, you could certainly win with the pizzas or pissaladiéres on page 132, topped with a good selection of tasty vegetables. And soup (page 110) is a dead cert. With home-baked bread on the side (page 128) you'll have one very happy veggy. "But what about tofu, lentil burgers and soya sausages?" you cry. Well, what about them? The cooking instructions are usually on the back of the packet, and many of them are quite edible. However, the idea of doing an imitation version of meat is mildly odd. Though the Americans do have a vegetarian thanksgiving dish called Tofurkey. Yes, it's tofu moulded into roughly the shape of a turkey roast. Brilliant.

Here's a rough guide: Classic vegetarians are exactly what you'd imagine. No meat, no fish, but eggs and dairy products like cheese are fine. Pescetarians, as they sometimes call themselves, will eat fish but no meat. And you may come across the occasional 'no red meat' type who will tackle chicken but not beef, lamb or pork.

On the hardline wing there are vegans, who won't eat meat, fish, poultry, eggs or dairy products, honey, or indeed anything of animal origin which includes a surprising array of colourings, thickenings and other minor ingredients in food. It's down to the local health food shop for you, then, where you'll find a reasonable selection of vegan-friendly substitutes for cheese, chocolate, ice cream, mayonnaise and even, er, haggis. McPeculiar.

And then you'll find the odd person on a special diet, either for religious reasons, due to food intolerances (see Hazard Warning opposite) or because they're trying to shift a few pounds or train for some extreme sport. If you're entertaining an Olympic weightlifter, good luck with the grocery bills.

So how to cater for one of these picky customers without just serving them a standard dinner with a space where the meat should be? Not that tricky, actually.

Obviously there are plenty of recipes in here that don't contain any meat. Try the vegetables section on page 53, the salads on page 100 and many of the things on page 82 (if you're roasting spuds, go easy on the goose fat, eh?).

But, you say, these are mere accompaniments. How about main meals? Well, apart from the fact that roast veg alone (page

⚠ HAZARD WARNING!

Proper allergies are a pretty unpleasant thing. Not the "I don't like courgettes much" sort, but the proper medical ones that involve carrying an adrenalin pen and watching out for stray ingredients in everything. Unless you enjoy watching your friends or relatives convulsing on your floor, you need to be extra careful when you're cooking, and always check the ingredients when you're buying something packaged.

- **If someone's allergic to shellfish, that includes prawns, lobster, crab and so on as well as mussels, cockles and oysters. Shop-bought fish dishes, particularly soups, will often contain these.**
- **Nuts can be a real nuisance to avoid. Cakes, biscuits and chocolate are suspect, and oriental stir-fries and curries are worth keeping a sharp eye on.**
- **Milk and eggs are reasonably common causes of trouble. Tricky to avoid, but use your common sense.**
- **Gluten (the substance that makes bread flour stick together into dough) is linked with a fairly nasty syndrome called coeliac disease. However, some places sell bread baked with spelt or buckwheat flour which is gluten-free. So are rice and potatoes – you don't need to miss out on tasty stodge.**

Pesto Genovese

Here's something that always works, whether you're a hardline vegan or a committed carnivore. Tasty and zingy, with plenty of flexibility and a dash of Italian style.

Difficulty | **Actual work** 10mins | **Total time** 20mins | **Serves** 4-6

TOOLBOX

- Food processor or mortar & pestle
- Baking tray
- Large saucepan

COMPONENTS

- 50g pine nuts
- 75g Parmesan cheese, Pecorino or similar very hard cheese (leave out if you're doing a vegan version)
- 4 cloves of garlic
- 125ml olive oil
- two handfuls fresh basil leaves
- salt & pepper
- 125g per person of your favourite dried pasta

METHOD

1. Put the oven on, 220C.
2. Fill the pan with water and put it on to boil. Add a pinch of salt and a splash of olive oil.
3. Spread the pine nuts out on a baking tray and bang them in the oven for 3-4 minutes. Keep a close eye – you want them toasted, not incinerated.
4. Peel the garlic. Put it and the pine nuts in the food processor and whizz until they're a thick paste. (if you're using a mortar and pestle, adding a teaspoonful of sea salt will help you grind the garlic).
5. Add the basil, whizz briefly. Chop the cheese into manageable lumps and do the same. Add a generous pinch of salt if you haven't already.
6. Whizz again, while dribbling the olive oil in slowly, making sure it mixes well.
7. Put your pasta in the boiling water until it's done. Drain, add a bit of black pepper, throw in the pesto and stir for a moment. Serve, eat. Try to avoid snogging anyone who hasn't already had pesto for a good couple of hours.
8. If you want to store surplus pesto, stick it in a jar, dribble a bit of olive oil on the top to keep the air out, then put it in the fridge. It'll last at least a fortnight.

Pesto pestle: the classic mortar method

ALTERNATIVES AND IDEAS

- This works as a topping on loads of things. Fish or pork chops, for instance. Hardly veggy, though. Oops.
- For a more veg-friendly idea, stick a large flat mushroom per person under the grill; 3 minutes on the underside, then 7-8 on the top. Get it out and dollop pesto on it, plus a twist of black pepper. Surprisingly steak-like.
- You can add roasted red pepper to your pesto (stick a red pepper on a gas burner or under a grill for 10 minutes, turning occasionally). Chillies are good too, but be cautious.
- Any nuts will work instead of pine nuts. Almonds, hazelnuts and pecans are good; walnuts are superb with the red pepper version above.
- You can also swap out the basil for another fresh herb. Oregano/marjoram, dill or parsley work well. Sage and rosemary are great too, but keep the quantities down to a tablespoonful because they can get a bit overpowering. Test it – you can always add more if it's a bit weedy.

CHAPTER 6
LIGHTS

Whether it's filling a gap between meals, kicking off a big dinner, or providing picking fodder for when you're not really hungry but just fancy a nibble, the mini-dish is a brilliant thing.

It's also a great tactical move if you've got a bunch of people coming round and you're still faffing in the kitchen – give them something light and tasty that you've knocked up in advance and it'll shut them up for ages while you finish off the main meal's masterpiece.

It's all about taste rather than stodge here: little savoury bits of this and that to make your taste buds go 'ping' rather than your trouser buttons. Quite a bit of this stuff is healthy; that's not really the point, but it's a very worthwhile side-effect. And it's always good to give the gigantic portions a miss once in a while and go for something lighter, particularly in summer.

But if you fancy something warming for the depths of winter, you can't beat a steaming bowl of soup either. And that's remarkably good for you, particularly if you knock up your own from fresh ingredients. So embrace the lighter side of life. Go on...

Retro rocket: prawn cocktail

It's more horribly '70s than a lime green Ford Capri, but a decent prawn cocktail is still a great thing. As, indeed, is a lime green Ford Capri (3000GT with twin headlights, please).

Difficulty	Actual work 10 mins	Total time 10 mins	Serves 2

TOOLBOX
- Two small bowls or cocktail glasses
- Flared trousers
- Paisley Bri-Nylon shirt
- Medallion (large)

COMPONENTS
- 1 lettuce
- 1 spring onion
- Quarter of a cucumber
- 200g of cooked, shelled prawns
- 5 tablespoonfuls of home-made mayonnaise (see opposite) or the same of shop-bought mayo, if you're in a hurry
- 1 teaspoonful of Tabasco sauce
- 1 tablespoonful of tomato ketchup – Heinz, not cheapo rubbish
- Juice of half a lemon
- A pinch of paprika

METHOD
1. Chop the lettuce, cucumber, and spring onion finely and pile them in the bottom of two small bowls or, to be flashy, large cocktail glasses.
2. Put the prawns on top.
3. Mix the mayo, ketchup, lemon juice, and Tabasco together.
4. Dollop it on top of the prawns.
5. Sprinkle the paprika on top.
6. For extra style points, hang a prawn over the edge of the dish and/or stick a thin slice of lemon in at a jaunty angle.
7. Open a Party Seven of Watneys Red Barrel and watch *The Sweeney* for a bit. No idea? Ask your Dad.

Classy glass: use a martini glass for retro chic

More '70s Excess

Firm favourites among the Abba-fancying crowd included the dead easy pasta salad, its cousin potato salad, and a half-grapefruit speared with cocktail sticks bearing cubes of processed cheese, tinned olives and/or pineapple chunks. You can probably work out how to make that last one yourself. If you must. But both pasta salad and potato salad are simple enough and still tasty. They rely on a dollop of mayonnaise (see p107) stirred into the cooked stodge, plus sundry other bits. Of course, if you're really going retro you should use salad cream, but for a lighter, more modern version, try cutting the mayo with a good splash of olive oil. Finely chopped garlic and chopped fresh chives are excellent with boiled new potatoes – small, crisp types like Jersey Royals or pink fir apples are very good – while pasta salad can work well with chopped red or green peppers, mild onions or shallots, tomatoes, garlic and basil. Add a tin of tuna if you fancy it as a main meal. Groovy.

The mayo clinic: easy mayonnaise

This is one of those slightly terrifying but satisfyingly impressive things to make. People are genuinely awed if you make your own mayonnaise, as it's got a reputation for being tricky. Actually, it's not hugely difficult, and it really does taste better than the shop equivalent.

Difficulty | **Actual work** 20 mins | **Total time** 20 mins | **Serves** 4+

TOOLBOX
- Food processor/ mixer or
- Whisk and large bowl

COMPONENTS
- 2 egg yolks
- 500ml of olive oil
- 1 teaspoonful of mustard
- Juice of half a lemon
- Salt and pepper

Mayo is also vastly useful for a whole pile of different dishes, either as a foundation (like prawn cocktail) or an add-on. It lifts baked potatoes, is great with chips (I blame the Belgians), and can be dolloped on all manner of other things like roasted asparagus, dressed crab or, yes, a burger (see page 65 for that one). Just remember raw eggs and pregnant women shouldn't be mixed.

METHOD
1. Put the egg yolks and mustard in a food processor or mixer and whizz on slow speed (you can do this manually with a whisk and a bowl, but it's a bit fiddly – prop the bowl somewhere so it doesn't move, otherwise you'll need three hands).
2. Drip the olive oil in very, very, very slowly while mixing. Take your time – this is the tricky part. Do it a drop at a time.
3. When it's starting to thicken you can speed up the oil a bit, but only to a dribble.
4. Eventually, you'll have used up all the oil and you'll have a bowl full of lovely mayo. Add a pinch of salt and pepper and a squeeze of lemon juice, fold it in and you're done.

ALTERNATIVES AND IDEAS
- The basic mayo is great, but you can add all sorts of other stuff too. Try a teaspoonful of finely chopped garlic or shallot; a pinch of chilli powder or paprika; a large pinch of chopped herbs like thyme, oregano or parsley; tomato ketchup (for prawn cocktail, see opposite) a splash of wine vinegar to make it more tangy... just experiment.
- You may well find that leaving it in the fridge for an hour or so will intensify the flavours of some add-ons.

⚠ HAZARD WARNING!
This recipe contains raw eggs. Of course, you're using decent quality free-range eggs, aren't you? Good. Also bear in mind that pregnant people should keep well clear of all raw eggs, due to the potential salmonella risk. Best keep Junior safe.

Gone chopping: crispy coleslaw

You can buy coleslaw, but if you make your own it'll be fresher, tastier, and crunchier. And it only takes a few minutes' chopping to come up with a crisp accompaniment or standalone salad. Knife work if you can get it.

Difficulty	Actual work 5 mins	Total time 5 mins	Serves 4

TOOLBOX
- Large bowl
- Sharp knife
- Big spoon

COMPONENTS
- A small white cabbage
- About three medium-sized carrots
- A mild salad onion
- Mayonnaise

METHOD
1 Cut the cabbage in half, lay it flat, then slice it thinly, first vertically then horizontally. Put it in a biggish bowl.
2 Chop the onion finely. Put it in the bowl.
3 You've probably guessed what you do with the carrots. Unless they're old or manky, no need to peel them – just wash, top and tail them, slice down their length, turn through 90° and repeat. In the bowl with them.
4 Add three to four tablespoonfuls of mayonnaise, salt, pepper, and a squirt of lemon juice. Stir well.

ALTERNATIVES AND IDEAS
- Alternatives include adding almost any crunchy veg, sliced finely – celery, fennel, beetroot, radishes, even apples or pears.

- Walnut pieces or sesame seeds (above) can work well too.
- A squirt of salad cream in with the mayo adds a bit more kick.

Semolina? With cucumber? Oh yes: couscous salad

Couscous is one of the easiest things to prepare. Stir in a bit of olive oil, pour on boiling water and stir again. Five minutes later it's ready. There's a more complete couscous recipe on page 71, but this is a great thing to do with leftovers from a huge couscous meal.

Difficulty   **Actual work** 5 mins **Total time** 5 mins **Serves** 4

TOOLBOX
- A biggish bowl

COMPONENTS
- 300g or so of cooked couscous
- Half a cucumber
- 2 tomatoes
- 2 small carrots or 1 large one
- 1 spring onion
- A glug of olive oil
- A handful of fresh mint leaves
- Salt and pepper

METHOD
1 If you're cooking the couscous from scratch, make sure it's cooled down to room temperature.
2 Chop the vegetables into 1cm or smaller chunks.
3 Chop the mint reasonably finely.
4 Mix them all into the couscous.
5 Pour on a glug of olive oil, add salt and pepper, stir.

ALTERNATIVES AND IDEAS
- Pretty much any crunchy veg will work, cut into small chunks. Try fennel, celery, red cabbage, beetroot (this will turn it a highly amusing colour), radishes, red onion and so on.
- Also try crispy fruit like apples and pears.
- Nuts to you – pine nuts and almond, walnut or pecan pieces to be exact. Try sesame, hazelnut or walnut oil too.
- Cooked veg can also be good; it's a fine way of using up last night's roast vegetables. Dice them and throw them in.
- For a more protein-heavy version, add a drained can of tuna or even crispy bacon bits – not exactly in the North African tradition, but what the hell. Which is exactly where you're going. Got a lonely, cooked, lamb or pork chop in the fridge? Cube it and add it.
- Go more Moroccan by adding spices. Try a pinch of cinnamon, nutmeg, turmeric or cumin. Not all at once. What do you think this is, Christmas cake?

Get dressed, love: salad dressing

Salad can be, let's face it, a bit dull. There's only so much lettuce and cucumber a man can eat before starting to hunger for a big bit of cooked meat. However, there's a quick and simple way to add some zing to your greens – dressing.

This can range from bog-standard basic to incredibly elaborate, but there's one thing to bear in mind with all of them – the quality of what you put in is crucial. Decent extra virgin olive oil and good wine vinegar will make it taste heavenly. Cheap cooking oil and chip shop malt vinegar will be utterly hellish.

BASIC
Splash on oil. Splash on slightly less vinegar. Done. The French call this a *vinaigrette*.

Well dressed: oil, vinegar, onion, garlic, herbs. That'll do

BASIC PLUS
Add a squeeze of lemon juice, a pinch of salt, and a generous twist or two of black pepper.

BASIC WITH A TWIST
Use walnut, hazelnut or sesame oil, or olive oil flavoured with garlic or chilli. Try balsamic (page 27) instead of wine vinegar.

CLASSIC
Chop a clove of garlic very finely. Put it in a small jar with a good solid screw top. Add a teaspoonful of mustard, a pinch of salt and pepper, a small splash of wine, a pinch of herbs (herbes de Provence, oregano, marjoram, parsley... see page 26), and a tablespoonful of vinegar. Then top up with oil until the jar's half to three-quarters full. Shake in the style of a mad Mexican maracas maestro for a good three minutes. You did make sure that top fitted well, didn't you? Otherwise you've just coated yourself and the entire room with salad dressing.

CLASSIC ALTERNATIVES
Now you know the theory, start experimenting. Use different oils; add lemon juice or Tabasco; go oriental with sesame oil and soy sauce; try Worcestershire sauce; use a shallot or spring onion instead of, or as well as, the garlic; put some capers in (great with grilled tuna); be creative. Stick roughly to those proportions, though, and you shouldn't go too far wrong.

CREAMY DRESSING
Sometimes you need something a little more hefty, so add 100ml of sour cream, crème fraîche or double cream to the classic version above. Or use mayonnaise, either home-made (page 99) or shop-bought.

CAESAR DRESSING
Mince four garlic cloves finely, chop up six anchovy fillets, and add to the creamy version. Stonking.

Tasty quickly:
fast snacks and starters

Sometimes you need to lash something together superfast, either due
to unexpected guest arrival, absentmindedness or sudden hunger.
Here are some ideas which you can rustle up in double-quick time.

CRUNCHY SALAD

This is more a concept than a recipe. You'll need these
basic ingredients:

- Any crunchy, sliceable salad vegetable: fennel, a big
  mild onion, a beef tomato, cucumber, a large carrot etc.
- Any hard cheese: parmesan, jarlsberg, emmental,
  gouda, cheddar, etc.
- A crispy, tart fruit: apple and pear are best.
- A dollop of decent oil: olive, hazelnut, walnut, sesame etc.
- Some balsamic vinegar (see page 27).
- Salt and pepper

Pick one from each category. Slice your veg thinly, do the
same with your cheese and your fruit. Now lay them, alternating,
in an overlapping circle on a biggish plate. Drizzle the oil and
vinegar lightly over them. Add a pinch of salt and pepper, and
there you go. Tasty, crunchy and speedy.

FISHY TALES: TONNO E FAGIOLI

Or tuna & beans, as it's more sensibly called. This really is
a great lazy dish. It involves a long and arduous process,
mostly opening two tins and chopping an onion. Result.

Components
1 400g tin kidney beans, 1 250g tin tuna, A smallish,
mild onion, A generous glug of olive oil, A handful of
fresh basil, A squeeze of lemon juice, Salt & pepper

Method
1 Open the tins. Drain the liquid from both; you
  don't need it.
2 Chop the onion finely.
3 Put everything in a bowl. Add a good glug of olive
  oil, salt & pepper – not too much salt, if the beans
  have already got some added; check the tin
  – lemon juice and basil leaves. Tear the basil
  leaves up a bit if they're big ones.
4 Mix. Eat. Practise saying 'fagioli'
  – fadge-ee-oh-lee. Then try to convince people that
  it's the name of an obscure Ferrari racing driver. It often works.

Roast your nuts

Components
250-500g unsalted mixed nuts, 125-250g unsalted
mixed seeds, 1 pinch cumin, coriander and/or
fennel seeds, 3 cloves garlic, unpeeled, 1 large
pinch dried rosemary, or three 5cm twigs of fresh,
1 large pinch sea salt or rock salt, 1 large pinch
ground black pepper

Method
1 Put the pan on a low heat. Throw in everything.
2 Leave it until it smells toasty, then stir. Keep
  stirring until it's evenly brown. Stop when most
  of it looks darkish brown, and before it starts
  to develop burnt bits.
3 Put it into a bowl, try to let it cool before
  digging in.

Alternatives & Ideas
- Instead of rosemary, try adding a teaspoonful of
  sesame oil, a teaspoonful of honey and a splash of
  soy sauce. You'll have to stir more often to stop it
  sticking or burning, but it's instant oriental style.
  Add a pinch of Chinese five-spice or Thai seven-
  spice for even more Far East grooviness.
- If you like it hot, throw in two or three whole chilli
  peppers. If you like it extra hot, chop them finely
  or use chilli flakes.

Cold fish, those Swedes: gravlax

Also known as gravadlax, gravlaks or, if you're Finnish, graavilohi, this actually means 'fish in a hole in the ground', but don't let that put you off. These days, you don't have to bury your salmon unless you really want to.

Difficulty   **Actual work** 20 mins   **Total time** 2-3 days   **Serves** 4-6

PART 1
TOOLBOX
- A large glass or ceramic dish
- A plate or board that fits in it
- A heavy weight
- Greaseproof paper

COMPONENTS
- A big piece of whole salmon, 500g or so
- 3–4 large bunches of fresh dill
- 2 teaspoonfuls of white pepper
- 2 teaspoonfuls of salt
- 2 teaspoonfuls of sugar

PART 2
TOOLBOX
- A mortar and pestle or a screw-top jar

COMPONENTS
- A tablespoonful of mild mustard – Dijon will work, German mustard or hot dog mustard is better
- 1 tablespoonful of sugar
- 2 tablespoonfuls of wine or cider vinegar
- 200ml of olive or groundnut oil
- 1 handful of fresh dill

GRAVLAX PART 1
1. Hack the dill into biggish bits and squash it with the flat of your knife to bruise it. Put about a third of it into the dish.
2. Mix the salt, sugar, and pepper together.
3. Cut the salmon into two pieces down the middle. Whip the backbone out if it's still got one; likewise any small bones.
4. Rub the salt/sugar/pepper mixture into the cut sides of the fish.
5. Put one piece in the dish, skin side down. Put about half your remaining dill on top. Then put the other piece on top of it, like a sandwich. Put the rest of the dill on top and around it.
6. Cut a piece of greaseproof paper to fit inside the dish, then put a plate or board on top, plus something heavy (a kilo or so) to weight it down.
7. Put it in the fridge for two to three days, taking it out at least a couple of times a day to turn the salmon over and pour the juices over the fish.
8. When you're ready, take the salmon out and slice it as thinly as possible with a very sharp knife. Then do Part 2...

GRAVLAX PART 2
1. Chop the dill very finely.
2. If you're using a mortar and pestle, put the dill in with the mustard, sugar, and vinegar. Stir well.

3. Dribble in the oil; carry on mixing so it forms a smooth, thick paste.
4. If you haven't got a mortar and pestle, no worries – put all the ingredients in a screw-top jar and shake like mad. It won't be quite as thick, but it'll be just as tasty.
5. Cover the salmon with the sauce. If you leave it in the fridge for half an hour it'll intensify the flavour, but you don't have to. Particularly fine eaten with brown bread, watercress, and a glass of cold Scandinavian lager.

Swede dreams: go Scandinavian with salmon

Nice to eat you: salad niçoise

It's a firm favourite in the South of France, but the locals have long wine-fuelled rows about what exactly goes into it and how to make it. Well, here's a simple version. No arguments, now.

Difficulty   **Actual work** 20 mins   **Total time** 20 mins   **Serves** 4

TOOLBOX

- A large bowl
- 2 saucepans; one small, one medium
- Sieve or colander
- Slotted spoon or drainer

COMPONENTS

- 500g new potatoes
- 1 Little Gem or Romaine lettuce
- 200g green beans (fresh or frozen)
- 70-100g jar or packet of black olives
- 4 eggs
- 1 200g tin tuna (in water, preferably)
- 250g tomatoes
- A splash of olive oil
- 2 cloves garlic
- Salt & pepper

METHOD

1. Fill both saucepans with water and put them on to boil.
2. While that's happening, wash and dismantle the lettuce. Chop the stem off and split it into its leaves; line your bowl with them.
3. Unless you're using baby new potatoes, cut them into quarters. No need to peel them.
4. When the water comes to the boil, put the potatoes in the bigger pan and the eggs in the smaller one. Bring them back to the boil then turn them down to a simmer. Check the time.
5. If your tomatoes are biggish, cut them into quarters. If you're using cherry tomatoes, halves will do.
6. Open the tin of tuna and drain off the liquid.
7. Cut the tops and tails off the beans.
8. 7-8 minutes after you put the eggs in, fish them out with a slotted spoon or drainer. Let them cool.
9. 10-12 minutes after the potatoes started cooking, throw in the beans.
10. 5 minutes later the beans should be done, and so should the potatoes. Drain them into a colander or sieve, then run cold water over them for a couple of minutes to cool them down.
11. Chop the garlic finely.
12. Peel the eggs and quarter them.
13. Assembly time. Throw everything into the lettuce-lined bowl, then splash a good glug of olive oil over it and give it a stir to separate the tuna and make sure it's all covered in garlicky oil.
14. There you go. Time to open a nice bottle of rosé and settle down to watch the Brigitte Bardot lookalikes promenading down the beach in the sunshine. What, you mean that doesn't happen in Doncaster?

ALTERNATIVES AND IDEAS

- You can make it even quicker by using a 300g tin of new potatoes instead. You can use tinned beans too if you insist, though they tend to be a bit slimy and tasteless.
- If you want a posher version use fresh tuna steaks, splashed with a little oil, salt, pepper and lemon juice then griddled or grilled for 3-4 minutes per side. Break the steaks into bite-sized chunks and add them to the salad. Don't worry if they're still a bit warm.
- Some of the salad dressings on page 102 would be great on this – try a red wine or red wine vinegar one, with herbs like finely chopped rosemary, thyme or basil.

Tapas: nibbles with attitude

Anybody who's been to Spain, or many restaurants here, knows how tapas works. Loads of small dishes are plonked in the middle, and everybody helps themselves. It's perfect party food. If you keep a few suitable things in the fridge it's jolly fine for a midweek lash-up.

BREAD AND OLIVES

Make your own bread (page 128). Make it more Spanish by using white flour and plenty of olive oil. But don't soak your own olives. It's a long-winded, unreliable pain. Buy them.

PIMIENTOS DE PADRON

Surprisingly obscure, but if you see a bag of these smallish (about 25mm), pointed, bright green peppers in the local supermarket, deli or ethnic shop, buy them. Fry them in decent olive oil until they start to scorch, then take them out, shake plenty of sea salt over them, and eat, holding them by the stalks, which you can discard. Mostly mild, but every tenth or so is hot. Russian Roulette, Spanish style.

PATATAS BRAVAS

Basically roast potatoes (page 82) served with a spicy tomato sauce (use the tomatoey pasta sauce recipe on page 67, but add a couple of chopped chillies along with the onion, and a teaspoonful of pimentòn towards the end; leave out the meat if you're feeling veggie). But the key ingredient, like a lot of Spanish food, is pimentòn – smoked paprika (see page 27). A perfect trick if you've got lots of leftover roasties.

ALBONDIGAS

Meatballs to you. The burger recipe on page 65 will work perfectly well, though you can use half and half pork and beef, plus a pinch or two of oregano, and make the meatballs smaller; golf-ball-sized is plenty. The patatas bravas sauce above works with these too.

GAMBAS AL AJILLO

Prawns with garlic. Use biggish prawns; cook them for a couple of minutes in plenty of hot, but not smoking, olive oil, add lots of thinly sliced garlic (at least a clove per person), then cook for two minutes more. Use a slotted spoon to put them in a bowl, pour over some of the garlicky oil, then sprinkle on a biggish pinch or two of finely chopped parsley. Use bread to mop up.

CHORIZO

Gorgeous spicy sausage. Buy soft rather than dry if you can, slice it about 10–15mm thick, then bang it on a hot griddle or dry frying pan. Give it three minutes, then turn it over for the same. It needs nothing else.

SALAD

It's up to you. The Spaniards have a liking for that rather odd 'Russian Salad' with grated carrot and the odd hard-boiled egg, but anything fresh and crisp will go well with tapas. Plenty of oil, sea salt, and lemon juice as a dressing is good.

DRINK

Yes. San Miguel beer, of course, out of large bottles. A chunky red Rioja will hit the spot. And if you're feeling flashy, there's a stonking and unusual white from the North of Spain called Albariño. That's Al-bar-een-yo, like a Brazilian footballer.

Ai caramba! Tortilla!

This chunky, delicious Spanish speciality, also known as the Spanish omelette, is more than enough for a meal. The only snag is that it takes at least 45 minutes, so it's not an instant snack. But it's well worth the wait and is just as good cold the next day, so make loads.

Difficulty | **Actual work** 20 mins | **Total time** 1 hr | **Serves** 4 - 6+

TOOLBOX

- Medium-sized frying pan, with lid (or anything that will cover it, like a large heatproof plate)
- Spatula
- Fork
- Large bowl

COMPONENTS

- About 3 large or 5 medium potatoes
- 6 eggs
- A biggish onion (preferably Spanish, of course)
- Olive oil
- A pinch or two of oregano, sage, or any herb you prefer

METHOD

1 Halve the potatoes, then slice them thinly (about 2–5mm).
2 Peel, halve, and slice the onion thinly.
3 Put a hefty glug of olive oil into the pan and heat it up.
4 When it's starting to spit, put in the potatoes and onions, stirring well to mix them together.
5 Add a sprinkling of salt and pepper.
6 Put the lid on, and turn it down as low as it'll go. Keep an eye on it in case it starts to burn, and shake or stir it occasionally.
7 Crack the eggs into the bowl. Add the herbs and mix with a fork for a minute or so, until it's all the same colour. You don't want to beat them too much or it'll go all frothy.
8 15–20 minutes after you put them on, the potatoes should be cooked. Test them with the point of a knife – if they're soft you're all set.
9 Tip them into the bowl with the eggs and herbs. Mix gently – don't make them into eggy mash.
10 Put another glug of oil into the pan, and put it on full blast again.
11 When the oil's spitting, put the egg/spud mix into the pan, then turn it right down. Flatten the top a little.
12 Leave it simmering. Run a spatula round the sides occasionally to tidy them up. It'll be at least 20 minutes, maybe closer to 30, before the bottom and middle are cooked, and the top's starting to look much less liquid.
13 Here's the flashy bit. Using the lid, or a large plate on top, turn the pan upside down. (See hazard warning below.) Then slide the inverted tortilla back into the pan. The spatula will be helpful here. Cook for another three minutes or so.

Cheat!

If you bottle out at stage 13, just stick the whole lot under a lowish grill for three minutes or so. It works, and nobody will ever know.

14 Turn the gas off and leave it to cool for 5–10 minutes. It'll coagulate into a springy, dense mass of tasty stodge. Estupendo!

ALTERNATIVES AND IDEAS

- You're welcome to try adding extra ingredients like sliced chorizo, ham, olives, prawns, roasted peppers, chillies, tuna, garlic, chicken, sweetcorn, tomatoes... your imagination (and larder) is the only barrier. But there are two rules:
- If you're adding uncooked ingredients, particularly chicken or prawns, stick them in with the potatoes at the beginning and make sure they're well cooked. Cooked ones can go in with the eggs halfway through.
- Keep the quantities small – a handful of anything will be plenty, or you'll risk ruining the consistency and ending up with a collection of small potatoey lumps instead of a large, neat tortilla.

⚠ HAZARD WARNING!

The chances of getting stage 13 dangerously wrong are high. Scalding olive oil, superheated egg and bits of slippery potato could go everywhere, including on you. Wear oven gloves and do it somewhere mess-proof, like over a big baking tray or a clean draining board.

The serious sarnie: filling sandwiches

Sandwiches have got to be edible without special tools. What are those enormous American-style sandwiches all about, exactly? If it's held together by a skewer, and you can't get it in your mouth without taking it to bits, it's no longer a sandwich, but a meal involving some bread.

That having been said, there are some spectacular things you can pack between two bits of loaf. Just remember that if you're dealing with bitty, slippery ingredients you need some sort of glue to make them sandwichable. Mayonnaise is the classic – see our recipe on page 99 – but other things can work too. No, not Araldite.

Here are a few ideas, but remember that a sandwich is a very individual thing. Tweak, edit, and remix at will.

- **Tuna and cucumber** – A great summer special. Try a squirt of lemon juice and plenty of black pepper.
- **Tuna and sweetcorn** – Mayo is the key here, otherwise you've got a sort of sweetcorn scattergun.
- **Ham and mustard** – Hand-carved ham is always tastier than machine-sliced. Something to do with the fibres, apparently. Use good ham and your favourite mustard, but don't overdo the mustard – it's not supposed to make you cry.
- **Ham and cheese** – Use Emmental or Gruyère, as they slice nice and thinly. Sliced dill pickles or gherkins can be a good thing.
- **Roast beef and horseradish** – If you know anybody who grows horseradish, beg or steal a bit of root from them and plant it in a bucket full of earth. It'll grow like mad and just-dug-up, freshly-grated horseradish is awesome. Exactly halfway between a condiment and a chemical weapon.
- **Brie and cranberry sauce** – Any French person would be horrified. Do you care? No, thought not.

- **Smoked salmon** – A good squeeze of lemon juice, plenty of black pepper, and that's all you need. Brown bread's good here. If you must have greenery, try watercress or rocket.
- **Peanut butter and jam** – Or jelly as the Yanks call it. One for the more sweet-toothed, but smooth PB with blackcurrant or strawberry jam can work. Also try PB and banana, or even honey.
- **The Elvis** – Bacon, banana, and peanut butter on toasted bread, fried in bacon fat. He's dead, you know.

Porky, bready, happy: bacon or sausage sandwiches

Apologies to butchers, but a great bacon sandwich is made (or ruined) by one thing – the bread. Home-made is best, of course (see page 128 for more on that), but a good fresh loaf from your local bakers will do.

Don't buy sliced plastic bread, unless you have a real yen for the cheap, greasy caff experience; it's sweet and gummy, and will leave you unsticking bits of soggy dough from your fillings for days. If you still need convincing, Google 'Chorleywood Bread Process'.

BACON

cooked to your taste, either thin and crispy or thick and soft – should be decent stuff, not the plastic-sealed type which is mostly water. Streaky will crisp nicely; back is more meaty and dense. Follow the method on page 150 and that should sort you out.

SAUSAGES

Thick, thin, herby, plain? It's up to you. One thing you should try to do, though, is halve them before you stick them in the sandwich. Cook them through in a well-greased frying pan or on the griddle, then whip them out of the pan, halve them, and give them a final minute, cut sides down, to get them slightly crisp. You can do the same trick if you prefer to grill them, but try not to let them dry out too much. Halved, they'll give a more manageable sandwich – one that's less likely to explode and ping hot grease into your lap.

Condiments

Mustard's good. Ketchup or brown sauce if you like. For a bit of oriental sweetness on sausages, try a splash of soy sauce and a light smear of honey. And horseradish can work on bacon too. Experiment. It's your sandwich, after all.

Like food, but you drink it: soup

Whether it's a light snack, a Thermos full of outdoorsy nourishment or a hefty winter warmer, the liquid meal otherwise known as soup can fill a gap like nothing else. Here are a few bowlfuls of ideas.

BASIC VEG SOUP

Fry a chopped onion in olive oil for 5 minutes. Add 500g of chopped root vegetables and a litre of water. Maybe a bay leaf and a little salt and pepper. Bring to the boil, then simmer for 30 minutes or longer. Could it be any simpler?

PEA AND HAM SOUP

Perfect for using up leftover ham from the recipe on page 88. Throw the bone in too. Or beg a ham bone and its attached scraps from your local supermarket's deli counter. They'll think you're mad, but it's dirt cheap and delicious. Fry an onion as above, then add a litre of water, ham bone and/or bits, 300g of split peas, salt and pepper, and a bay leaf. Cook for an hour until the peas are soft.

PEA AND HAM II

Try the recipe above, but leave out the split peas and use a 500g bag of frozen peas instead. After 30 minutes, take the ham bone out and whizz the soup briefly. Put it back in the pan and give it another ten minutes.

Soup gets a bad reputation; the bog-standard tinned versions like tomato, cream of mushroom or chicken are at best a bit average and at worst deeply dire, often featuring a weird metallic aftertaste and mouth-puckering levels of salt.

But if you make your own you'll find that doesn't have to be the case. Tasty, hearty, and healthy, home-made soup is a whole different thing. Stick it in a Thermos and take it out with you, or serve it in a bowl with home-baked bread on the side and you'll discover why it's such a great meal.

It's as straightforward as you like too. Yes, you can construct an elaborate and long-winded recipe involving many techniques and gadgets, but you really don't have to. If you've got a stick blender (see page 14) that might make life easier for some of these, and some soups are good blended or whizzed in a food processor, but it's all up to you and how lumpy or smooth you like your soup.

Here are some easy ones.

Like Leeks? Almost any veg will make great soup

PEA AND HAM ADD-ONS

Carrot, celery, and leeks are all good with ham too. Dice them finely and throw in with the onion.

FISH SOUP

There's a stonking recipe for this on page 72.

CREAM OF CHICKEN SOUP

Leftover chicken is great for this. Start with the onion as usual, then add a chopped stick of celery and/or a leek, then at least a litre of water. Sage or thyme is nice too. If you're using the remains of a roast chicken, bung it in, bones and all (not the stuffing), boil, then simmer for at least 40 minutes. Then pour it through a colander into a bowl or big jug to catch the big bits. If you can be bothered, you can dig out the bigger, more edible bits and put them back into the soup at this point. Put it back in the pan, stir in 125ml of double cream and give it another five minutes.

TOMATO SOUP

Chop and cook an onion, a stick of celery, and a couple of carrots in olive oil. After a few minutes, add a couple of cloves of garlic. Chop 500g of fresh tomatoes roughly, then throw them in, followed by a litre of water. A little dried thyme, oregano or rosemary won't hurt, plus salt and pepper. Boil, then simmer for about an hour. When the tomatoes have gone soft, whizz it briefly, then put it back in the pan. Taste it – you might find a teaspoonful of sugar is good, and don't skimp on the black pepper. Then give it a few minutes to reheat. Stir in 125ml of cream at the end if you like. You can use a couple of tins of tomatoes if you're out of fresh ones.

SWIFT SPANISH SOUP

Start with cooking the onion as usual but add about 125g of chorizo (see page 106) and, after three or four minutes, four cloves of garlic, sliced. After another couple of minutes, throw in a drained 400g can of chickpeas, a can of chopped tomatoes, a bay leaf, a good pinch of dried oregano, and either a teaspoonful of pimentón or paprika (see page 27), a pinch of chilli flakes, or half a chopped red chilli. Careful, now. Simmer for 20 minutes.

CURRIED LENTIL SOUP

This will have terrible side-effects tomorrow, but it's lovely. Cook an onion in oil for five minutes. Then add a litre of water, 200g of lentils, and a pinch each of cumin, coriander, turmeric, and chilli flakes. Cook for 30 minutes, by which time the lentils should be very soft. Just before serving, stir in two tablespoonfuls of yoghurt and a handful of chopped fresh coriander.

AND THERE'S MORE

If you've read this list, you'll be starting to realise that there's a basic formula at work here. Cook an onion and maybe a few other veg until they start to soften; add water (or stock if you like); throw in the main ingredients; cook until done. In some cases you then whizz it or add cream, yoghurt, or fresh herbs. Now you know the one-size-fits-all recipe, off you go. Make soup out of anything you like. Except, possibly, chocolate cake or next door's cat.

CHAPTER 7
SWEET RUNNING

There's a school of thought that says puddings just aren't manly. And as for cakes and biscuits, they're definitely women's work.

This is cobblers. Which, coincidentally, is the American version of crumble. Even if we don't mention Spotted Dick, which is inarguably the most masculine dish on any menu anywhere, a good pud is a real achievement.

If you're cooking for a potential girlfriend she'll be pretty impressed by your skill with a starter and very complimentary about a well-crafted main course. But make a pudding and she'll be all over you like lumpy custard.

And if you're catering for kids, you'll win their little hearts with a great dessert. Plus you can use it as a very effective bargaining counter in the never-ending Vegetable Wars: 'No carrots, no afters...'

There's also great potential for cheating in the dessert department. While home-made everything is a nice idea, nobody's going to take umbrage if the custard, ice cream, jam and so on are straight from the local supermarket. Many of the best desserts are a swift assembly job involving little effort but huge rewards.

Biscuits and cakes, meanwhile, are the sort of thing you can lash together quickly while doing something else, but will brighten your day and everybody else's. Take a tin of home-baked biscuits to work and you'll suddenly discover that even grumpy old Janet from Accounts will become your new best friend. Go on, unleash your sweet side.

A bit peaky: mastering meringue

It's not too difficult, but for some reason people find it a bit scary. Just be careful about a couple of things and you'll be fine. You can make some superb things with it, too, like pavlova or lemon meringue pie (see below), and the Baked Alaska on page 115.

Difficulty | **Actual work** 20 mins | **Total time** Variable | **Serves** 4 - 6

TOOLBOX

- Large mixing bowl and whisk or mixer
- Small bowl

COMPONENTS

- 3 egg whites
- 125g of caster sugar
- A pinch of salt
- 2 drops of vanilla essence (optional)

METHOD

1. Make sure your bowls are clean and dry. It won't work if they aren't.
2. Crack the eggs and pour the whites into the small bowl (see page 46 for more details). Make absolutely sure that there isn't any yolk in with them – that's another failure factor.
3. Put the egg whites into the mixing bowl and whisk like mad until they're white, fluffy, and stand up in stiff peaks. It shouldn't slop when you tilt the bowl.
4. Add the salt, and vanilla essence if you like.
5. Whisk in the sugar gradually. Don't overdo it, or it'll collapse again.
6. Add to your recipe and cook. There are several different ways of doing this...

PAVLOVA (& STANDALONE MERINGUES)

1. Cook long and slow. 130°C for at least one and a half hours is the way to go. It won't hurt to turn the oven off and leave the meringue in it for a while afterwards either.
2. For a fruit pavlova, line a flat baking tray with greaseproof paper, dollop the meringue into the middle, then spread it out to the edges, making a sort of nest shape. Cook as above, then fill with whipped cream and fresh fruit.
3. For standalone meringues put tablespoon size dollops onto greaseproof paper and cook as above.

LEMON MERINGUE PIE

1. Put the oven on at 180°C.
2. Make pastry (see page 116) or buy some. Line a pie dish with it. Put it in the oven, filled with greaseproof paper and some lentils or beans, for 15 minutes. Then ditch the beans and paper and put it back for another ten. It should be light golden brown. Take it out and turn the oven down to 160°C.
3. Make the filling. Grate the rinds of three lemons (preferably unwaxed) into a saucepan. Squeeze the lemon juice in, then add 200ml of water. Bring to the boil.
4. Mix a tablespoonful of cornflour with a small amount of cold water, then add to the pan and stir in. Simmer for about three minutes until it starts to set.
5. Beat three egg yolks until they're frothy, then stir in to the lemon mixture. Heat for three minutes – very gently unless you like lemony scrambled egg.
6. Let it cool for five minutes, then pour into the pastry case.
7. Dollop the meringue on top, squidging it with the back of a spoon to make peaks.
8. Put it in the oven for 20 minutes, or until the tips of the peaks are starting to go brown.

Very cool. Also hot: Baked Alaska

This is really an assembly job, but the finished product is ridiculously more impressive than any single part. Make this and you will be cool forever. And hot. Simultaneously.

Difficulty   **Actual work** 30 mins **Total time** 2 hrs + **Serves** 4 - 6

TOOLBOX
- An ovenproof plate
- A decent-sized freezer

COMPONENTS
- Half a home-made sponge cake (see page 122) or a shop-bought sponge flan case
- Meringue mixture
- A large tub (500ml) of ice cream
- 3–4 tablespoonfuls of jam
- 1 tablespoonful of brandy or rum (optional)

METHOD
1 Clear plenty of space in your freezer.
2 Get the ice cream out of the freezer.
3 Put the sponge on the plate.
4 Dollop the jam on top and spread it around.
5 Dig the ice cream out of the tub and put it in a rough mound on top of the jam.
6 Stick it all in the freezer.
7 Make the meringue.
8 When it's stiff and peaky, get the cake/ice cream construction out of the freezer.
9 Spread the meringue over the whole thing, making sure it's all well covered.
10 Put it back in the freezer for at least an hour. Longer won't hurt – next day is fine.
11 Fifteen minutes before you want to eat it, put the oven on at 220°C.

12 When the oven's warmed up, stick it in for no more than five minutes. Three might do – check if the meringue's starting to go brown on the peaks. If so, it's done.
13 For extra cool, heat a ladle of brandy or rum over the hob the moment it comes out of the oven, then light it and splash it (carefully) over the pudding. Flaming ice cream! Brilliant!

Arctic Roll

This is a variation on the theme, where you use a Swiss roll (see page 123) filled with ice cream and jam. It's a swine trying to roll up a warm Swiss roll before the ice cream melts, but if you're quick and brave it's possible. It's easier to slice and serve, too.

So it's good pie from me: perfect pastry

So why make your own? Well for a start, it'll be fresher, won't have preservatives or other additives in it, and it's really very little hassle to do. Plus all-butter pastry, made with a decent free-range egg, is delicious. Here's a classic no-frills recipe for shortcrust pastry.

Difficulty   **Actual work** 20 mins   **Total time** 1 hr   **Serves** Variable

TOOLBOX

- Food processor or mixer (see page 13)
- Smallish jug, mug or bowl
- Cling film
- Rolling pin
- Pie dish or flan tin (that's the one with the detachable bottom)

COMPONENTS

- 250g of plain flour, plus a little extra for flouring the worktop
- 200g of butter, plus a dab extra for greasing the pie dish
- 1 egg yolk
- 3 tablespoonfuls of cold water

METHOD

1 Put the flour and butter in the food processor or mixer. Whizz until it looks like fine breadcrumbs.
2 Mix the egg yolk and the water together.
3 Add to the mixture and pulse until it all squidges together into one lump.
4 Take it out, put it on a well-floured board and make it into a round dollop.
5 Wrap it in cling film, then stick it in the fridge for at least half an hour. Longer is fine, even overnight. It can be frozen too – just make sure you defrost it well before you use it.
6 Then get it out, put it on your well-floured worktop or board, flour a rolling pin, and roll it flat. Then put it into your pie dish, greased with a little butter, and trim the edges with a knife. Don't forget to leave enough for a lid if you're doing a full pie. After that, the world's your oyster. Or oyster pie.

ALTERNATIVES AND IDEAS

- If you want a sweeter pastry, try adding 50g of icing sugar and using milk instead of water. You could also throw in a pinch of cinnamon, nutmeg or allspice. Great for apple pie.
- For a professional look, brush beaten egg yolk or milk thinly over the top of your pie before baking. It'll go nice and glossy.
- For some types of sweet pie you'll need to bake it blind. No, that doesn't mean shutting your eyes and slamming it in the oven. It means baking the pastry on its own first, lined with baking parchment or greaseproof paper, and with a few handfuls of dried beans, lentils or similar inside to keep it in shape. Give it 15 minutes at 190°C with the beans in, then take them and the paper out and keep baking it until it's a light, biscuity colour. After that, it's filling time – see below.

- If you're doing a pasty or a meat pie, head over to pages 136 - 139 .
- Puff pastry is more work, but useful for some things like meat pie toppings, sausage rolls or apple strudel. Double the amount of butter above, and don't mix it as smoothly; leave bits of butter showing. Then make it into a lump and chill in the fridge as above. When you roll it out, fold it over itself at least three times, roll it flat, fold it again, and so on about five or six times. You should end up with lots of layers, and when it's baked you'll get fluffy, buttery puffiness.
- Filo pastry (also known as phyllo) is like super-thin, multi-layered puff pastry with oil instead of butter. It's good for samosas, spring rolls, savoury parcels, and that sticky-sweet Greek stuff, baklava. It's also an absolute pig to make. Unless you've got the patience of several saints and the touch of a concert harpist, just buy it off the shelf.
- Apple pie filling is easy – just peel, core, and slice 750g of apples and stick them in your pie, mixed with 100g of brown sugar and a pinch of nutmeg, cinnamon, and/or cloves. If you want it mushier, put it all in a saucepan with 100ml of water and cook it on low for 20 minutes.

Packet pastry

There's a type of pastry which takes very little time and almost no skill to prepare, will work for every recipe, and is amazingly difficult to mess up. It's the type that comes in a packet from the local shop. And you know what, it's absolutely fine. The big names, like Jus-Rol, Saxby's or filo pastry specialists Antoniou are readily available and convenient.

Crumbs! That's easy: apple crumble

Crumble is yet another variation on pie – it's basically sweet pastry, but without the liquid and the last stage of mixing. And it's very straightforward indeed.

Difficulty   **Actual work** 15 mins   **Total time** 1 hr   **Serves** 4

TOOLBOX
- Food processor or mixer
- A deep bowl or dish – must be ovenproof

COMPONENTS
- 250g of plain flour
- A pinch of salt
- 150g of brown sugar
- 200g of butter
- 500g of cooking apples
- 50g of brown sugar
- A pinch of cinnamon, nutmeg, allspice or ground cloves

METHOD
1 Put the oven on at 180°C.
2 Whizz the flour, salt and butter until it looks like breadcrumbs.
3 Add the sugar and give it one quick final whizz.
4 Peel and core the apples (see page 45). Put them in your bowl or dish, cover them with the sugar and spice, and give it a quick stir.
5 Pour the crumble on top, making sure it's roughly even.
6 Put it in the oven for 45 minutes. Done. Excellent with custard (see page 119).

ALTERNATIVES AND IDEAS
- Pretty much any soft fruit will do. Pears are great if you add about 25g more sugar, plums (stoned, man) are good; apricots (ditto) are fine; gooseberries, blackberries and so on work too.
- Add a handful of nuts or mixed fruit to give it extra vroom.
- Or try a mix – apple and blackberry, plum and almond, redcurrant and weasel (maybe not that one, then). But test out your own favourite fruits.

Cool as anything: no-bake cheesecake

This is dead straightforward and pretty reliable. It doesn't make a huge cheesecake, though, so double everything (and use a bigger tin) if you're starving or have hungry guests coming. The biggest problem you'll find, though, is not eating all the biscuits before you start.

Difficulty | **Actual work** 25 mins | **Total time** 1 - 2 hrs | **Serves** 4 - 6

TOOLBOX
- Saucepan
- Plastic bag or clean tea towel
- Mixing bowl and spoon (or food processor/mixer)
- Whisk (or hand mixer)
- Medium-sized (18cm) cake or flan tin – it would save aggro if it's got a removable bottom or spring-clip sides
- Kitchen foil

COMPONENTS
- 250g of digestive biscuits (half a large packet)
- 100g of butter
- 450g of sugar
- 400g of cream cheese
- 4 tablespoonfuls of lemon juice
- 250ml of whipping cream

METHOD
1 Melt the butter in a saucepan. Slowly – don't let it burn or go brown. Turn it off when it's liquid.
2 Add 50g of sugar to the butter, then stir it in.
3 Put the biscuits in a bag or a folded, clean tea towel. Smash them up with a rolling pin or similar heavy weight. Or use a food processor.
4 Add your biscuit crumbs to the pan, then stir them in.
5 Line the tin with the buttery, crumby mixture. Use the back of a spoon or the bottom of a glass to pack it down well. Then put it in the fridge.
6 In a bowl (or a food processor/mixer), beat the cream cheese, the rest of the sugar and the lemon juice together.
7 Whip, or whizz, the cream until it's stiff. Fold it in to the mixture, gently so it doesn't go sloppy.
8 Take the crust out of the fridge and put the filling into it. Smooth it down a bit, then put it in the freezer, covered with foil, for at least an hour – two wouldn't hurt.
9 Take it out, run a knife round the edge to loosen it, then put it on a serving dish or plate and stick it in the fridge.

ALTERNATIVES AND IDEAS
- Add 150g of chocolate, melted then allowed to cool, before the cream. Chocolaty and gooey. Or try 50g of cocoa powder, roughly swirled through it.
- Dump half the lemon juice and add 2–3 drops of vanilla extract.
- Add the grated rind of a lemon to your biscuit mixture for more lemoniness.
- Add a teaspoonful of ground cinnamon to the biscuit base, for that American-style flavour.
- Top with soft fruit: sliced strawberries, blackcurrants, kiwi fruit, whatever. Nothing too crunchy, though, or it'll disintegrate when you try to eat it.
- Use Oreo cookies for the crust. Or try wholemeal Hovis digestives and brown sugar. Or HobNobs. Or ginger biscuits. Use your imagination.

Who are you calling cowardy? Real custard

You can buy custard in a pot or carton from the local shop and it's mostly absolutely fine, particularly the posher ones (not soymilk custard, though – that's disgusting slop). But sometimes you might fancy making the real stuff, which is even nicer than shop custard.

Difficulty | **Actual work** 10 mins | **Total time** 10 mins | **Serves** 4

TOOLBOX

- Medium-sized saucepan
- Bowl and whisk
- Wooden spoon

COMPONENTS

- 500ml of whole milk (if you've only got semi-skimmed, add 50ml of single cream)
- 3 egg yolks
- 25g of sugar
- 1 tablespoonful of cornflour
- 1 vanilla pod or three drops of vanilla essence/ extract

METHOD

1 Put the milk (and vanilla pod if you're using one) in the pan and put on a low heat.
2 Put the egg yolks, sugar, and cornflour into the bowl and whisk them thoroughly.
3 By this time, the milk should be simmering. Don't let it boil or burn. Whip out the vanilla pod, and pour the milk into the bowl while whisking briskly.
4 Keep whisking until it's smooth, then pour it back into the pan. Add vanilla extract or essence. Keep the heat low and bring it back to a simmer while stirring it with a spoon.
5 Slop it into a jug and serve it immediately. It'll get a skin after a few minutes cooling, but some people like that bit. If you're not one of them, try putting a saucer on top of the jug.

Cheat!

Steamed pudding is a nuisance to cook from scratch – it takes ages and can easily turn into a rubbery football. But decent shop-bought ones last forever – they often come in tins or can be frozen, and, brilliantly, can be microwaved in mere seconds. Keep a few, plus a carton of long-life custard or some ice cream, in the back of the cupboard or freezer for emergency dessert when you've got unexpected guests, when something's gone badly wrong, or when you're just feeling particularly piggy.

Dark and deadly: chocolate mousse

This is one of those dishes with a built-in limit. No matter how lip-smackingly fantastic it is, you'll find yourself unable to eat more than a bowlful, because it's so stomach-bogglingly rich. Lovely, though.

Difficulty | **Actual work** 15 mins | **Total time** 1 hr 15 mins | **Serves** 4

TOOLBOX
- Medium saucepan
- Wooden spoon
- Bowl and whisk

COMPONENTS
- 150g of really decent dark chocolate
- 150ml of double cream
- 2 eggs
- 1–2 tablespoonfuls of your favourite sweetish alcohol – rum, brandy, Grand Marnier, Cointreau, whatever (no, not Bacardi Breezer)

METHOD
1 Put the cream in the pan and put it on a medium heat.
2 Chop the chocolate finely.
3 When the cream comes to the boil, turn it off, add the chocolate and stir well until it's melted.
4 Add the alcohol.
5 Break and separate the eggs. Add the yolks to the pan and beat in.
6 Whisk the egg whites until they're white and frothy, then stir it in gently, bit by bit, until the mixture's as light as possible. Not too hard or you'll knock all the air out.
7 Put it in a bowl, then stick it in the fridge for an hour or so to set. Or you can use little glasses or coffee cups, in which case you could bung an almond, walnut or a small biscuit on the top of each one. Very classy.

Choc and awe: use good dark chocolate

It's a fruit fool

An alternative to the mousse is a fruit fool. Stew some fruit (gooseberries or rhubarb are good) either in the microwave for 10 minutes or on a low heat on the hob for 15-20 minutes. When stewed, mix in sugar until it's sweet enough for your taste. Stir in 200ml of custard (out of a carton is fine). Whip up a small pot of double cream until stiff and fold the fruit mixture into the cream. Put into small bowls or one large bowl and chill in the fridge for a couple of hours.

Snack yourself silly: basic biscuits

Biscuits are so easy you wonder why McVities ever made any money. Plus it's as flexible as you like. Invent your own flavour of biscuit and win... an unusual biscuit

Difficulty	**Actual work** 20 mins	**Total time** 1 hr	**Serves** Loads

TOOLBOX

- Food processor or mixer
- Cling film
- 2 baking sheets or trays
- Cooling rack or grid

COMPONENTS

- 90g of butter
- 90g of caster sugar
- 200g of plain flour
- Half a teaspoonful of baking powder
- Half a teaspoonful of vanilla essence
- 1 egg
- A little extra butter for tray-greasing

METHOD

1 Beat the egg.
2 Put everything into a food processor or mixer and whizz until it forms a paste.
3 Put a large sheet of cling film on your worktop.
4 Scrape the mixture on to the film and, wrapping the film around the paste, roll into a log shape. When you have a reasonable size log, screw the ends of the plastic up (Christmas-cracker style) and place in the fridge for at least 30 minutes. Longer is fine, overnight is OK.
5 Put the oven on at 180°C.
6 Grease two baking sheets. Lightly smear butter on them with a bit of kitchen roll or a butter wrapper.
7 Take the log out of the fridge and carefully remove the cling film. Cut the roll into slices with a sharp knife. It should make about 20. Place, spaced well apart, on to the baking sheets.
8 Cook for ten minutes or until slightly coloured.
9 Take them out of the oven and allow to cool for two minutes before placing on to a cooling rack. Try not to eat them all before putting into an airtight tin.

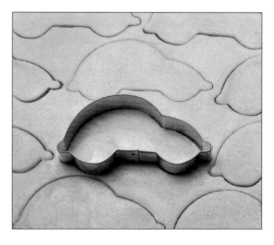

ALTERNATIVES AND IDEAS

- Chocolate version – Replace 55g of flour with 55g of cocoa powder.
- Really chocolaty cookies – Just before placing on the cling film, add 75g of chopped chocolate (white, milk, or plain and bitter). If you make them thicker they're great with ice cream and/or soft fruit as a dessert. Cook for a bit longer if making giant cookies, say 15 minutes.
- Lemon biscuits – Add the grated rind of a lemon to the basic mixture and replace the vanilla essence with a few drops of lemon essence or the juice of half a lemon.
- Cherry – Add 75g of glacé cherries, rinsed of their sticky coating, dried, and cut into quarters. Add at the same stage as the chocolate pieces (see above).
- Spiced up – The possibilities are (almost) endless: experiment at will. Just don't add curry powder, but mixed spice is fine.
- Instead of rolling mixture into cling film, you can roll out flat on a floured surface and use a cutter.

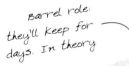

Barrel role: they'll keep for days. In theory

Victoria's secret: the classic sponge cake

This is one of the simplest and easiest recipes. It's so straightforward you only need to know one quantity – the weight of the eggs. Clever. It's also a great recipe to keep kids occupied, and then stickily full, for a while, as there are millions of possible decoration and filling options.

Difficulty | **Actual work** 20 mins | **Total time** 45 mins | **Serves** 6 - 8ish

TOOLBOX
- Large mixing bowl and wooden spoon or mixer
- 2 round cake tins, about 20cm across
- Skewer
- Wire rack or cooling tray

COMPONENTS
- 4 eggs
- Caster sugar (see below for quantity)
- Self-raising flour (and again)
- Butter (yes, here too)
- A couple of drops of vanilla essence (optional)
- A sprinkle of icing sugar (for the top, if you're not going to ice it)
- A large dollop of jam and/or cream (for the filling)

METHOD
1 Get the butter out of the fridge.
2 Put the oven on at 180°C.
3 Smear butter inside the cake tins. Be generous, otherwise you'll have a sod of a job getting your cake out intact. You could use greaseproof paper too if you've got really old and shonky non-non-stick tins.
4 Weigh the eggs, in their shells. Then here comes the clever bit – the other ingredients should weigh exactly the same as the eggs. If they weigh 226g, you'll need 226g of butter, 226g of flour, 226g of sugar... get it? Brilliant.
5 Put the sugar in your bowl. Weigh the butter and cut it into 2–3cm lumps. Add that and mix until it's creamy. This will be easier if your butter's not too cold.
6 Crack the eggs, one at a time, and beat them in.
7 Keep beating and add the flour.
8 If you like, drip in a couple of drops of vanilla essence. Not essential, but nice. Mix in.
9 Divide the mixture between the two tins.

10 Stick it in the oven. After 20 minutes, stick your skewer in. If it comes out wet, they're not done yet. Test again in five minutes.
11 When the skewer comes out dry – likely to be 25–30 minutes – take the cakes out of the oven.
12 Let them stand for five minutes, then carefully run a knife round the outside and turn them upside down on to a wire rack. With luck, they'll pop neatly out. This may not happen. If not, try giving the bottom of the tin a sharp tap or two. Or bite the bullet and try to ease them out with your knife or a small, flat spatula. If they do leave a chunk behind, pick it out of the tin and stick it back. Nobody will notice once it's filled and iced, particularly if you put the tatty one on the bottom.
13 When they're cool, dollop your favourite jam on top of the lower half, and whipped or clotted cream if you're feeling piggy, then add the top half and sprinkle some icing sugar on. Sifting it through a sieve gives a more professional effect.

"we are not a mousse": Victoria sponge

ALTERNATIVES AND IDEAS

- Chocolate sponge is easy – just stop weighing the flour about 50g before you've reached the right weight and top it up with cocoa powder.
- Lemon sponge – add a tablespoonful of lemon juice with the eggs, and/or lemon essence. You could add some finely chopped lemon zest for even more lemoniness.
- Marble cake is flashy but simple. When the cake's done, divide your mixture into two. Add colouring to one half (or both, for extra pizzazz). Food colouring's good, or a couple of tablespoonfuls of cocoa powder mixed in. Then fill the cake tins with alternate dollops of each half. When you've used it all up, take a knife and swirl it through the mix a few times. Bake as before – you should end up with a thoroughly psychedelic cake. Top with brightly coloured icing and hundreds and thousands for a deeply trippy experience, man.
- Swiss roll is straightforward, but timing's important. Make half the quantity above (two eggs), and use a flat tin, well lined with buttered greaseproof paper or baking parchment. It'll only take 10–15 minutes to cook. When it's done, immediately turn it out on to a piece of greaseproof paper, sprinkled with icing sugar, slightly bigger than your roll. Cut the edges off, and make a shallow cut (not all the way through) 1cm or so in from the nearest short edge. Spread it with jam, but not all the way to the edge. Then use the shallow cut to start rolling it up, and carry on until you've got a neat roll. If you wait until it's cooled to do this, though, it'll crack. Now use it for your Arctic Roll (see page 115).

I should cocoa: chocolate sponge

Basic icing

- 250g of icing sugar
- 1–2 tablespoonfuls of warm water

METHOD
1 Beat the water into the sugar until it's hit the right consistency.
2 Warm water makes it shinier.
3 If it's too dry add water, but only a tiny amount, as it goes a long way. Too wet? Add more sugar.

Butter icing

- 250g of icing sugar
- 125g of butter (ideally unsalted)
- 1 tablespoonful of milk

METHOD
1 Beat the butter until it's soft, then start adding the sugar.
2 Towards the end, add the milk.
3 If it's too dry, add more milk; too wet, add more sugar.

As nutty as a... great fruit cake

This is a very fine thing at any time of year, but it's also the basis of a stonking Christmas cake – make it a few weeks in advance and drip-feed it alcohol at regular intervals and it'll be on particularly good form. A bit like many of the relatives you're likely to have round at Christmas.

Difficulty 🥄🥄🥄 | **Actual work** 30 mins | **Total time** 3 - 4 hours | **Serves** 8 - 10

TOOLBOX

- Deep round cake tin (approx 20cm diameter), ideally with spring-clip sides and/or a removable bottom
- Large mixing bowl and wooden spoon or mixer
- Baking parchment
- Skewer

COMPONENTS

- 250g of butter
- 250g of brown sugar (dark muscovado or Demerara is good)
- 250g of plain flour
- Half a teaspoonful of baking powder
- 4 eggs
- 75g of ground almonds
- 1kg of chopped nuts, dried fruit, candied peel, dried banana, coconut, cranberries, sultanas, figs... whatever you fancy
- Juice of 1 lemon
- A glass of brandy

METHOD

1 Put the oven on at 150°C.

2 Butter your cake tin, then butter enough baking parchment to line the tin and do so. This will stick like an absolute sod if you're not careful to keep it well greased.

3 Chop all your bits of dried fruit, nuts etc into smallish (around 5–10mm) bits.

4 Beat the butter and sugar together until they're fluffy.

5 Add the eggs, one at a time. Keep beating.

6 Add the nuts and fruit, brandy, and lemon juice, and mix them in well.

7 Gently mix in the baking powder and flour. Make sure it's well mixed, but don't go mental.

8 Stick it in the oven for two hours. Then poke it with a skewer. If it comes out dry, it's done; if not, bung it back. Depending on your oven, the sort of fruit you've used, and many other factors including the weather in Bulgaria and the price of peas, it could take another hour or more. It won't be hurried so keep calm.

9 Take it out of the oven and leave it to cool in the tin. Don't try to get it out until it's pretty much cold. Then be gentle. You may have to run a thin-bladed knife round the edge.

10 Put it in a tin or airtight container – an old biscuit or chocolates tin is ideal. Every few days, spike the top with a skewer and dribble in a bit more brandy (or whatever you've got lying about – sherry, rum or whisky can work too). It'll last months, but three weeks to a month is just fine.

The Xmas factor: Christmas cake

To make a proper Christmas cake, of course, you'll need to ice it, and bang on a plastic robin or some such nonsense. But icing won't stick to a big squidgy fruitcake, which is why people use a layer of marzipan between the cake and the icing, and jam as glue under that.

Difficulty	Actual work 20 mins	Total time 20 mins	Serves 8 - 10

COMPONENTS

- 200g of brown sugar
- 200g of icing sugar
- 400g of ground almonds
- 2 eggs
- A splash of brandy
- 1–2 drops of vanilla or lemon essence
- Pot of jam (apricot is favourite)

You can buy pretty decent marzipan ready-made, but don't buy the very cheap stuff, as it's tooth-rottingly sweet and tastes of nothing except a faint whiff of disinfectant. Marzipan should be sweet but almondy. And a bit of brandy never hurts.

METHOD

1 Put the brown sugar, icing sugar, and ground almonds in a bowl or a mixer.
2 Beat the eggs and mix them in.
3 Add a splash of brandy and a drop or two of vanilla or lemon essence.
4 Beat it until it's a solid dough. If it's too dry, add more brandy. If it's too wet, bung in a few more almonds.
5 Plop it on to a board dusted with icing sugar and roll it out until it's a flat sheet. Cut a circle about 2cm bigger than your cake.
6 Spread your cake with a thin layer of jam then bung the marzipan on top. If the top's risen so it's dome-shaped, cut a slit from the middle to the edge of the marzipan so that it fits.
7 Roll the rest of the marzipan into a long strip and fit it round the edge. Crimp the top and sides together. Using more than one bit's fine; the icing will cover most minor bodges.
8 Then leave it for a couple of days to dry, otherwise the icing won't work.
9 After that, use the royal icing recipe above and get creative. Remember that reindeer are surprisingly difficult to draw with an icing nozzle, though.

Royal icing

- 250g of icing sugar
- 2 egg whites
- 1 tablespoonful of lemon juice

METHOD

1 Beat the lemon juice and egg whites together.
2 Add the sugar and keep beating.
3 Keep this somewhere airtight if you're not going to use it immediately, or it'll set and you'll end up with a brick.
4 This has raw egg in it, so it's best not to serve it to anybody pregnant.

Frosty the snowman: if you really must

CHAPTER 8
OVENDRIVE

Of all the big, impressive gadgets you can have in the kitchen, the oven is definitely a contender for top spot. Yes, it's only a steel box with a door and pitifully few knobs on the front, but it gets really, properly, crisp-your-own-face hot.

And the best thing you can do with it is bake stuff. Roasting's good, but if you master the art of baking you are truly a Jedi knight of the kitchen.

That's because it's usually seen as being tricksy and difficult to master. Any oaf can slam a big bit of meat in for an hour and a half at gas mark 5, then get it out looking like a proper roast. Satisfying, tasty, but somehow slightly obvious.

But baking starts with apparently unpromising raw ingredients like flour and water, and produces a fantastic loaf, a pie like Mum made, a professional-looking pizza or rustic pasta that would impress any Italian. Sheer magic.

But here's the best bit – it's dead easy.

Yes, there are bread enthusiasts (doughspotters?) who get all worked up about the right kind of yeast, the ambient temperature and the perfect crust, and drive everybody around them mad by filling the airing cupboard with buckets of fetid yeasty slop and driving 400 miles to buy artisan-ground rye flour from a semi-derelict watermill in deepest Wales. But you don't have to be one to make great bread.

Likewise, pies are just common sense. Pasta's easy if you've ever played with Play-Doh. And pizza is no problem either – apart from being an excuse to get your oven as hot as it'll go and do some really scorching stuff.

So turn the big knob on the front of the oven to 11 and off we go...

Bake it like a man: bread

The one tricky thing about baking your own bread is finding the time. It's one of those things that's best done in bits, in between other stuff, over a few hours. But the total amount of work is only about 20 minutes; there are just a few longish gaps between the various parts.

Difficulty | **Actual work** 15 mins | **Total time** 2 hrs | **Serves** 12+ slices

TOOLBOX

- Food processor or mixer (an old Kenwood Chef with a dough hook works very well – see page 13)
- Measuring jug
- Baking tray, loaf tin, or pizza stone (page 14)
- Cling film
- Wire mesh cooling tray (or clean grill pan rack)

COMPONENTS

- 650g of strong bread flour
- 400ml of water
- 15ml of oil (about a tablespoonful) or 15g of butter (about a thumb-sized lump)
- 1 sachet (7g) of instant yeast
- 1 teaspoonful of sugar
- 1 teaspoonful of salt

METHOD

1 Put the kettle on.
2 Put everything except the water in the food processor or mixer and mix until the oil or butter's absorbed and it's looking slightly breadcrumby.
3 Mix 200ml of boiling water with the same of cold, so it's warmish.
4 Rev up the mixer again, and trickle the water in gently, waiting until one splosh is absorbed before adding the next. When you're done, after about five minutes, it should be clagged together into a smoothish ball. If not, leave it going for another minute or two. Sometimes you may need to add more water if it's not turning to dough, but give it a good while before deciding. More often you may have to add a little more flour, if it's still wet and soupy. Always add carefully, a little at a time.
5 Leave it in the bowl and wander off for a while. If you're using a mixer, you'll need to cover the bowl with cling film (wipe a bit of oil on it to keep it from sticking) to keep it airtight. Food processors are usually pretty well sealed anyway. Try to keep it out of cold draughts in both instances, though. If you're making a batch, turn the first one out into a lightly oiled bowl and cover as above, then start again with your next loaf.
6 Come back in 30 minutes to see how it's doing. If it's doubled in size (in a smallish food processor that'll look dangerously bulgy), you're ready for the next step. If not, keep coming back every ten minutes or so until it's big enough.
7 Tip it out of the bowl and on to a well-floured board or worktop (don't throw away the cling film yet).

8 Give it a pounding. You're trying to knock the air out and squash it back to its original size, more or less. This is the step where you can do elaborately impressive proper baker-style kneading, if you've got someone to impress. Or just wallop it randomly for about five minutes. Sprinkle more flour underneath if it starts to stick.

9 Once it's well beaten up, shape it roughly into the sort of loaf you like and put it into its final home – on a floured baking tray, in a loaf tin, or leave it on the floured board if you're using a pizza stone. Cover with oiled cling film; possibly the bit you've saved from the mixer bowl. A damp tea towel will also work.

10 Put the oven on as high as it'll go (probably 250°C).

11 Leave the loaf for another 30 minutes or so to rise. You can bung it in the fridge or anywhere cold if you want to really slow it down, so you can go to the pub or wherever for a couple of hours.

12 When it looks a good size, cut a slash or two in the top with a very sharp knife, and sprinkle with flour if you like.

13 Stick it in the oven, which should be seriously hot, then immediately turn it down to 220°C. Do this quite carefully; don't hurl it in and then slam the door, or you'll knock the gas out of it and end up with a doorstop.

14 After 30 minutes, pull it out and tap the bottom. If it sounds hollow, it's done. If not, pop it back for another five minutes, then test again.

15 Put it on a wire mesh rack or similar to cool. DON'T be tempted to hack off a slice yet; all the gas will escape and it'll go flat and soggy. Wait at least an hour. Sorry. It's worth the wait, though.

Breadmaking

Breadmaking can be messy. But when you clean up, use a dry cloth first to catch stray flour, then *cold* water to wash your doughy tools. Hot water and flour makes an amazingly strong glue, which will cover everything in sight including you, and can only be scraped off with a sharp knife and a great deal of care. If you've left it a bit long, soak the dried-on dough in plenty of cold water.

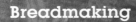

Knead more ideas: advanced bread

If you've taken off your dough-basher's L-plates, it's time to experiment with some more adventurous bread. Here are a few tips and tricks to make you into a true lord of the loaf.

- **Tins** – Put your dough into a tin if you want that tidy toaster-shaped slice.

- **Rolls** – At step 8, cut the dough up into however many rolls you want. Continue for the rest of the recipe, but cut the cooking time to 15 minutes.

- **Breadsticks** – Same principle, but cut the dough into flat sheets, then slice to the size of a drinking straw or a pencil. Spread on several trays and bake for ten minutes.

- **Small stuff** – If this is too much loaf, try 500g of flour and 300ml of water. Reduce the other ingredients roughly to suit, but you can still use one sachet of yeast; it may just rise a bit faster.

- **Crust tweaking** – Some bakers believe Vitamin C improves the crust; try crushing a 500mg tablet (not an orange-flavoured one) into the mix at step 2.

- **Water injection** – Most commercial bread is baked in a steam oven. You can get a similar effect by placing an oven-safe bowl or tray of boiling water at the bottom of the oven. Or open the oven every ten minutes or so and spray the sides and top with a plant squirter. Remember to empty the Baby Bio out first.

- **Flour power** – Obviously this is the crucial ingredient. So be picky. Try to use good-quality flour, preferably organic. And if you're anywhere near a working mill, even better. Firstly, they're fascinating, impressive bits of machinery, and secondly, they generally grind extremely good flour.

- **Floured up** – Try different types. Nowadays, you can get smoked flour, kamut (a sort of yellowish Middle-Eastern grain which is very good for bread), granary, wholemeal, rye, French, and many more. Mess about all you like, provided you stick to mostly strong bread flour (normal plain flour doesn't make a decent dough). But you could add 100g or so of fine pasta flour to give a silky texture to a white loaf. Some flours are drier than others, particularly granary and wholemeal, so you may need to add slightly more water.

- **Oil change** – Try varying the type of oil you use. Butter is classically British and olive is pleasantly Continental, but sesame or even hazelnut oil can be great for a brown loaf.

- **Sweet success** – Try swapping the sugar for maple syrup, honey, treacle, or pretty much any mild-flavoured sweet stuff.

- **Seedy business** – Sesame or poppy seeds are good on top of a loaf. Or get adventurous with fennel or caraway seeds.

Painless deep pan: perfect pizza

It's the classic Italian fast food, but it's very easy, and satisfying, to make at home. Home-made pizza is one of the finest things you can eat. Domino's? Who needs 'em?

Difficulty | **Actual work** 25 mins | **Total time** 1.5 hrs + | **Serves** 2 - 4

TOOLBOX

- Food processor or mixer (an old Kenwood Chef with a dough hook works very well – see page 13)
- Measuring jug
- Cling film
- A thin, rimless baking sheet or bakers' peel (see page 14)
- Pizza stone or unglazed quarry tile (also on page 14), or possibly a large cast-iron griddle pan

COMPONENTS

- (Makes one large pizza or two small ones)
- 250g of strong bread flour or Italian Type 00 (pasta) flour
- 150ml of water
- 30ml (about 2 tablespoonfuls) of olive oil
- 1 sachet (7g) of instant yeast
- 1 teaspoonful of sugar
- 1 teaspoonful of salt

METHOD

1 Put the kettle on.

2 Add 75ml of boiling water to the same of cold, so it's warmish.

3 Mix the yeast, oil and sugar into the warm water and give them five minutes or so to mix properly.

4 Put the flour and salt into the bowl of your mixer or food processor. Start it up on a slow speed and gradually add the liquid.

5 The dough should end up silky and bouncy, like a giant marshmallow. If it's too wet, add a little more flour; too dry, add a splash of water.

6 Put your ball of dough into a lightly oiled bowl (the easiest method is usually to drip a bit of oil in and wipe it round with a bit of kitchen towel) and cover it with oiled cling film or a damp tea towel. Leave it somewhere warmish for an hour or so, until it's doubled in size.

7 Plop it out on to a well-floured worktop or board – marble's supposed to be best for this, but anything will do – and squish it around to knock the air out of it.

8 Cut it in as many pieces as you want pizzas (the quantities above will make two medium-sized ones), roll them into a ball, and either wrap them in cling film and put them in the fridge until they're needed or use them right away.

9 About half an hour before you want to eat, put the oven on as high as it'll go, and if you have a pizza stone or quarry tile, put it on a low shelf.

10 Get the dough out of the fridge, flatten it out to a suitable size and shape – be careful it's not too big for your tray or stone – making sure the edges are a little higher than the rest, and put it on a well-floured, thin, rimless baking sheet or baker's peel. Add topping (see below).

11 Bake until it's crispy and browned. Depending on your oven temperature, this could be as little as five minutes, but 10–15 is more usual.

Puzzling over pizza

Pizza, even more than bread, is the subject of fierce debate. Making the perfect pizza is a subject that causes endless angry arguments – many of them about what the perfect pizza actually is in the first place.

Americans prefer a chewier, deeper crust, Italians like it thin and crispy. Then there's the French who, as usual, have their own version that loses the cheese and usually adds anchovies and olives. They call it *pissaladière*, and claim, if anybody's listening, that they invented the whole idea. Of course.

If you go online and search for pizza recipes, you'll soon find yourself in a weird world of dangerously modified ovens, yeast mixes purloined from local restaurants, tomatoes flown in from the Marzano Valley and gaggles of bulgy-eyed lunatics who claim to have discovered the ultimate pizza. One restaurant in New York even had the water of Naples analysed so they could reproduce it exactly...

But, basically, there are three equally important elements to good pizza. Get these right and it's easy and tasty:

- The dough – fresh and bouncy
- The topping – sparse but tasty
- The heat – as high as your oven can manage

Perfect pizza: the topping

There are as many favourite toppings as there are Italians. Maybe more. But here's how to put together your own ideal slice of pizza perfection.

Difficulty	**Actual work** 30 mins	**Total time** 30 mins	**Serves** 2 - 4

TOOLBOX

- Sharp knife
- Can-opener
- Medium saucepan
- Spatula or wooden spoon

COMPONENTS

- 3 tablespoonfuls of olive oil
- 2 cloves of garlic
- Half an onion or 1 shallot
- 1 tin (400g) of peeled, chopped tomatoes
- Half a teaspoonful of dried oregano or 1 handful of fresh basil leaves
- Salt and pepper
- A pinch of sugar (optional)

METHOD

1 Pour the olive oil into the pan. Put on a medium heat.
2 Peel and finely chop the onion or shallot.
3 Add to the pan, stir.
4 Peel the garlic and smash the cloves with the side of your knife blade.
5 Add to the pan.
6 After about five minutes, when the onion and garlic have started to soften, add the tomatoes and stir.
7 Leave to cook for 15 minutes on a low heat, stirring occasionally.
8 Add the dried oregano, if you're using it, and salt and pepper to taste. You can also add a pinch of sugar if the tomatoes you're using are slightly bitter. Give it another five minutes.
9 If you're using fresh basil, chop or tear the leaves (some say this helps them keep their flavour) and add them right at the end.
10 Use the mix as a base layer on your pizza, spreading thinly with the back of a spoon, then add your favourite extras. For instance mozzarella cheese, pepperoni, prawns, olives, anchovies, rocket, a whole egg (just break it on top of the pizza before you put it in – it'll be perfectly cooked when it comes out), ham, cooked chicken or bacon, mushrooms... whatever you fancy.
11 Try splashing a trickle of olive oil on the top just before it goes into the oven. Add a sprig of basil after it comes out for extra flashiness.

Topping tip

Remember, sparse is best. Topping overload will make your pizza into an inedible, half-cooked mush.

Veg: go sparse but crisp and tasty

Meat: salami's classic. Try chorizo too

Cheese: thinly grated but now powdered

Sauce: not too much. It's not soup

Base: home-made (p131) is best

Extreme pizza tricks

...and there's more. Just when you thought it was safe to go back in the kitchen, here are some ideas to turbocharge your pizza, from simple to seriously scary.

PISSALADIÈRE

At risk of offending every French person, it's much the same as pizza. Try making it in an oblong baking tin with the tomato sauce topped with a criss-cross pattern of anchovies, dotted with pitted, halved black olives, a light dusting of chopped rosemary, and a generous splash of olive oil. Nice, as they say in Nice.

CALZONE

A stuffed, folded pizza, like a giant Italian pasty. Make the pizza as usual, but for the topping use a mixture of:

- 50g of mozzarella, in 1cm cubes
- 25g of ham, ditto
- 25g of salami, ditto
- 25g of ricotta cheese, crumbled
- 1 egg
- A pinch of oregano
- Salt and pepper

Mix it all together, then dump it on one half of the pizza. Fold the other half over, crimping the edges. It'll take a few minutes longer than a standard pizza to cook, but it's hugely filling. Other fillings will work too – just experiment.

⚠ HAZARD WARNING!

The griddle-pan method described below involves shifting incredibly hot, heavy objects, so is fearsomely dangerous. Wear stout oven gloves and be super-careful. Test that your griddle pan will fit in the oven before you start!

THE GRIDDLE-PAN METHOD

Loopy genius chef Heston Blumenthal may well be to blame for this method of getting enough heat to cook pizza properly. Put a cast-iron griddle pan on the stove, on a high heat. Meanwhile, put your oven's grill on as high as it'll go. After 20 minutes put the hot griddle pan, upside-down, on the middle shelf of the oven and give it another five minutes under the grill. By this time, everything will be red hot. Then slide your pizza gently on to the underside of the griddle pan, close the door and stand well back. But don't wander off: a pizza can cook in as little as two minutes using this trick.

HAND-MADE DOUGH

This is messy but fun. Dump the flour and salt in a pile on the worktop, and make a well in the middle. Pour the liquid into the well and gradually mix the flour in using a fork or your fingers until your dough achieves the right consistency. Then complete from step 6 of the recipe.

Italian styling: manual pasta

This could be the ultimate Italian recipe. Messy, sticky, complicated and with plenty of possibilities for hysterical handwaving. But also stylish, tasty and filling. Molto bene!

Difficulty 🥄🥄🥄🥄 | **Actual work** 40 mins | **Total time** 1 hr 15 mins | **Serves** 4 - 6

TOOLBOX

- Large area of clean worktop or flat marble slab
- Rolling pin
- Cling film
- Clean broomstick(s)
- Tea towels
- Chairs
- Large pan

COMPONENTS

- 500g of flour (pasta flour, often called 'Tipo 00', is best; fine plain flour will work), plus a bit more for flouring the worktop
- 5 large eggs – free-range, organic or local; quality is important
- A pinch of salt
- A splash of olive oil

METHOD

1 Weigh the flour.
2 Mix in the salt.
3 Make the flour into a mound on your worktop, with a hollow in the middle.
4 Break the eggs into the middle of the mound, working them in as you go with your fingertips.
5 When it's all one lump, keep kneading until it's smooth and silky to the touch.
6 Wrap it in plenty of cling film so it's airtight and stick it in the fridge for half an hour.
7 Flour your work surface very well. Get the dough out of the fridge. Cut off a lump about the size of a tangerine, then squash it flat with your hand. Rewrap the rest and put it back in the fridge.
8 Flour the rolling pin, then get rolling, first one way then the other. If it starts to stick, dust more flour. You're aiming for a thin sheet about 30cm square. Then fold it in half and roll again; repeat at least four times until you've got a long, thin sheet that's 1–2mm thick.
9 Dust with flour yet again, then roll into a cylinder and slice thinly – 5–8mm slices for tagliatelle, 1–2mm for spaghetti.
10 Hang your pasta over a clean broomstick, dusted with flour, to dry. Prop it between two chair backs. Or use the chairs themselves, or any clean, horizontal edge. One of those ceiling-mounted clothes hangers would do fine. Use floured tea towels on the table if nothing else is available.
11 Now get another chunk of dough out of the fridge and repeat until you've used it all.
12 By this time, your kitchen will look like a nightmare of dangling pasta, flour, tea towels and mess. Don't worry.

Pasta della casa 16v turbo

This is a really good case for buying a flash gadget or two. Firstly, pasta dough is a lot easier to mix in a food processor or powerful mixer (see page 13), and secondly, a pasta machine (page 14) will save a lot of grief. Plus pasta machines are shiny, with lots of exciting mechanical bits, and styled like part of a 1930s Alfa Romeo. And they're not pricey – a cheapish one can be found for £12–£15. A classier make like Imperia will cost you under £50, with several extra add-ons too. Electric ones are available, but they're about the price of a used Lamborghini, and just as dubious on reliability and practicality. You can get attachments for various mixers that claim to be pasta makers, but they look more like something you'd use for Play-Doh.

You can also buy a pasta drying rack, which looks like a rather overcomplicated wooden swastika, if you get very serious.

13 Put a big pan of water on to boil. Add a pinch of salt and a splash of olive oil.
14 When it boils, add the pasta. It'll cook very fast – three minutes should be plenty.
15 Add sauce (see page 67), or just butter and black pepper. Eat. You'll need the energy for cleaning up...

SEMI-AUTOMATIC

The same as manual pasta however throw flour, salt, and eggs into your food processor or mixer, and let it run until they form a neat ball of smooth dough.

Faster pasta: the mechanised version

...and now the same thing, but with extra added machinery. A pasta machine's a fantastic gadget and once you've learnt how to work it you'll be the Enzo Ferrari of tagliatelle.

Difficulty | **Actual work** 30 mins | **Total time** 1 hr | **Serves** 4 - 6

TOOLBOX

- Large area of clean worktop or flat marble slab
- Food processor or mixer
- Pasta machine
- Cling film
- Pasta dryer
- Large pan

COMPONENTS

- As for manual pasta

METHOD

1 Weigh the flour as above.
2 Throw flour, salt, and eggs into your food processor or mixer, and let it run until they form a neat ball of smooth dough.
3 Wrap it in plenty of cling film so it's airtight and stick it in the fridge for half an hour.
4 Flour your work surface very well. Get the dough out of the fridge. Cut off a lump about the size of a tangerine, then squash it flat with your hand. Rewrap the rest and put it back in the fridge.
5 Put it through your pasta machine, on its widest setting. Run it through four times, then fold it in half and repeat. Do this three times.
6 Now start reducing the width between your pasta machine's rollers, one click at a time, putting the pasta through twice at each setting. Stop one from the thinnest if you're making most types of pasta; for very thin spaghetti or similar go all the way.
7 Now run it through the cutting attachment on your pasta machine, slicing it to your chosen width.
8 Hang it on your pasta dryer (or broomstick contraption, see above). Work quickly, as it dries fast.
9 When the dough's all finished, follow the instructions for manual pasta from step 13 onwards.

Pasta mastery: just add sauce

And it's good pie from me: steak and ale pie

This is perfect for a warming autumn or winter dish. Or, in fact any time when you want to eat a great pile of tasty stodge accompanied by beer. Which is most of the time.

Difficulty | **Actual work** 30 mins | **Total time** 2.5 hrs | **Serves** 4

TOOLBOX
- Deep stewpan or large saucepan
- Slotted spoon or drainer
- Pie dish

COMPONENTS
- 300g of shortcrust pastry (see page 116)
- A glug of olive oil
- 1 medium onion
- 1kg of braising steak
- 2 carrots
- 500ml of your favourite ale (plus extra for drinking)
- 2 tablespoonfuls of plain flour
- 1 tablespoonful of mustard
- 500ml of stock (see page 57) or water
- 1 pinch of dried thyme
- Salt and pepper
- 100ml of milk or water or 1 beaten egg (for pie crust glaze)

METHOD
1. Glug enough oil into the pan to cover the bottom and put it on a medium heat.
2. Chop the onion into roughly 1cm chunks and put into the hot oil.
3. Cut up the steak into 2cm chunks and add it to the pan, bit by bit so it browns.
4. Cut the carrots into 1cm slices and add to the pan. Stir.
5. Add the flour and stir so it thickens up the juices.
6. Pour in the beer gradually and keep stirring.
7. Once the beer's all in, add the mustard, thyme, and a pinch of salt and pepper. Stir it in.
8. Top up with stock or water until you've got a rich, but not too thick stew – some liquid will evaporate as it carries on cooking.
9. Turn down to the lowest simmer you can manage, then leave for 1½ hours. Test any extra beer to make sure it's up to your high standard.
10. Put the oven on at 180°C.
11. Using a slotted spoon or drainer, lift out the meat and veg and put into the pie dish. There should be enough to form a pile higher than the edges of the dish, which will stop the crust flopping. Spoon over the gravy until the dish is full.
12. Roll out your pastry until it's bigger than the pie dish. Put it on top, press it down round the edges, then engrave any flashy decorative pattern you like into it, making sure there's at least a 2cm slit or hole somewhere for steam to escape.
13. For extra style, brush or wipe milk or beaten egg over the top of the pastry.
14. Put in the oven for 25–30 minutes until it's golden brown.
15. Drink beer, eat pie. Say 'I should really open my own pub one day.' Forget all about the idea by next morning.

ALTERNATIVES AND IDEAS
- Add more stuff – Other things that would happily go into this basic recipe include diced bacon (add it before the steak), mushrooms, potato, turnip, swede, parsnip, celery or garlic. You could swap the thyme for rosemary, add a bay leaf or two (fish it out before putting the crust on), swap the mustard for horseradish or Worcestershire sauce, even add cumin, chilli powder or paprika, and generally customise to your heart's content. Just keep an eye on the quantities so you don't have far too much filling, and don't go overboard and make it into a confusing array of far too many flavours. Aim for simplicity.
- Lamb and redcurrant – This is a sneaky variation on the lamb shanks recipe on page 70. Swap the steak for stewing lamb, and instead of using beer, throw in a glass of red wine and extra stock or water. Put in half a 300g jar of redcurrant jelly instead of mustard, and use rosemary instead of thyme.

And it's good pie from him: chicken and ham

Another variation on the crusty classic; this one's a creamy chicken and ham variety, which is a bit quicker to cook but just as likely to leave you satisfyingly full.

Difficulty | **Actual work** 20 mins | **Total time** 1.25 hrs | **Serves** 4

TOOLBOX
- Deep stewpan or large saucepan
- Slotted spoon or strainer
- Pie dish

COMPONENTS
- 300g shortcrust pastry (see page 116)
- 500g chicken
- 500ml water or stock
- 2 carrots
- 1 leek
- 1 pinch of thyme
- Salt and pepper
- A glug of olive oil
- 250g cooked ham (preferably as one lump or big bits, rather than sliced)
- 1 onion
- 2 tablespoons of plain flour

METHOD

1 Put the chicken, cut into 2-3cm lumps, into a pan with the water or stock, two chopped carrots, a sliced leek, a teaspoonful of dried thyme and a pinch of salt & pepper. Bring to the boil then simmer for 20 minutes.

2 Put the oven on at 180°C.

3 Lift the chicken and veg out with a slotted spoon and put them in your pie dish. Add ham, cut into 1cm chunks, and mix in.

4 Put a glug of oil into a saucepan, then cook a chopped onion for 5 minutes. Add two tablespoonfuls of flour, stir in well, then gradually add the stock from the pan.

5 When you've got a thickish sauce, pour it over the chicken and ham mixture and mix a little.

6 Add the crust (see step 12 of the steak and ale pie recipe opposite) and bake for 25-30 minutes.

Pied off: A crusty rant

Pubs have done many good things over the years. Serving beer mostly, though providing a venue for dominoes also counts as a public service. However, there's one terrible thing that pubs – or more accurately big chain pubs that serve pre-packaged cook-chill food – have done. They've ruined the pie.

That thing they serve which comes in an oval pottery dish, topped with a weirdly inflated pastry crust, is not a pie. It's a stew with a pumped-up biscuit sat on it.

So to save the proper pie, you'll have to make your own. Which is, luckily, a whole lot easier and quicker than burning down The Old Dog and Bucket as a protest against pie crime.

Pie but not really: shepherd's and cottage

The difference is that one's lamb and one's beef. You can probably guess which. But they're basically the same thing – minced or diced meat with a layer of mash on the top. Which sounds a bit dull, but tastes great.

Difficulty | **Actual work** 20 mins | **Total time** 45 mins | **Serves** 4

TOOLBOX
- Stewpan, casserole or biggish saucepan
- Pie dish
- Medium saucepan for mash

COMPONENTS
- 500g of beef or lamb: good-quality mince or finely diced meat
- 1 large onion
- 2 carrots
- 1 400g tin of chopped tomatoes
- 250ml of water or stock (see page 57)
- A glug of olive oil
- A teaspoonful of dried thyme (beef) or rosemary (lamb)
- Salt and pepper
- 750g of potatoes

METHOD
1 Put a glug of olive oil into your pan and put it on a medium heat.
2 Chop the onion into 1cm bits. Add to the pan and cook for five minutes.
3 Add the meat and cook until browned – about 7–8 minutes. If you're using cheap mince, stop to slap yourself about a bit (see rant at the end of page 66's chilli recipe), then pour off some of the excess fat.
4 Add the carrot and tomatoes. Stir in.
5 Pour in stock or water, stirring well. Add the herbs and a pinch of salt and pepper. Turn down to a simmer.
6 Put the oven on at 190°C.
7 Make your mash – see page 89.
8 By the time that's done, your meat will be ready. Pour it into your pie dish. If it's very sloppy, use a slotted spoon to fish out the meat and veg first, then pour over enough stock to keep it moist but not soup-like.
9 Spoon the mash on top. Make a pretty pattern with a fork, or scrawl rude words in it with a dirty thumb. Up to you.
10 Put in the oven for 20 minutes, or until it's nicely brown and starting to go crispy at the edges.
11 If there's any stock left in the pan, that'll make good gravy with a little more water. Otherwise, see page 77.

Ask a piskie: Cornish pasties

They're a bit of old Cornish folklore that you can eat. And much tastier than chewing a lump of Tintagel Castle. Also remarkably portable – handy when you're down a tin mine.

Difficulty | **Actual work** 20 mins | **Total time** 1hr 20 mins | **Serves** 4

TOOLBOX

- Rolling pin
- Smallish dinner plate
- Baking tray

COMPONENTS

- 500g shortcrust pastry
- 400g decent steak
- 1 biggish potato
- 1 medium swede
- Salt and pepper
- A splash of water or milk

METHOD

1 Put the oven on at 180°C.

2 Roll out enough shortcrust pastry (see page 116) to be slightly larger than a smallish dinner plate. You should get four out of 500g of pastry.

3 Place said plate on your pastry and cut round it. That's the casing. For extra Cornish cred, save the scraps to make pastry initials to stick on each one.

4 For the filling, take the steak and dice it into 1cm cubes. Peel and dice a biggish potato and half a medium-sized swede.

5 Lay a quarter of the vegetables on top of one side of your first pastry circle. Put a quarter of the steak on top. Give it a good pinch of white pepper.

6 Wipe some water or milk round the edge of the ingredient-covered side. Fold the pastry over and crimp it firmly. You're looking for a good tight seal, so make sure it's solid.

7 Brush or wipe milk on the pastry. If you're initialling them, due to style or paranoia, use milk to stick your letters on. Cut a 2cm slit somewhere to let steam escape.

8 Repeat to make three more.

9 Put them in the oven for 1 hour. If they're starting to look too brown, put a bit of greaseproof paper or foil on top.

10 Eat with a pint of rough scrumpy, or maybe Doom Bar, a very decent bitter brewed by Cornwall's Rock Brewery.

Crimped style: like an edible Jiffy bag

A portion of pasty history

Like much of English folklore, the Cornish pasty is surrounded by myths, legends, and bits of half-remembered, unreliable nonsense. Should the seam be on the side or the top? Was there ever really a version with meat at one end and fruit at the other? Is it the same thing as a clanger? Was the shape designed for aerodynamics, so they could be hurled accurately down a tin mine? And if you put carrot in yours, will the locals burn you alive on the village green?

If you must know, the best authorities (and there is actually a body called the Cornish Pasty Association) claim that the Cornish version is a side-seamed, all-savoury affair, unlike the similar Bedfordshire Clanger (and some Welsh variants) which could include jam or fruit. The aerodynamics theory, sadly, is nonsense. But including carrot will definitely get you deported from the Duchy of Cornwall by an angry mob wielding flaming torches and sharp scythes.

If you want further information, head to the Internet, where there's an hilariously trainspotterish pasty culture. The Wikipedia pasty page alone is longer than some whole countries' entries.

But unless you're part of the Tamar Valley CPA, it's a free world and you can do what you like. So here's a pasty that will hit the spot, even if the spot isn't anywhere near Penzance.

CHAPTER 9
FITNESS FUEL

There's more to food than just stuffing your face and slumping on the sofa to snooze it off, you know. Not that there's much wrong with that, but we all need a bit of exercise, if only so that we can fit through the kitchen door without needing a thick coating of margarine and a good shove.

So here are a few ideas that will help you keep lean and mean without forcing you to eat nutritious, energy-intensive products with all the taste and appeal of Polyfilla.

Whether you're getting a few miles in on the bike, hitting the pavement for a good long run, rowing, canoeing or swimming, endurance sports demand a lot from your body. The only way to keep performance up and avoid that dreaded moment when you run out of energy is to keep eating slow-release foods that keep your muscles supplied with a good trickle of vital nourishment.

If you're more of a sprinter, though, you'll need a very different type of nutrition – quick hits of full-on power fuel to give your muscles a turbo boost. And the last thing you want is something big and stodgy sitting in your stomach like a lead medicine ball.

So choose your fuel carefully. And even if you're not really the sporty type but want something that might help you shift the odd pound, this chapter will come in handy too. Charge yourself up and get going.

Tasty performance: a fit dinner or two

If you're just an average athlete, you won't need umpteen thousand calories a day. Unless you're competing in the World Flab-Wobbling Championships. But the same rules apply to you as to any professional – get a good balance of protein and carbs.

So here are a few ideas for healthy food that you can mix and match according to your chosen sport. They'll also help keep your weight down and your energy levels up, so you don't have to be a steely-thighed sports maniac to give them a go.

1 Griddled protein

Put a cast iron griddle pan on a high heat and let it get really hot. Hover a hand 5cm or so over it – you should really feel the heat coming off it. Take a tuna steak, splash one side lightly with olive oil and a pinch of salt and pepper. Bang it on the griddle for three minutes. Splash the top with olive oil, salt and pepper, then flip it for another three.

■ This also works with skinless chicken breasts. Use a sprinkle of herbs – rosemary, thyme, sage, oregano or mixed – with the olive oil and salt and pepper. Give it 5–6 minutes a side. Rare tuna is good; rare chicken isn't recommended.

2 Carb cooking

Potatoes are a good healthy source of carbohydrate. Bake them by sticking them in an oven at 190°C for an hour, or give them ten minutes in the oven, as hot as it'll go to crisp them, then microwave them at full power for five minutes, then leave to stand for another five. Make sure you cut a slit in them or they'll explode. Eat with olive oil, though a little butter won't kill you.

3 Beans means energy

Another healthy source of energy-transporting carbohydrate; but shop-bought tinned baked beans tend to be heavy on the salt and sugar. Make your own by soaking 500g of dried haricot beans overnight, then frying a chopped onion, two chopped rashers of bacon, and two chopped cloves of garlic in a big pan or casserole. Put the oven on at 160°C. After five minutes add two tins of chopped, peeled tomatoes, a tablespoonful of treacle, a bay leaf, and a splash of Tabasco or other hot sauce. Bring it to the boil, then put it in the oven for a couple of hours. Taste, add anything else you think it needs (including liquid if it's looking dry), and check the beans are done. This will keep in a jar in the fridge for ages.

4 You may also like

More healthy foods tucked away in this book include:
■ **Pasta** – page 55
■ **Rice** – page 55
■ **Chops** – page 84
■ **Roast veg** – page 83
■ **Thai curry** – page 92
■ **Roast nuts** – page 103
■ **Couscous salad** – page 101
■ **Tonno e fagioli** – page 103
■ **Home-made pasta** – page 134
■ **Pesto** – page 95
■ **Porridge** – page 153
■ **Smoothies** – page 167

Fast food: the athlete's diet

If you're heavily involved in sport, you'll already know that feeding yourself properly has a big impact on performance.

You'll also know that different sports demand different types of nutrition. Power sports need protein, sprinters wolf sugar and other quick-release sources of energy, and endurance events demand stodge – loads of carbohydrates.

So here are some great examples of sportsmen's fodder. You may find that your 20-minute commute to work doesn't burn up quite as much as Lance Armstrong's four-hour mountain ascent, though, so go easy on the quantities...

THE SUPER-ENDURANCE DIET

Michael Phelps, multiple world and Olympic champion swimmer, divulged his daily diet to the BBC a little while ago. Here you go. And remember, this is every day:

- **Breakfast** – Three fried egg sandwiches; cheese; tomatoes; lettuce; fried onions; mayonnaise; three chocolate-chip pancakes; five-egg omelette; three sugar-coated slices of French toast; a bowl of grits (that's American corn-based porridge); two cups of coffee.
- **Lunch** – Half a kilo of enriched pasta; two large ham and cheese sandwiches with mayonnaise on white bread; energy drinks.
- **Dinner** – Half a kilo of pasta, with carbonara sauce; large pizza; energy drinks.

That's at least 10,000 calories a day, but he burns 1,000 calories an hour training. Don't try this at home, kids.

THE TOUR DE FRANCE DIET

Lance Armstrong and his colleagues put out vast amounts of power during their gruelling stage races, but endurance and recovery are a priority too, as well as the occasional easily digestible energy boost during the race itself and plenty of liquids. This is what was on the menu for Team Columbia's boys during one particularly tough mountain stage on the 2009 tour:

- **Breakfast** – 1 banana, 150g of muesli, 150g (uncooked weight) of pasta, 1 croissant with chocolate, 200g of mixed fruit, 300ml of orange juice, 300ml of soymilk, coffee.
- **Pre-race snack** – 150g of pasta, 500ml of water.
- **During the race** – 4 energy bars, 100g of fruit cake, 4 litres of carbo drink, 4 sachets of energy gel, 400ml of Coca-Cola, 2 turkey sandwiches, 1 litre of water.
- **Post-race** – 500ml of recovery drink, 1 turkey sandwich, 1 energy bar, 330ml of Coca-Cola, 100g of fruit cake, 400ml of water.
- **Dinner** – 200g of mixed vegetables, 200g of pasta, 250g of chicken breast, 100g of sauce, 350g of plain yogurt, 150g of mixed fruit, 800ml of water.
- **Pre-sleep** – 100g of gum/sweets, 25g of chocolate, 500ml of water.

THE SPRINTER'S DIET

Usain Bolt, the world's fastest man, has little need for endurance; if he's doing his job, it's all over in ten seconds. His diet's pretty relaxed, though it keeps close to a ratio of 60% protein, 30% carbohydrate and 10% fat, and the quantities are huge:

- **Breakfast** – Jamaican dumplings made of flour, water, butter and milk, plus a large helping of starchy yams.
- **Lunch** – Brown rice, wholemeal bread, and protein such as tuna or snapper.
- **Dinner** – Brown rice, plus chicken, pork or beef. And, very occasionally, junk food like burgers or chicken nuggets.

Cheap fuel: home-made energy bars

You'll see energy bars in sports shops, wrapped in little foil packets and with a head-spinning price tag attached. Make your own instead of exercising your credit card.

Difficulty | **Actual work** 15 mins | **Total time** 35 mins | **Serves** A whole team

TOOLBOX

- Large saucepan
- Baking tray
- Baking parchment or greaseproof paper

COMPONENTS

- 100g of butter
- 100g of honey
- 100g of brown sugar
- 50g of fruit spread (that's the stuff like thick gooey jam; apricot's good, pear and apple work too)
- 150g of jumbo oats
- 50g of chopped nuts (walnuts, hazelnuts, almonds, pecans etc)
- 100g of dried fruit (chopped apricot, banana, pineapple, apple, figs, dates and/or sultanas, raisins, currants etc)
- 100g of seeds (sunflower, sesame, linseed, pumpkin etc)

METHOD

1 Heat the oven to 180°C.
2 Line your baking tray with parchment/paper and grease it with a smear of butter.
3 Put the butter, honey, fruit spread and sugar in a pan and heat gently, stirring, until it's dissolved and the sugar's starting to go claggy (technical term) and thicken up the mixture.
4 Mix in the rest of the stuff, making sure it's evenly distributed.
5 Spoon it into the tray, smoothing the top down.
6 Put it in the oven for 20 minutes. Keep an eye on it – if it's going too brown, cover it with a bit more parchment or some foil.
7 Let it cool before getting it out of the tray and slicing it up into pocket-sized chunks. Store somewhere airtight. Look forward to your next ultra-marathon test of stamina.

Beating 'the bonk'

There are some sports that demand long-term nourishment: marathon running, mountain biking, and anything with the phrase 'long-distance' in the title. You can argue for the inclusion of watching the full 90 minutes of a tedious second division game if you like, but medical experts are still undecided on that one.

However, if you don't keep your blood sugars topped up, you'll get into a state cyclists charmingly term 'the bonk'. You hit a brick wall of lethargy, feebleness, and fatigue, and suddenly even the effort of turning the pedals becomes too much. It's not nice at all, and the only remedy is eating something sweet, for a quick energy hit, and then topping up properly with something more long-lasting to get you home.

The way to avoid this is to eat little and often and combine processed sugars, which give you a fast but short-lived boost, with fruit sugars, which are slower to get into the bloodstream, and some starchy and/or protein-rich stuff. Which happens to be roughly the make-up of energy bars, and that's why they work. But they're expensive, even if you don't buy them from a specialist sports shop.

So make your own – it's pretty straightforward, plus you know exactly what's gone into them, and you can mess about with the recipe, provided you keep the ingredients very roughly in proportion, to include your favourite sort of healthy bits and pieces.

Tastes better than it sounds: fruit leather

If you're looking for a concentrated, healthy hit of energy you can't get much better than fruit. But in its natural form it's mostly heavy, bulky, and fiddly, so here's a neat way of packaging it up to cart about with you.

Difficulty | **Actual work** 25 mins | **Total time** 14 hrs + | **Serves** You, for months

TOOLBOX

- 2 baking trays with rims
- Baking parchment or greaseproof paper
- Medium saucepan (not aluminium – use steel or non-stick lining)
- Medium-sized bowl
- Sieve (that fits in the bowl)

COMPONENTS

- 1kg of fruit – apples, blackberries, cranberries, pears, apricots, peaches, kiwi fruit or whatever you like
- 150g of honey
- Juice of 1 lemon

From this

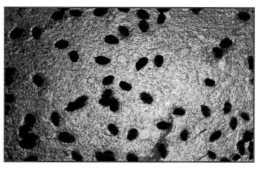

METHOD

1 Put the oven on, as low as it'll go – 50–60°C.
2 Peel, stone, or core your fruit and chop the bigger ones into lumps no bigger than 3cm.
3 Put them in your saucepan, add the lemon juice, and cook very slowly, for about 20 minutes or until they go mushy.
4 Line your baking trays with one big piece of parchment/paper each.
5 Squish the fruit through the sieve into the bowl.
6 Add the honey and mix well.
7 Now spread the mixture very thinly over the parchment. Use the back of a spoon to make sure it's even and about 5–8mm deep.
8 Put it into the oven and leave it there overnight, or for at least 12 hours. It'll be done when it's completely dry and peels away from the parchment easily.

9 Cut it into strips and put it into something airtight. It'll last ages – months at least. Just grab a bit when you need a light, durable snack, and wrap it in a bit of cling film if you're likely to get muddy. That means you, mountain bikers.

To this

Eat yourself fitter: no-hassle diets

If you have a little trouble squeezing into your trousers occasionally, there's a simple answer. Eat less. Well, maybe it's not quite that simple. 'Eat less of the wrong things, eat more of the right things' would be closer. (And don't forget to get a bit of exercise).

But what are the right and wrong things? If you've made it this far into this book, you'll be well on the way to finding out – because cooking your own food rather than buying it as a ready meal or from the local takeaway/burger joint is a fine way to make sure that you're eating a good variety of fresh, decent-quality ingredients rather than accidentally ingesting a load of added salt, sugar, fat, and other unwanted gubbins.

Those non-optional extras are what really pile on the pounds, not to mention clogging up your arteries and doing your system all sorts of other damage. And they're mostly put there by food manufacturers to cheaply bulk up their products, mask the taste of low-quality ingredients, or simply give an unappetising bit of food an instant, if fake, boost with salt, sugar, and monosodium glutamate (MSG), which stimulates the appetite while doing you very little good at all. Then there are 'trans fats', colourings, chemical flavour enhancers...

Rant over. But you get the idea. Get fresh, get healthier.

QUICK FIXES
Here are some simple things you can do tomorrow which are guaranteed to help you lose weight and get healthier. It's that easy.

1 Eat less meat
Instead of treating your main meals as a big bit of animal with a small amount of other stuff on the side, swap the proportions. Make the meat a tasty addition, and cook more vegetables.

2 Add fish
Fish are a fantastic thing. They're low in bad fat, and oily fish like tuna and mackerel contain so-called 'good fat', which lubricates joints and even boosts the brain. Swap fish for meat a couple of times a week.

3 Stop snacking
It's the between-meals stuff that often causes trouble. If you must nibble, have a handful of nuts (see page 103) or a bit of mixed dried fruit. Stock up on some decent snacks like tins of olives, sesame seed bars, or even a bit of raw carrot.

Nuts to you: snack fodder

4 Get out a bit

Walk to the local shops (see page 30) instead of getting in the car and doing the supermarket run. That way you won't be tempted down the crisps aisle either. Double result.

5 Cut down on the booze

A pint of beer has roughly the calorific value of a cream cake. Try to remember that next time you're off to the pub. And have a glass of milk or juice before you go, so you don't do that thirsty first pint slurp.

start right: muesli's marvellous

9 Get started

Breakfast, many nutritionists say, is vitally important. Yes, it's a time when most of us are sprinting to get out of the door, but if you can wolf down a bowl of something fairly healthy (not sticky, brightly-coloured kids' rubbish) it'll get your system working and prevent the mid-morning munchies.

6 Keep it varied

Boredom's a terrible thing. Try to switch between types of food. Yes, you might like bread and cheese, but why not try hummus (see recipe below), crab pate, a bit of smoked mackerel, and maybe crackers or crispbread instead of the bread. Mix it up a bit and be adventurous.

7 Fill your freezer

You're bound to overdo it on the portions sometimes when you cook, so bung the leftover bits in the freezer in one-portion bags or containers. In the time it takes some lunatic on a moped to deliver a dodgy pizza, you could have defrosted something decent.

8 Easy on the heat

If in doubt, undercook vegetables. They're nicer with a bit of crispness to them anyway and all the vitamins and minerals won't get sucked into the cooking water and thrown away. And many, like carrots and potatoes, keep much of the healthy stuff just under the skin, so just give them a swift scrub instead of peeling them. It's easier too.

Make this. It's nice

Home-made hummus is dead straightforward if you've got a food processor or blender. Open a 400g tin of chickpeas and drain the liquid into a bowl or cup. Then stick the chickpeas in your food processor with two cloves of garlic, a pinch of salt, the juice of half a lemon, a good glug of olive oil and two tablespoonfuls of tahini – sesame seed paste that you can get from most supermarkets and any health food shop. Add about a quarter of the chickpea liquid and whizz. If it looks dry and crumbly, add a little more liquid. It should be creamy and smooth. Stick it in a bowl, and if you want a little extra middle-eastern pizzazz, sprinkle chopped parsley, black pepper or oregano on top, with a splash of olive oil. Eat with warm pitta bread, or anything you fancy.

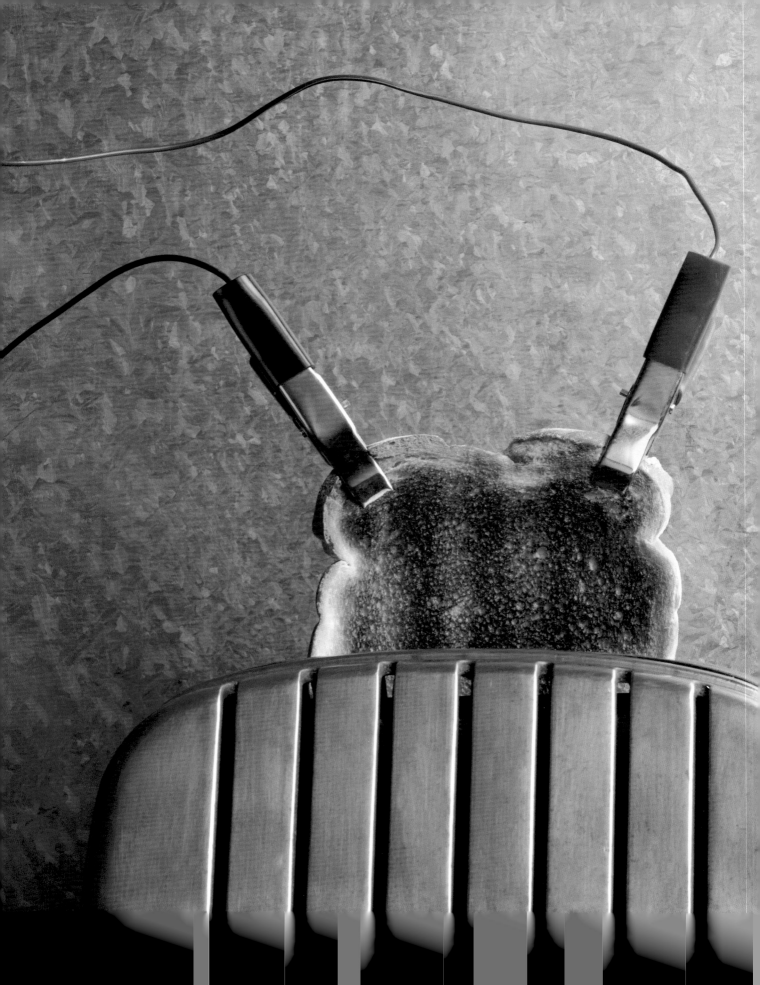

CHAPTER 10
HOT STARTING

Some people don't understand the importance of a decent breakfast. Italians, for instance. They seem to think that one tiny, super-strong coffee will keep them going until lunchtime. It's no wonder their cars are notoriously unreliable. You wouldn't be able to wire up a complicated electronic ignition system either if you were twitchy, irritable and starving.

You could argue that the classic Full English/Builder's Breakfast goes too far the other way – how do builders actually get up a ladder after fried eggs, bacon, sausage, black pudding, beans, fried bread, chips and a mug of tea with six sugars? But there's nothing to beat it once in a while, particularly after a heavy night.

The first meal of the day can be the best meal of the day. Allow yourself a bit of time, maybe on a weekend morning, and a long lazy breakfast can stretch into brunch and beyond, fuelling you up for a bracing afternoon walk to a country pub or just an enjoyably uneventful day with the papers.

Or you can opt for a quick pre-work top-up to get you off to a flying start; it's tasty, healthy, and guaranteed to stop those mid-morning munchies.

So don't miss out on your morning feast. Here are loads of ways to make your first bite a bit of all right rather than a rush job. Make waking up hungry a reason to celebrate with our breakfast bonanza.

Begin with a bang: the classic breakfast

You wouldn't want to scoff a full English every day unless your job involves lifting two-ton steel girders. But once in a while it's the finest thing you can eat. Here are the simple assembly instructions for the classic blowout.

THE FULL ENGLISH – YOUR PICK'N'MIX MENU

This classic is several dishes, really, all thrown on to a plate together. Which is why your local caff will do a great version; they're set up with all the industrial toasters, griddles, pans and so on you need. At home, it's fairly complex and rather heavy on the washing-up, but incredibly satisfying.

You'll notice the word 'fried' crops up rather a lot. If you go for the traditional full-fat heavy-on-the-lard version more than very occasionally, you're heading straight for the health equivalent of a train crash. Be careful out there.

Here are the component parts. Pick and choose your favourites.

- **Bacon** – see opposite.
- **Eggs** – see page 54
- **Sausages** – see page 109
- **Beans** – for great home-made ones see page 142, or use top-quality tinned ones, not watery cheapo rubbish.
- **Black pudding** – you really don't want to know how this is made. But it tastes great, fried in very little oil on each side until it's crisp.
- **Hash browns** – grate three potatoes and an onion into a bowl. Tip out any juice. Add a pinch of salt and pepper, then break an egg into it and mix well. Spoon the mixture into a hot, lightly oiled, frying pan and make it into your favourite shape. Flip it after a couple of minutes; when it's brown and crispy on both sides it's done.
- **Mushrooms** – the big flat Portabella mushrooms are tasty, grilled with a dab of butter or fried until the juices start to ooze out of them. Or slice the little ones and fry in a little oil with plenty of black pepper.
- **Tomatoes** – slice them in half and fry them cut side down until they start to go wrinkly. Or cook them in a hot oven for about 15 minutes.
- **Fried bread** – does what it says on the tin, cooking wise. If you want the full 'doctors advise against this' unhealthy version, you could fry it in lard, dripping or even goose fat. Then go for a long, energetic walk before your arteries clog up completely and you die.
- **Bubble & squeak** – this is really a way of using up leftover mash and veg, so making it from scratch is a nuisance. Fry an onion lightly in oil, mix the potato and veg together and bung it in. Shape it into a cake or several, and flip over when it's brown and crispy.
- **Accompaniments:** Mustard, brown sauce, ketchup, even pickle all have their fans. But try to stick to trustworthy brands. That well watered-down vinegary liquid of the type you find in dodgy caffs will do it no favours.

FROM RASHER WITH LOVE: CRISPY BACON

Like cat-skinning, there's more than one way to cook bacon. But there's definitely one way not to do it, if you want it crispy and tasty – and that's too fast, too hot. Slow and gentle is the way to cook perfect bacon.

- **Frying pan** – put the bacon into a cold pan, then heat it up on low to medium. Don't rush it. If fat starts to build up, drain it off, and turn the rashers often. If the edges start to turn black, it's too hot; turn it down. It'll take around 15 minutes.
- **Griddle pan** – much the same method, but the ridges on the pan will let the fat drain, which should give you crisper bacon.
- **Grill** – again, slow and gentle. You might want to put foil under the grid, as it can get messy.
- **Microwave** – put a piece of kitchen towel on a microwaveable plate, lay the rashers in a single layer on top, then gently put another bit of kitchen towel on top. Don't squish it down or it'll stick. Put it on for four minutes, then check it – another minute or two may be needed, depending on the number of rashers and how powerful your microwave is.
- **Oven** – line a big roasting tin or baking tray with foil, then lay the rashers in it. Bake at 180°C for 10 to 15 minutes, depending on how crispy you like your bacon. If too much fat builds up, drain it off. Watch out, it's hot and slippery.
- Barbecue, George Foreman Lean Mean Grilling thing, wood fire, nuclear reactor, Primus stove – yes, all possible, provided you stick to the Golden Rule of Bacon: steady as she goes.

Breaking a few eggs: the omelette

Omelettes are delicious, quick, and easy, but they're one of those basic recipes which can be added to, tweaked, and customised until they're a fantastically complex feast. Start simple, then get adventurous.

Difficulty | **Actual work** 10 mins | **Total time** 10 mins | **Serves** 4

TOOLBOX
- A smallish frying pan or omelette pan
- Spatula

COMPONENTS
- 2 eggs
- 50g butter
- splash of olive oil
- 1 tablespoonful milk
- salt & pepper

Somewhere along the way you could find yourself up to trying a potato (or Spanish) omelette – also known as a tortilla, which is on page 107 as well.

There's also a lot of controversy in cooking nerd circles about the perfect pan to use; some say a smallish, steep-sided cast-iron frying pan is perfect. Other rather more sensible people say that the best one is whatever you happen to own. If you become a real omelette enthusiast, you can invest several hundred pounds in a specialist triple-walled Paris-made copper-bottomed Teflon-coated weapon, but then people will walk out of the room, humming loudly, when you try to tell them all about it.

Let's start with a basic omelette.

METHOD
1 Put a thumb-sized lump of butter and a splash of olive oil into a smallish frying pan and put it on a medium heat.
2 Crack two eggs into a bowl and beat them with a fork. Add a tablespoonful of milk and a pinch of salt and pepper and stir in.
3 Pour the mixture into the pan. Cook it until it starts to set, pushing the edges in with a spatula occasionally so they don't stick.
4 Fold it in half with the spatula, then tip it on to a plate and eat.

VARIATIONS AND IDEAS
This could go on forever, as there are about four million opinions on the perfect omelette. But here are a few ideas:

- Try breaking the eggs directly into the pan and briskly stirring in the milk. Some say this makes it lighter. Watch out for bits of eggshell, though.
- Use chicken stock (page 57) instead of milk for a richer taste. Or use water if you want it lighter.

- The point when the omelette's starting to set is when you should add fillings. Throw them on top, then fold the omelette, turn down the heat and let it cook for a minute or two. Try the following, all in small bits:
- Cheese: grated cheddar is good, but anything will do. Smoked cheese can be very fine.
- Chopped spring onions, peppers, cooked ham, leftover roast chicken, peas, sweetcorn.
- Pre-fried onions, garlic, bacon bits or even thinly sliced sausage.

French toast
Also known as eggy bread or even gypsy toast, it's fried rather than toasted. This is great for a bunch of people – it's perfect post-party food.

1 Break three eggs into a wide bowl. Beat them with a fork. Add 125ml of milk and a pinch of salt and stir.
2 Put a couple of thumb-sized lumps of butter into a frying pan and put on a medium heat.
3 Take as many slices of bread as will fit in the pan and dunk them in the eggy mixture until they're soaked.
4 Transfer them to the pan and fry until brown. Then do the other side.
5 Repeat until the mixture is used up and everybody is completely stuffed.
6 For a more American version, add a pinch of cinnamon and anything up to a teaspoonful of sugar to the mixture. Serve with maple syrup and/or crispy bacon. Squeal like a piggy, y'all.

Straight from Route 66: Yankee pancakes

You may think you know what a pancake is – it's exactly the same batter as Yorkshire puds, but cooked thinly in a hot frying pan, then flipped. But there's an American variation. And being American it's bigger, fluffier, stodgier, and sweeter. Put on your Stetson and get cookin'.

Difficulty | **Actual work** 5 mins | **Total time** 5 mins | **Serves** 4 folks

TOOLBOX
- Large mixing bowl and whisk
- Smaller bowl or jug
- Small bowl or saucepan
- Frying pan
- Ladle

COMPONENTS
- 2 thumb-sized lumps of butter
- 1 egg
- 150ml of milk
- 150g of self-raising flour
- 2 tablespoonfuls of sugar
- 1 teaspoonful of baking powder
- A pinch of salt

METHOD

1 Melt half the butter – put it in a bowl in the microwave for 15 seconds, or melt it in a small saucepan over a low heat. Let it cool for a minute or so.

2 Beat the egg with a whisk, then whisk in the milk and the melted butter.

3 Put the flour, sugar, baking powder and salt in a large bowl, then mix in the egg/milk/butter mixture. Mix until it's smooth.

4 Put the rest of the butter into a frying pan and heat over a medium heat. When the butter's melted, dump a ladleful of the batter in. Give it two minutes or so, then flip the pancake over and cook the top. You can always flip it back if the first side is a bit pale. As the pan heats up, they'll cook faster. They should be fairly fluffy and thick, unlike the Euro version.

5 Eat with maple syrup and crispy bacon for the true USA flavour. Or put some blueberries or other smallish fruit in with the mixture.

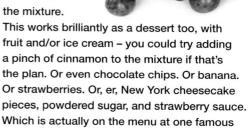

This works brilliantly as a dessert too, with fruit and/or ice cream – you could try adding a pinch of cinnamon to the mixture if that's the plan. Or even chocolate chips. Or banana. Or strawberries. Or, er, New York cheesecake pieces, powdered sugar, and strawberry sauce. Which is actually on the menu at one famous American pancake chain. Goshdarn it.

Great Scot: perfect porridge

It's difficult to think of a better winter breakfast than porridge (or porage if you live Up North). Warming and nutritious, it's also quick to make and amazingly cheap, if you go easy on the added extras.

Difficulty   **Actual work** 5 mins   **Total time** 5 mins   **Serves** 2

TOOLBOX

- Cup
- Medium-sized saucepan
- Wooden spoon

COMPONENTS

- 1 cupful of porridge oats
- 2 cupfuls of water

METHOD

1. Put a cupful of porridge oats into a medium-sized saucepan.
2. Using the same cup, add two cupfuls of water.
3. Bring to the boil, then turn down to a simmer, stirring so it doesn't stick.
4. After three or four minutes it should be at your perfect consistency. Don't let it cook for ages or it'll turn into a brick.

VARIATIONS AND IDEAS

- Use milk instead of water. Or half and half.
- Add a pinch of salt.
- Stir in a lump of butter at the end.
- Add a teaspoonful (or more) of sugar. Brown is good.
- Add a tablespoonful of honey.
- Add a squirt of maple syrup. Not cheap, but luxurious.
- Add a dollop of yoghurt.
- Stir in a pinch of cinnamon, nutmeg or mixed spice.
- For a chocolate version, add a tablespoonful of cocoa powder at the beginning, or cheat and use chocolate milk.
- Throw in a handful of strawberries, blackberries or similar. Maybe a dash of honey as well.
- Throw in a handful of dried fruit or nuts.
- Soak the porridge oats overnight before cooking the lot as above.
- Use the microwave – four or five minutes on high, stopping it occasionally to stir. Use a non-metallic bowl.
- Try any combination of the above. Or none of them.

Bandidos' breakfast: huevos rancheros

This is a fine traditional Mexican dish. But like many Mexican traditions – revolutions, drug wars, and wearing sombreros for instance – it needs a dash of bravery. Do you have the *cojones* to tackle a chilli-fuelled breakfast? Well do you, gringo?

Difficulty 🥄🥄🥄   **Actual work** 15 mins   **Total time** 25 mins   **Serves** 4

TOOLBOX

- Medium or large frying pan
- Medium saucepan

COMPONENTS

- 2 glugs of olive or corn oil
- Half an onion
- 3 cloves of garlic
- 1 red or green chilli, mild or hot – your choice
- 400g tin of chopped tomatoes
- 2 eggs per person
- 2 large soft tortillas or wraps, or 4 small ones
- A handful of grated Cheddar or similar hard cheese

METHOD

1 Put a glug of oil in the saucepan and put on a medium heat.
2 Chop the onion finely and put it in the pan.
3 Chop the garlic and add that to the pan. Fry for two minutes. Stir a bit.
4 Chop the chilli finely (see the hazard warning on page 91) and bung that in too. Fry for another minute.
5 Add the tomatoes and cook for 15 minutes.
6 Put a glug of oil in the frying pan and put on a high heat. When the oil's hot, fry the tortillas for a few seconds on both sides and put them on warm plates.
7 Fry the eggs in the frying pan for two to three minutes. Don't splash oil on them or flip them as you might do for 'normal' fried eggs. You don't want the top too cooked.

8 Put the eggs on top of the tortillas. Pour on the sauce – the hot sauce will cook the top of the eggs. Add a pinch of salt and pepper and sprinkle on the grated cheese.
9 Serve, accompanied by a mariachi band and at least two bottles of tequila (optional).

Indian? For breakfast? Blimey: kedgeree

This was a traditional Victorian breakfast, back in the days of the Raj, when we ruled India and nicked whatever we liked, including some rather excellent food.

Difficulty   **Actual work** 10 mins   **Total time** 25 mins   **Serves** 4

TOOLBOX
- A medium-sized saucepan with a lid

COMPONENTS
- Pack of smoked mackerel
- 1 onion
- 2 thumb-sized lumps of butter
- 1 cupful of basmati or long-grain rice
- 1 pinch of curry powder (optional)
- 1½ cupfuls of water
- 3 hard-boiled eggs (see page 54)
- 75g of frozen peas
- Juice of half a lemon
- 1 sprig of fresh parsley
- Salt and pepper

The Victorians made it with smoked haddock, but it's a great thing to rustle up with some of that smoked mackerel that every corner shop seems to have, with a sell-by date of many years hence. If you've got any leftover rice knocking about, you can do a good version of this in about five minutes. It also makes a superb lunch or dinner.

METHOD
1. Put half the butter in your pan and put on a medium heat.
2. Chop the onion finely and put it in the pan. Fry it for three minutes.
3. Add the rice, plus curry powder if you fancy the trad Indian style. Fry for a few seconds.
4. Add the water. When it comes to the boil turn it down to a slow simmer, then put the lid on and leave it for 15 minutes.
5. Cut up the eggs into rough eighths, chop the parsley, cook the peas and flake the fish.
6. After 15 minutes, check the rice. If it's still hard, leave it for another few minutes. If it's soft, stir in the other ingredients including the rest of the butter, put the lid back on, and put it back on the heat for five minutes.
7. Don your finest Victorian morning coat and enjoy.

VARIATIONS AND IDEAS
- If you prefer to use smoked haddock, or any other fresh fish, poach it in a pan of boiling water for 5 minutes before, er, fishing it out, letting it cool for a few minutes and flaking it. Don't throw the poaching liquid away – use it instead of water to give the rice extra fishy loveliness.

Bony but bonny: kippers

These are just herrings, salted and smoked. But while you might balk at the idea of herrings for breakfast, kippers are a fine traditional treat. Serve them hot by grilling them for 5 minutes, then dolloping on a pat of butter, a twist or two of black pepper, and/or a squeeze of lemon. You won't need salt, they're already salty enough.

You can also microwave them by putting them on a (non-metal) plate and blasting them at full power for two or three minutes. You might want to put some clingfilm over the top, though, otherwise they'll spit and hence make your microwave smell fishy for ages.

They're also excellent toast topping or sandwich filling if you peel off the skin and flake or mash them with butter.

Watch out for local varieties, too – bloaters, bucklings and the closely related arbroath smokies or finnan haddie (actually haddock). One final tip – if they're cold smoked they need cooking; if they're hot smoked they don't.

A nice cuppa: English tea

In the view of some English tea snobs, there are two types of people – milk-in-first and tea-in-first. Firstly, they really need to get out more. And secondly, it's all a matter of personal taste anyway. Even if you care.

Mugging up: the perfect cuppa

GUIDELINES FOR THE PERFECT CUPPA

- Make it in a proper teapot with good-quality tea leaves.
- The pot should be warmed first by pouring a little boiling water in and leaving it to stand for two minutes.
- The pot should then be emptied.
- The tea (one teaspoonful per person, plus one extra 'for the pot') should be put in.
- Then the water should be put in, by this time just off the boil so at the optimum temperature.
- It should be left to steep for at least five minutes.
- It should be poured through a strainer into a cup with the milk already in the bottom, so the milk doesn't denature, which makes it taste odd.
- If you take sugar, it must be white sugar.

Alternatively, you can do like the rest of us – throw a teabag in a cup with some milk and hope for the best.

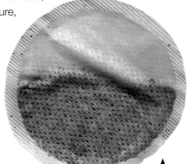

Handy bag: quick and easy

HERBY, THE LOVE CUP: ALTERNATIVE TEAS

While you might put herbal teas strictly into the hippy sandal-wearing vegetarian category, some of them are very good at times. Here's a quick guide to a few. You can buy teabags in most places these days, but some of them, like mint, are easy to make just by pouring water on a sprig of the fresh stuff. If there's some growing in your garden (above pet peeing height, of course) snip off a bit and boil it up for a free treat.

- **Mint (or Peppermint)** – The classic drink of North Africa and Turkey. You can either drink it very sweet from a tiny glass, like the natives do, or have a teabag in a normal-sized mug, when you'll find it's great after a big meal for settling down the digestion and chilling out.
- **Fennel** – Much the same digestive effect, but you may prefer the aniseedy, liquoricey flavour. Or hate it. Whatever.
- **Rooibos (or Redbush)** – South African stuff with a distinctive flavour, though you can often find it mixed with vanilla or other spices. One big advantage is that it's caffeine-free, so it's good last thing at night or when you're starting to get twitchy through too much coffee or standard tea.
- **Fruit tea** – There are too many to list, so try a selection. The lemony ones can be very refreshing.
- **Chamomile** – Some people swear by it for aiding sleep. Some swear that it smells of cat widdle. The flowers, if you can find them, are more pleasantly fragrant.
- **Other variations** – Some varieties contain the sort of spices you'd associate with mulled wine, or possibly fruitcake – cinnamon, nutmeg, even coriander or black pepper. These are usually very good as an alternative warming winter drink. And you can always slam in a tot of rum to liven things up a bit.

Espresso macho: coffee gadgetry

There's nothing quite as cool as a bit of Italian machinery. Yes, it might not always work terribly well (ask any owner of a 1970s Lancia) but it generally looks fabulous, makes a great noise, and is ludicrously powerful if slightly dangerous.

That's exactly why everybody loves an espresso machine. It's basically a big reservoir of superheated water under pressure and has a valve that, when you pull the lever or press the button, noisily blasts a jet of steam through compressed ground coffee and into the cup, where it forms that classic tiny, dark brown, super-strong coffee with an oily froth on top.

You might think it's been around forever, but actually the espresso machine as we know it was only invented in 1903, when some genius called Luigi Bezzera came up with the idea. And espresso as we know it didn't arrive until 1946, when the all-important pressure valve was perfected.

So do you need a proper espresso machine at home? They do look great, they make an impressive whooshing noise, and there are plenty of knobs, dials, tampers, and filters to fiddle with. But many of the affordable kitchen-sized ones don't get enough pressure up to make a really good espresso, or are finicky when it comes to the fineness of the grind or the temperature it comes out at. Sadly, unless you've got a fortune and lots of time, it's probably better to leave real espresso to a proper barista.

However, there are plenty of other gadgets available, and many of them make a very good cup of coffee indeed:

■ **Coffee grinder** – An essential buy if you're serious about your brew. They vary from tiny hand-cranked things (a bit like hard work) to industrial-sized hoppers with umpteen adjustments. For most purposes a basic electric one is fine, though you may have to work out the perfect grind by trial and error. Keep your coffee beans in the fridge or freezer and grind to order, and it'll always be fresh.

■ **Stovetop espresso maker** – or *macchinetta*. A substitute for an espresso machine. You fill the bottom with water, screw a filter full of coffee and a jug on top, and put it on the hob. These can make a very decent cup of coffee; it's not quite real espresso, but it's rich and strong, if occasionally a little muddy.

■ **Cafetière** – or 'French press', as Americans call it. This is a simple jug with a plunger inside. You pour water on the ground coffee, leave it to brew for a few minutes, then push the plunger down to trap the grounds. This can make very reasonable coffee, once you work out how long a particular blend takes to turn into decent coffee, how hot the water should be (just off boiling is a good place to start), and how much coffee to use. Can be a bit fiddly to clean, but makes an easy, straightforward coffee.

■ **Filter** – A basic filter on top of a jug or coffeepot is good and reliable, though having to pour water through it bit by bit can demand a little patience. Worth it, though.

■ **Electric filter coffee machine** – These are fine, usually, though after a while their pipes can get blocked with limescale or other debris. And their ability to keep coffee hot is a mixed blessing – after a while it tastes of scorched car tyres.

■ **Capsule or pod coffeemakers** – New(ish) on the market, these use a little coffee module that slots in the front and gives you, in theory, a perfect cup every time. Many do in fact give you good results, but they're not terribly cheap.

There are many other systems that have been tried over the years – the percolator, the office-style Kona machine with its bulbous jugs (oo-er), the twin-reservoir flip machine, the Turkish or Greek coffee boiler, the Chemex system, and so on. If you'd like to become an obscure coffee bore, there's plenty to go at here. Most, though, have disappeared for a very good reason – they're complicated or make coffee that's just not very nice. Apart from the Turkish version, that is, which is headbangingly strong and gritty, with a good half being solid sediment – and just excellent if you're in the mood for some supersonic wake-up juice.

The daily grind: keep your beans fresh

CHAPTER 11
FLUID CHECK

No matter how good your food is, it's always improved by a little liquid to accompany it. Well, not quite always. Eminent scientists are still trying to decide exactly how bad for you the classic lager/kebab combination is. But pick your drinks wisely and they'll lift any meal to true brilliance.

That doesn't necessarily mean a bottle of 1964 Château Poncy, either. While decent wine's a great thing, there's much more to matching food and drink than just plumping for the most expensive alternative.

Beer's versatile and can work brilliantly with a whole range of food (even desserts); cider is an underused British great, and especially fine in summer; non-alcoholic juices and smoothies will see off the toxins in style; and there's much more.

How about an aperitif to kick off with, or a dessert wine, liqueur or spirit to finish off a meal perfectly? Or a classic cocktail for that sophisticated moment?

While it's safe to say that nothing goes with an alcopop (except possibly a bucket), there's a place for almost every other drink you could imagine, and probably several you can't. The only rules are experiment, enjoy, but don't get too excessive – particularly before or during cooking. Not if you like having a full set of undamaged fingers, that is. Sharp knives and alcohol don't mix. Ask any knifethrower.

Remember, be careful out there. Just not too careful. Where's the fun in that?

Before, after, whatever: aperitifs, digestifs, and cocktails

Top and tail your meal with one of these ever-so-sophisticated ideas. If you want to wear a white suit and adopt a Roger Moore accent as well, do feel free. That would be raather maaahvellous, daaahling.

COCKTAILS

This isn't really the place to go into a full dissertation on cocktails; there isn't the spare 300 pages you'd need to list and explain them all. However, a Martini or a gin and tonic to loosen up your guests before dinner is a fine thing if you're feeling like a bit of cool sophistication. Here are five old favourites that'll get you in the mood. If you've got a cocktail shaker and a proper measuring cup it'll help; if not, just use roughly the proportions here, measured with a tablespoon or whatever, and stir with a straw or cocktail stick:

- **Gin and Tonic** – 2 units of gin, 5 of tonic, a slice of lemon.
- **Martini** – 2 units of gin, 1 of dry vermouth (Martini, Cinzano etc), a twisted slice of lemon or an olive or a cocktail onion.
- **Champagne cocktail** – 1 unit of brandy, 6 units of champagne, 1 teaspoonful of sugar, a dash of lemon juice.
- **Bloody Mary** – 1 unit of vodka, 8 units of tomato juice, black pepper, a dash of Tabasco sauce, a dash of Worcestershire sauce, a slice of lemon. A teaspoonful of grated horseradish or a stick of celery optional.
- **Caipirinha** – 2 units of cachaca (a South American spirit; you can also use 1 unit of tequila and 1 of white rum), 1 lime, cut into small pieces, 3 teaspoonfuls of caster sugar. Mix well. Best with crushed ice – wrap it in a clean tea towel and hit it with a rolling pin.

APERITIFS

Something simple to get the taste buds going is a traditional and pleasant start to a relaxed meal. Some like a small glass of dry white wine or rosé as a palate-cleanser, those with expensive tastes prefer champagne. You could also try:

- **Kir or Kir Royale** – White wine (or champagne in the Royale version) with a splash of cassis, a blackcurranty liqueur.
- **Ricard, Pernod, or any other pastis** – Served in a small glass with a jug of water on the side, so you can water it down to your taste. If you like aniseedy, liquorice flavours it's great. If not, not.
- **Sherry** – A traditional Spanish aperitif. If it's very good, very cold sherry this is excellent. Again, if not, not.
- **Vermouth** – This herby fortified wine, served over ice, is an Italian speciality. An acquired taste, but worth acquiring.

DIGESTIFS

There is a theory that white spirits go better at the beginning of a meal, brown ones at the end. This may or may not be true, but the classic things to drink after a blowout do seem to be dark-coloured and moody.

- **Brandy or Cognac** – Only the posh French one is allowed to be called Cognac, but other brandies, such as Spanish, can be perfectly decent. Very cheap stuff of any nationality will be rough, though.
- **Armagnac** – A variation on Cognac, but a very pleasant one.
- **Whisky, or whiskey** – Irish and American versions are supposed to be spelt with the extra 'e'. Single malts are best, aged is good; you can pay an absolute fortune if you're picky, though. Easy on the ice – too much will kill the taste.
- **Grappa** – A lethal clear spirit that Italian restaurants tend to dole out with dangerous abandon. Can be added to an espresso to make *café corretto*, or 'coffee done properly'.

The big match: drink and food

Take a look at this food and drink chart and you'll get an idea of what usually goes best with what. These are just suggestions – ideas of what most people seem to think works. Nobody's going to throw a wobbler if you prefer a chunky red wine with your fish and chips.

Some of these might overlap, but try a few options. And never drink something you don't fancy because somebody says it goes with a certain kind of food. If you don't like it, don't drink it. It's your stomach, after all.

And don't be afraid to vary these according to sauces or ingredients. While a very dry wine might be great with some sorts of fish, if it's cooked with lots of spices or rich sauce something less acidic – maybe even a red or rosé – will probably do the job better.

Global tip

One useful tip is that the native drink of an area often goes with the local food. Try a chunky Italian red wine with meaty pasta dishes, for instance, a light Indian lager with curry, or a pint of Guinness with an Irish stew.

Food type	Drink
Barbecues	Tinnies of ice-cold lager, cobber.
Burgers	Beer (or red wine if you're feeling flash).
Cheese	Chunky red wine, port, maybe dessert wine.
Chicken	White wine or light red.
Chilli con carne	Light beer, and plenty of it.
Chinese food	Fruity white wine, or lager.
Couscous	Lager or very dry rosé. Or mint tea.
Desserts	Sweet wine or port. Dry red can work.
Eggs	Tricky with wine. Try beer.
Fish	Dry white wine.
Fish and chips	Fruity white wine, if you're posh. Or lager.
Indian curry	Lager, maybe medium white wine or even red.
Lasagne	Medium red wine.
Meaty stews	Red wine, real ale or Guinness.
Pasta	Red wine, unless it's a fishy sauce then white.
Pizza	Beer always works. But red wine's good too.
Pork/ham	Cider or light red wine.
Roast meat	Rich red wine or ale.
Seafood	Medium white wine.
Tapas	Spanish wine or beer.
Thai food	Lager or medium white wine.

I'm getting leather, fish, wet dog: wine unwound

Sadly, food and drink is one area that seems to attract pretentious gits. And wine is probably the worst of all. If you piled up all of the over-excitable, frilly, pompous nonsense that's been written about wine, you'd have a heap the size of Everest.

Luckily, you don't have to be a top-class berk to enjoy wine. And the basics of it are simple enough for anybody to grasp and enjoy. If you do want to slurp, gargle, and spit like the pros, go ahead. Seems like a waste of good wine, though. So here are some of the most common wines and a swift guide to what they're like.

REDS

From?	Known as?	What's it like?
Italy	Chianti, Barolo Valpolicella	Hefty, chunky and often high in alcohol.
Spain	Rioja	Also on the heavy side.
France	Burgundy, Bordeaux	Medium but variable. Posher versions can be quite rich.
France/USA	Pinot Noir, Syrah	Lightish, fruity, summery.
Australia	Barossa	Enormously heavy, strong, headbanging wine. Great with a barbie, though. Of course.
Australia	Cabernet Sauvignon, Merlot	Those Aussies do like a big, chunky wine. Often high in alcohol too (14–14.5%).
Argentina	Malbec	Big, dark, full-flavoured.
Chile	Cabernet Sauvignon, Merlot	Less heavy than the Aussie versions; medium to full-bodied, often fruity.
USA	Zinfandel	Very variable, but tends towards the full-bodied, extrovert end of things.
South Africa	Pinotage	A good one is rich and fruity, a bad one rough and sour.

WHITES

From?	Known as?	What's it like?
France, New Zealand, Chile, Argentina	Sauvignon Blanc	Fresh, fairly neutral, dry. A good solid choice.
USA, Australia, South Africa, Chile	Chardonnay	The famous Bridget Jones wine. Can be sickly and overpowering. Avoid anything with 'oak' on the label; it'll be like chewing a plank.
France	Chardonnay, Viognier	Usually much subtler and tasty without being overdone.
Germany	Riesling, Gewurztraminer, Liebfraumilch	A decent, fairly pricey one of these will be flowery and fresh. A cheap one will be like sugary paint stripper. Low in alcohol.
Italy	Pinot Grigio, Frascati, Soave	Pleasant if well chilled but usually a bit thin and weedy.
France	Muscadet	Dry, chalky, crisp.
Portugal	Vinho Verde	Slightly fizzy, refreshing.
South Africa	Chenin Blanc	Medium-dry, middling.

Basket cases: supermarket wine is usually pretty decent

FIZZ

- If you're buying proper champagne or anything French, look for the word 'brut', or dry. It's a bit crisper than the sweet ('doux') stuff.
- Other fizz, like Spanish Cava, French Crémant or straightforward 'sparkling wine' from elsewhere, is usually perfectly respectable and cheaper. Again, try to go for something dry, because sweet cheap fizz can be like supercharged Lucozade.
- Italy's Prosecco is usually a bit more refined and tasty, but can be sweetish, so is best drunk very cold.
- English sparkling wine is amazingly good, if you can find it. The South of England has much the same climate as the French champagne regions, you know.

ROSÉ

- Look for a strong but subtle colour. If it's brownish or fluorescent lipstick pink, it's usually rubbish.
- Very pale rosé can be good, though – if it's called 'gris' the colour's supposed to be light and transparent.
- A comedy bottle is not necessarily a problem – many rosé varieties traditionally come in a tall, pointy bottle.

SWEET AND SO ON

- Usually found in half-bottles, as you'd have to be a sugar addict to get through a whole one.
- Sauternes, Muscat (not to be confused with Muscadet) and Sauternes are all worth looking out for.
- There's a quite mad Canadian drink called ice wine, which is made by letting the grapes freeze. Obscure but good.
- Sherry is a bit of a specialist taste (hello, Grandma), but a really, really dry sherry, drunk ice-cold with salty roast almonds, can be very fine.
- Port's much the same. In small quantities with blue cheese it's great. In large quantities you'll have a hangover that would flatten a rhinoceros.

ABSOLUTELY CORKING

Opening a bottle of fizz without spraying it everywhere, F1-style, is easy. Here's how.

1 Peel off the foil and, carefully, untwist the wire cage round the cork. If the bottle's been shaken this is where it could go pop, so go slowly.

2 Hold the cork firmly and – here's the trick – turn the bottle, not the cork. Have a glass ready close at hand.

3 When the cork lets go, pour an inch into the first glass, then repeat for the others. Then go round again to top them up when the bubbles have subsided.

The real man's choice: beer and cider

Though the more snobby types used to look down their noses at it, beer is one of the most varied and useful drinks to match with food. Plus it's cheap and usually reliable.

REAL ALE, OR BITTER

This label covers a whole raft of brownish beers, from mass-produced big brands, via stuff that comes in a can with a 'widget', to one-man-and-a-dog operations brewing exquisite local ales. This has become even more popular in recent years, partly thanks to greater numbers of pubs featuring guest beers and enthusiastic support from a network of fanatics. It's the traditional thing to drink with British food in a British pub. And also works well inside British food like steak and ale pie or beef and beer casserole.

What's more, there's been a boom in smaller craft brewers, both in Britain and further afield, making everything from beautifully crafted variations on the classic styles to frankly mental concoctions that push the boundaries of what it's actually possible to wrestle down your throat.

At its best, beer is just as subtle and complex as the finest wines and, though the worst of the beardy real ale bores can be a bit off-putting, it's well worth taking seriously. Here's a very rough guide to the major styles:

Hop along: this is what's in your beer

PORTER, OR STOUT

Best known through Guinness, though other brands like Beamish or Murphy's have their fans. Some say that this thick, creamy, dark liquid contains tastes of coffee, chocolate, or even tar. Others prefer their beer to taste of beer. Lovely stuff, though, and nobody should ever go to Dublin without tasting a pint in its natural habitat. Also extremely good with another Irish speciality, oysters.

LAGER

Often bland, light, and fizzy, but it's refreshing when served cold and won't get in the way of food. The better brands, and even more so those from smaller brewers, can have quite distinctive characters. German lager is often tart and sharp, Danish and Dutch creamier, while big American and Australian brands can be a bit weedy. If you avoid the mass-produced stuff, though, there's a huge range to choose from, and even the Americans have a decent selection of interesting beers like Sierra Nevada Pale Ale and San Francisco's Anchor Steam Beer. Belgium, though, is the Holy Grail for enthusiasts. Some bars in Brussels have more than 1,000 bottles on their list, ranging from wacky things like fruit beers to impossibly strong speciality beers, brewed in musty cellars by mad monks and with all the subtlety of a baseball bat. Drink carefully. It's a natural partner for curries and anything spicy, and can also wash down bready or stodgy food like pizza or burgers rather well.

WHEAT BEER, OR WEISSBIER

A relative newcomer here – the best-known is the fragrant Hoegaarden, but many German and Belgian brewers do a variation. It's cloudy, often with sediment, and sometimes served with a slice of lemon. Not really one for the session drinker, though, as it's strong and remarkably filling. A glass is good with seafood or chicken stews in a Belgian style, however, and its sharpness can cut through the stodge factor of German-style dishes featuring pork, cabbage, and potatoes.

Barley? Really: and this goes in too

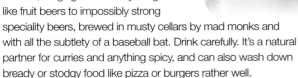

CIDER

This is on the way up – after a good few lean years, one of our best native drinks is definitely coming back. As far as my taste buds are concerned, the sweet variations you get over ice in a pub (Strongbow, Magner's, Gaymer's etc) aren't a patch on the drier, more tasty traditional ones like Weston's, Sheppy's, Addlestone's, or Aspall's. The last two are popping up on draught occasionally, which is a fine thing, particularly in summer when cider can be superbly refreshing. Another tasty type of cider is made in northern France: sometimes known as Normandy Cider or Cidre Breton, it's sharp and dry but very good served cold. You may well run across cider in Northern Spain too, but very little of that has sneaked across here yet. Cider is excellent with pork or ham, either drunk with it or used to cook it in. It can also be very good with savoury fish dishes like whitebait or deep-fried prawns.

Scrumpy

You may well run across the variant of cider known as scrumpy – often bright orange, rough, sweet, strong, and sold in a plastic flagon. If you drink this, your future health is entirely your own lookout. Some are perfectly palatable; some are an evil combination of gullible tourist souvenir and powerful weed killer. However, if your ambition is to win the World Headache Championships, go for the cheapest you can find.

Juiced up:
non-alcoholic alternatives

There are times when you don't want to get, er, juiced up.
So lay off the booze, keep a clear head, get healthy, and
try making your own juices and non-alcoholic drinks.

Get squeezing: fresh fruit is stupidly healthy

FRUIT JUICE

The first thing about making your own juice from fresh fruit – and this also applies to smoothies (opposite) – is that you'll need a powerful juicer or blender. Just as important as its ability to handle the chunkier bits of fruit, though, is how easy it is to clean. The process will get messy; there's no way round that. So if you've got a machine that comes apart into easy-to-rinse bits or can be bunged straight into the dishwasher you're on to a winner. If you have to spend hours trying to winkle strawberry pips or orange pulp out of tiny nooks and crannies every time, though, you'll end up sticking the thing in a cupboard and forgetting all about the whole idea. So, given a user-friendly juicer, what to put through it? Almost anything. But like smoothies, stick to a fairly standard repertoire to start with – apples, oranges, strawberries, blackcurrants, bananas – and then start to experiment, gradually, with more unusual or exotic fruit like papayas, mangoes, passion fruit and so on. After that, the sky's the limit.

CORDIALS

These are really just posh squash – they're concentrated fruity drinks that you add plenty of water to. But they come in quite a few unusual, more adult, flavours like elderflower, aromatic lime, ginger and lemon grass, or spiced berry, which can form the basis of an interesting drink, either non-alcoholic or alcoholic. If you're going the healthier route, try topping them up with sparkling water, or for an even more grown-up variation, use soda water and add a slice of lemon or sprig of mint.

OLD-SCHOOL FIZZ

There's been a bit of a resurgence in one-time playground drinks recently, but made to the taste of those who are well out of short trousers. Proper cloudy lemonade, dandelion and burdock, boutique cola, root beer, and most of all ginger beer, have made quite a comeback. They're a fine alternative if you're off the booze – ginger beer made by Fentiman's, James White and Australian company Bundaberg, among others, has quite a kick to it and is definitely not for the kiddies.

BOTTLED WATER

In most areas of the UK, something quite acceptable comes out of the tap. You can buy a water filter, either built into a jug or the more extreme plumbed-in kind, if your supply isn't quite up to scratch. Still bottled water is a very expensive way of buying H2O. However, if you want it fizzy you'll have to go that way. Some of the Continental brands, though, like Badoit from France or San Pellegrino from Italy, are very definitely different from standard tap water – their mineral content is high, and they have a distinctive tang. Whether that's good or bad is up to your palate – and, of course, your budget.

Thick and super-fruity: smoothie secrets

There's an old, and slightly bizarre, catchphrase that goes 'The answer's a lemon'. Well, in the case of making smoothies, the answer's usually a banana.

Look at the ingredients in any commercially made smoothie, and you'll usually find that bananas are high up the list, even if it doesn't taste particularly bananaish. The reason for this is that their texture and fairly bland flavour are ideal for making up the bulk of a smoothie and giving it that thick, smooth feel. A good trick here is to freeze the banana first, which will make it extra creamy. If you really don't like bananas (or don't have any) a good alternative is thick yoghurt – or just have your smoothie a little less, er, smooth.

The other thing you'll need is a blender. A decent, powerful one will do the job even if you're using tricky, tough things like ginger or carrot. But make sure it's easy to clean, as things will inevitably get messy. And chop up your fruit into small enough chunks to fit through the feed tube before you start.

Exact measurements are tricky, as all fruit varies in size a bit. But a good formula to start with is two handfuls of fruit or whole fruits plus one glass of juice. So, for instance, blend together:

- 1 banana
- 1 handful of blackberries, blueberries or strawberries
- 1 glass of apple juice

Colourful crush: get a red fruit fix

Or how about, for a bigger one:

- 1 handful of strawberries
- 2 ripe peaches, skinned
- 1 banana
- 2 glasses of orange juice

Or, for non-banana eaters:

- 2 handfuls of strawberries
- 1 small pot of plain yoghurt
- 1 small glass of orange juice

As with everything, taste before serving. You may want to add a tablespoonful of sugar or honey if it's too sharp, or a squeeze of lemon or lime juice if it's too bland.

Once you've become a master of the art of smoothie-making, try going a little further with the ingredients. For instance, try:

Ginger, Lemon grass, Carrot, Wheatgrass juice (extra healthy), Acai berries, Avocado, Cucumber

In fact, the sky's the limit. Nearly. When you come up with a successful recipe for a meat smoothie, do let us know.

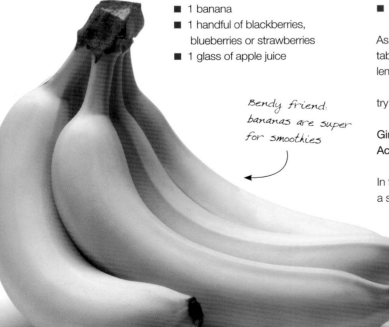

Bendy friend: bananas are super for smoothies

Fault diagnosis

Symptom	Reason/s	Remedy
My food comes out of the oven black and smoking.	You've overcooked it. Whoops...	Check the recipe. Try a lower heat or less time.
My food still comes out of the oven black and smoking.	Your oven's too hot or your kitchen timer's too slow.	Buy or borrow an oven thermometer – test to see if your thermostat's accurate. Check your timer against a reliable clock.
I keep burning things in my frying pan.	They're probably catching on the pan.	Is it non-stick? Check the coating isn't flaking off. Use a good layer of oil.
When I fry things, they come out soggy.	The oil's not hot enough.	Make sure the pan's very hot before starting to cook. Chuck in a tiny piece of onion – it should sizzle and spit.
Quite a few recipes start by frying an onion. But I don't like onions.	People are strange.	Try using fennel, celery, garlic, or missing that step out. It'll be fine.
I try to chop vegetables fast like the chefs on TV, but I keep nicking myself.	Too much speed, too little accuracy.	Don't try to keep up. It's not a race. Keep your fingertips tucked in and your knife sharp (page 16), and don't rush it.
I always make too much food and throw loads away.	Poor portion control.	Weigh everything and be frugal. Buy some freezer bags and store leftovers.
I always come back from the shops with stuff I don't need.	Disorganised shopping.	Plan ahead. Make a list (page 29) and stick to it. Don't shop when you're hungry.
I've left a pan on and the contents have burnt.	Being flaky or distracted.	If you're lucky, only the bottom layer will have burnt. Don't stir it. Carefully spoon the top three-quarters or so, avoiding any burnt bits, into a new pan and carry on. Add more liquid.
I've got a pan with a load of burnt stuff stuck to the bottom.	See above.	Use a wooden spoon to scrape as much as you can into the bin. Then soak it in hot water and scrape the soggy residue out every hour or so until you can get in there with a scrubbing brush or pad.
I've tried the deep-fried turkey recipe on page 60 and burnt my house down.	Bad luck, poor judgement, or extreme drunkenness.	You can't say you weren't warned. Tell the insurance company it was a meteorite strike.
My flatmate is addicted to chillies and makes everything too hot.	Poor flatmate choice.	Keep a pot of plain yoghurt in the fridge. Stir it into any offending dishes or keep it handy as a side dish/extinguisher.
I've just tasted my stew/soup and it's far too salty.	Cack-handed seasoning.	Chop a couple of potatoes into smallish lumps and throw them in. Cook for another 15 minutes and they should soak up most of the salt.
I've made some bread dough and forgotten the yeast.	Absent-minded baker behaviour.	Flatbread's fine, but if you want it to rise, you'll need to knead in the yeast as soon as you can.
My burgers/meatballs keep falling apart. They're turning back into mince.	Loose mixture.	Bung another egg in. They can vary in size, and a coarse mixture can need more gluing.
My gravy's full of lumps and bits of undissolved flour.	LGS, or Lumpy Gravy Syndrome.	Just push it through a sieve. Nobody will care. Next time, make sure you mix the flour well with the meat juices before adding the water.
My stir-fries always end up sloppy, soggy, and greasy.	Too little heat, too much time.	Don't wimp out with your wok. Keep the heat high, keep the food moving, and keep the cooking time short.
I've made and eaten a dish with lots of garlic. But I've just found out I've got a job interview/hot date in an hour.	Adventurous seasoning bites back.	Chew a sprig of fresh parsley. That'll freshen your breath naturally.
I read this book and got keen on cooking. Now I'm a rich, world-famous chef. Should I buy the Ferrari or the Aston Martin?	Far too much enthusiasm.	Get both and donate the spare one to the author in a gesture of gratitude.

Conversion tables

All these conversions are very close, but not necessarily accurate to several decimal points, so be careful. Also, many recipes (not ours) won't work if you mix imperial and metric, as the two use slightly different quantities. Beware. Also, the speed of light is exactly 299,792,458 metres per second. That might come in handy one day.

OVEN TEMPERATURES

Gas Mark	°C	°F
1	140°C	275°F
2	150°C	300°F
3	170°C	325°F
4	180°C	350°F
5	190°C	375°F
6	200°C	400°F
7	220°C	425°F
8	230°C	450°F
9	240°C	475°F

If using a fan oven you will need to reduce the oven temperature slightly (check your oven manual).

VOLUME

Imperial	Metric
2 fl oz	55 ml
3 fl oz	75 ml
5 fl oz (¼ pint)	150 ml
10 fl oz (½ pint)	275 ml
1 pint	570 ml
1 ¼ pint	725 ml
1 ¾ pint	1 litre
2 pint	1.2 litre
2½ pint	1.5 litre
4 pint	2.25 litre

WEIGHTS

Imperial	Metric
½ oz	10 g
¾ oz	20 g
1 oz	25 g
1½ oz	40 g
2 oz	50 g
2½ oz	60 g
3 oz	75 g
4 oz	110 g
4½ oz	125 g
5 oz	150 g
6 oz	175 g
7 oz	200 g
8 oz	225 g
9 oz	250 g
10 oz	275 g
12 oz	350 g
1 lb	450 g
1 lb 8 oz	700 g
2 lb	900 g
3 lb	1.35 kg

LIQUID CONVERSIONS

Imperial	Metric	American
½ fl oz	15 ml	1 tbsp
1 fl oz	30 ml	⅛ cup
2 fl oz	60 ml	¼ cup
4 fl oz	120 ml	½ cup
8 fl oz	240 ml	1 cup
16 fl oz	480 ml	1 pint

DIMENSIONS

Imperial	Metric
⅛ inch	3 mm
¼ inch	5 mm
½ inch	1 cm
¾ inch	2 cm
1 inch	2.5 cm
1¼ inch	3 cm
1½ inch	4 cm
1¾ inch	4.5 cm
2 inch	5 cm
2½ inch	6 cm
3 inch	7.5 cm
3½ inch	9 cm
4 inch	10 cm
5 inch	13 cm
5¼ inch	13.5 cm
6 inch	15 cm
6½ inch	16 cm
7 inch	18 cm
7½ inch	19 cm
8 inch	20 cm
8½ inch	21.5 cm
9 inch	23 cm
9½ inch	24 cm
10 inch	25.5 cm
11 inch	28 cm
12 inch	30 cm

Glossary

This isn't an index. It's a rough guide to some of the more obscure, foreign, or technical terms you might run across – because, hopefully, this book will have got you interested enough in cooking to explore further and try a few more experimental things.

A la plancha A Spanish style of griddling, where they heat a big flat sheet of steel until it's sizzling, squirt a bit of olive oil on to a bit of fish or meat, then slam it on quickly. Tasty, but impractical at home (unless you live in a restaurant in Madrid).

Andouillette French sausage made out of the more revolting bits of a pig. Sort of halfway between black pudding and haggis. A good one – look for the AAAAA badge – is meaty and chewy. A bad one tastes like a pig's bum. Be careful.

Antipasti An Italian phrase meaning 'starters', usually a number of little dishes like Spain's tapas; olives, bits of roasted pepper, cheesy nibbles, bits of ham or salami all work.

Au gratin Something with cheese and/or breadcrumbs on top, then baked or grilled to brown the top. Dishes with mashed potato on top like fish pie (page 75), shepherd's pie or cottage pie (page 138) work well, and you can also do it with veg like leeks or potatoes in a creamy sauce (see béchamel, below).

Au poivre Literally, with pepper. Often used to mean a green peppercorn sauce, usually found alongside steak. Also sometimes just means that the steak's been coated in crushed peppercorns before cooking, which is a fine idea.

Béchamel A creamy sauce. See the lasagne recipe on page 68 for a version. Also used in moussaka, and can be great to pour over a dish full of sliced vegetables – top with grated cheese and put in the oven for 25 minutes or so.

Bloater People who've eaten too much béchamel sauce. But also a lightly smoked herring, a variation on the kipper.

Braising A cooking method for meat where you seal it first by frying it very hot in almost no oil, then add liquid and put it in a slow oven for ages. The lamb shanks on page 70 are one example.

Bresaola Beef, but cured and sliced like ham. Cow ham, if you like. Very tasty in a sandwich or salad.

Broiling What Americans call grilling. They think grilling is what you do on a barbecue.

Caper A medium-sized green berry, usually found in jars of vinegar or water. A bit of an acquired taste, but can be great with fish. There is actually a caperberry plant, but cheap ones are sometimes actually nasturtium seeds.

Caramelised Crispy and brown. See 'Maillard Reaction' below for techy details, but it's what makes a lot of things tastier.

Chowder An American thick soup/creamy stew. Clam chowder is one of the finest reasons to visit Boston. Apart from Sam Adams Pale Ale, of course.

Cilantro What they call coriander in the USA and Mexico.

Confit A method where pieces of meat (usually duck or goose, sometimes chicken or pork) are cooked very slowly in their own fat. They end up succulent, melt-in-the-mouth soft and incredibly tasty. You can sometimes buy jars of duck confit in posh supermarkets.

Consommé Thin, very meaty clear soup. A sort of snooty stock, really.

Court-bouillon A posh phrase for cooking liquid; often used for poaching fish. It's basically water, wine, a few bits of veg like carrot, onion, leeks or celery, herbs, and a bit of salt and pepper, boiled for half an hour or so. Then you throw away all the lumpy bits and you've got a flavoursome basis for your fish dish.

Croque-monsieur A hot ham and cheese sandwich. Might have grilled cheese on the top, might be toasted, or might even have a creamy sauce on it.

Cups The ridiculously confusing American system of measurement. A cup of flour isn't the same as a cup of sugar, or milk, or … etc. Very silly indeed. If you need to use this a lot, you'll have to get a special measuring cup. Otherwise, there are quite a few conversion tables online. Be prepared to do some maths, though.

Eggplant Strange American name for an aubergine.

Entrecôte A cut of steak – you may know it as sirloin, or if it's still attached to the bone, T-bone steak.

Feta Squeaky, white, Greek cheese. Good grilled or cubed and sprinkled into a salad.

Flash-fry Exactly as it says – get the pan extremely hot, then wallop in your meat or fish very quickly. Use very little or no oil, and be prepared for plenty of smoke and noise.

Glaze To give something a shiny, often sweet, coating. Brushing beaten egg on to pastry is one example; using a dollop of honey or maple syrup on a roast ham is another.

Gnocchi Little Italian blobs of potato, which are cooked like pasta and do exactly the same job. They're a nice change, but enormously filling, so don't go overboard on the quantity.

Gumbo A New Orleans stew, often made with prawns, sausage, chicken, celery, and peppers, and served on rice. May well be confused with…

Jambalaya Another New Orleans dish, but closer to paella or risotto (see page 74). The meat, prawns and sausage are cooked in rice with plenty of stock, and often tomatoes and onions.

Jerusalem artichoke A lumpy, knobbly root vegetable with a pleasant smoky flavour. Great in stews, or baked in the oven in a creamy sauce. Has two disadvantages. First, it's tricky to peel because it's so knobbly. Second, it causes massive and uncontrollable farting a few hours later. Perfect if you're making dinner for irritating, pompous relatives.

Jus Posh gravy. It's literally the meat juices, reduced and possibly with a splosh of wine added, and maybe a little flour to thicken it.

Langoustine A big prawn. Like a trainee lobster.

Lardons Bacon bits. Great to fry gently for a few minutes so they start to release their fat, then you can cook the rest of your stuff in that. Beef stews or chicken dishes are particularly good with them.

Maillard Reaction The scientific term for what makes food taste good – the process in which heat makes the starch turn to sugar. The tasty brown crispy bits on the outside of roast things are the most obvious example. Discovered in 1912 by Louis-Camille Maillard, who is almost certainly no relation to the author of this book but had the most splendiferous moustache.

Mandolin A small stringed instrument, often found in bluegrass music. Also a sort of slicer, which in the right hands can chop veg thinly and quickly. In the wrong hands, it can also efficiently slice knuckles, finger ends and thumbs.

Marie Rose sauce The pinkish mayonnaise you get with prawn cocktails. Often just mayo, ketchup and a splash of Tabasco and lemon juice.

Marsala/Madeira Horrendously sweet and sickly fortified wines, from Italy and, er, Madeira respectively. Almost undrinkable unless you're desperate, but excellent for adding to desserts like tiramisu and trifle.

Mezzaluna A half-moon-shaped knife, sometimes with its own saucer-shaped chopping board, used with a rocking motion for chopping herbs and other things finely. Not everybody finds them comfortable or useful, but some swear by them.

Mise-en-place Cheffy French term that just means 'getting your stuff together'. Useful when you're making things like stir-fries: chop all the ingredients first and lay them out neatly, so you have them to hand when it's time to wok'n'roll.

Mutton An old sheep. Tastier but tougher than lamb, but hard to get hold of nowadays. Makes a superb stew.

Pak Choi/Bok Choi Chinese cabbage, as it's sometimes called. A teardrop-shaped leafy vegetable, great in stir-fries.

Pancetta Italy's version of bacon. Not usually smoked, and quite fatty, but cooks well.

Parson's nose The weird diamond-shaped bit of a chicken below its bottom. There's a little bit of meat on here, but it's hardly worth bothering.

Pesto A sauce, usually made with oil, garlic, nuts, cheese, and herbs. The classic, Pesto Genovese, uses basil, parmesan, and pine nuts, but you can make it with any similar ingredients. Easy in a food processor, but a mortar and pestle will be more satisfying and chunky.

Pimento Pepper – red, yellow, or green sweet pepper, but hot chilli peppers also count.

Prairie oysters Bollocks. Or testicles, to be more medical. Usually those of a young bull (which makes them bullock bollocks, probably), floured and deep fried.

Prosciutto Italian ham. Thin, pink, and often served raw. Also known occasionally as Parma ham, but let's not get into Italy's regional arguments or we'll be here all week.

Pumpkin Otherwise known as squash. Very fine when de-seeded, chopped into chunks and roasted. Also makes good soup.

Purée To whizz something very finely, until it's creamy and lacking in lumps. Or can describe the actual creamy stuff itself.

Ratatouille A classic French dish where you stew Mediterranean vegetables – peppers, aubergines, onions, garlic, courgettes, tomatoes and so on – in plenty of olive oil.

Reduce Used of liquids, it just means to boil them until they've thickened and, um, reduced in volume.

Rösti Germany hasn't given an awful lot to world cuisine, but these grated potato cakes are a worthwhile effort. Just stuff a few potatoes through a grater, mix them with butter or oil, add bacon, onions or cheese if you like and salt and pepper, form into flat cakes and shallow-fry. It's a sort of Teutonic tortilla (see page 107).

Saffron A ridiculously expensive spice – that's because it's handpicked crocus stamens. More costly than gold, weight for weight. It does give Spanish and some French cooking a special taste, though, so it might be worth investing in a small jar.

Salsa Sauce, in other words (and a dance, of course). But often used for the tomatoey, peppery sauces that go with Mexican or Spanish food.

Saucisson sec French version of salami. Not to be confused with British sausage, as the results could be disastrously chewy.

Sauté To shallow-fry in oil. Many, many dishes start by sautéing onions and garlic, which softens them and mellows the flavour out a bit.

Shrimp What Americans call prawns. If you run across shrimp in Britain, they may well be the lovely, crunchy native brown shrimp which you eat whole with a bit of mayo and brown bread.

Spatchcock Something you do to a chicken. No, not what you think. It's a complex bit of prep where you dissect a chicken, spread it open and insert two crossed skewers to keep it flat. A bit of a faff to do yourself, but if you're thinking of grilling or barbequing a chicken it's a good way to make sure it cooks evenly, and you can find them ready-done in some supermarkets.

Squash See pumpkin above. Not to be confused with the insipid watery fruit drink. But why would you?

Sweetbreads Not to be mistaken for prairie oysters (see above), even though the term is sometimes applied to lamb's testicles. They're actually the thymus glands of a young lamb, and both cheap and tasty if shallow-fried.

Tandoori The classic Indian restaurant style, named after the clay Tandoor oven you're supposed to use. Actually, if you marinade a bit of chicken or lamb overnight in yoghurt, cayenne pepper, garlic, cumin, chilli, ginger and any other spices you fancy, then stick it on a skewer and grill or bake it, you'll get a fairly decent, if not fully authentic, result.

Terrine Often used as another word for pâté, but in essence it's a squarish, deep dish that you fill with layers of finely minced meat, fish, vegetables or whatever, then cook by standing it in boiling water. When it's cool you put a weight on the top to keep it solid, then leave it in the fridge for a couple of days. Takes a while, but nice for a special occasion.

Tripe Cow's stomach lining. Sounds disgusting, looks disgusting, feels far worse, but is excellent for adding beefiness to gravy, stock or soup.

Vinaigrette Salad dressing – at it's simplest it's just oil and vinegar, but if you add a teaspoonful of mustard, finely chopped garlic, a splash of wine, herbs and salt and pepper you've got a fast and reliable dressing. Use decent ingredients, put it in a jam jar and shake. Make sure the lid's on tight, though...

Wasabi Japanese condiment, somewhere in the horseradish/mustard direction, but fiercely hot. It's a weird luminous green colour, which is just the shade you'll go if you accidentally snort some into your sinuses.

Information station: other sources

While this book is, of course, utterly brilliant you might want to journey even further into the food universe. So here are a few suggestions.

■ **Anthony Bourdain –** *Kitchen Confidential*
If you want to know what real chefs get up to, including violence, drug abuse, and horrible hygiene stories, this is great. Bourdain, a New York chef, makes Gordon Ramsay look like an effete poseur. Funny, fast, and eye-opening.

■ *The Dairy Book of British Food, Women's Institute Cookbook, Mrs Beeton, The Reader's Digest Cookery Year etc*
These are exactly the sort of books you'll find in your local charity shop, or on your Mum's shelf. And they're great for simple, no-nonsense versions of British classics. No lemon grass, no drizzling with olive oil, no bloody balsamic vinegar. Get one, and you'll use it all the time.

■ **Elizabeth David –** *South Wind Through the Kitchen*
Though often unfairly lumped in with umpteen twee, mumsy cookbook knitters, Mrs David was a game old girl who liked a drink, a series of highly unsuitable men, and good Mediterranean food. She was a great writer and her recipes are simple, tasty and readable.

■ **Jeffrey Steingarten –** *The Man Who Ate Everything* **and** *It Must've Been Something I Ate*
He's the food writer for American *Vogue*, but despite that, Mr S is funny and clearly obsessed with food. His story about making perfect pizza, from the second book, is worth the price alone ('A blackened disk of dough pocked with puddles of flaming cheese. I had succeeded...!').

■ **Carina Norris –** *The Haynes Food Manual*
Yes, it's a plug for one of our own books. But the lovely Carina has put together a fine reference book if you're interested in the health and nutrition side of food. It's got all the facts, neatly arranged in, er, bite-sized chunks.

■ **Prosper Montagné –** *Larousse Gastronomique*
The legendary ultimate reference book to French food, and proof that the French will eat absolutely anything. Like this: 'Roast Camel's Hump: Only the hump of a very young camel is prepared in this way. Marinate the meat with oil, lemon juice, salt, pepper, spices. Roast in the same way as sirloin of beef. Serve with its own gravy and watercress.' Also mentions otter: 'Its flesh, which is oily and leathery, has a horrible taste.' A million otters sigh with relief.

■ **Editoriale Domus –** *The Silver Spoon*
First published in 1950, it's every Italian housewife's guide to the classic dishes, and it's recently been published for the first time in English. Apart from some annoying celebrity chef recipes at the back, it's brilliantly clear and straightforward.

MAGAZINES

Delicious is the best of the High Street food magazines, though it can still be a bit frilly and girly occasionally. *Olive* is similar, and Jamie Oliver's self-titled *Jamie* magazine is appropriately 'pukka!' Posher and more pompous, but occasionally worth a look, is *Waitrose Food Illustrated*. *BBC Good Food* magazine will turn you into your Mum.

WEBSITES

BBC Food (www.bbc.co.uk/food) has tons of recipes, techniques, and ideas. Some annoying celebrity chef nonsense here and there, but we've all paid for it, so you might as well use it. And it's very easy to search. Channel 4 (www.channel4.com/food) also has a pretty decent food website. Beware of American sites when Googling, though; their measures and often ingredients are very different.

Index